The Death of Glory

Also by Robin Neillands

MILITARY HISTORY

The Dieppe Raid: The Story of the Disastrous 1942 Mission

The Battle for the Rhine, 1944: Arnheim and the Ardennes – The Campaign in Europe

The Old Contemptibles: The British Expeditionary Force, 1914

Eighth Army: From the Western Desert to the Alps, 1939–1945

The Bomber War: Arthur Harris and the Allied Bomber Offensive, 1939–1945

The Battle of Normandy, 1944

Attrition: The War on the Western Front, 1916

The Great War Generals on the Western Front

A Fighting Retreat: The British Empire, 1947–1997

In the Combat Zone: Special Forces since 1945

By Sea and Land: The Royal Marines Commandos, 1942–2003

The Raiders: The Army Commandos, 1940–1945

D-Day, 1944: Voices from Normandy (with Roderick de Normann)

The Conquest of the Reich, 1945

Wellington and Napoleon: Clash of Arms, 1807–1815

The Dervish Wars: Gordon and Kitchener in the Sudan

The Desert Rats: 7th Armoured Division, 1940–1945

The Hundred Years War

The Wars of the Roses

The Death of Glory

The Western Front 1915

ROBIN NEILLANDS

JOHN MURRAY

First published in Great Britain in 2006 by John Murray (Publishers)
A division of Hodder Headline

The moral right of the author has been asserted in accordance with the Copyright, Designs and Patents Act 1988.

I

A CIP catalogue record for this title is available from the British Library

ISBN-13 978-0-7195-6244-0
ISBN-10 0-7195-6244-9

Typeset in 11.5/14 Monotype Bembo by Servis Filmsetting Ltd, Manchester

Printed and bound in Great Britain by William Clowes Ltd, Beccles, Suffolk

Hodder Headline policy is to use papers that are natural, renewable and recyclable products and made from wood grown in sustainable forests. The logging and manufacturing processes are expected to conform to the environmental regulations of the country of origin.

John Murray (Publishers)
338 Euston Road
London NW1 3BH

This one is for Imogen Patricia Walker
Born 1 September 2005
With much love from her grandfather

Contents

Illustrations

The Publishers would like to thank the following for permission to reproduce illustrations: Plates 1 (Q 11728), 6 (Q 7629), 7 (Q 70069), 8 (Q 53650), 11 (Q 485), 12 (Q 58364), 13 (Q 380), 14 (Q 49217), 15 (Q 382), 16 (Q 49220), 17 (Q 49208), 18 (Q 90288), 19 (Q 28947), 20 (Q 49750), 21, 22 (Q 48951), 23 (Q 51647), 24 (Q 50418), 25 (HU 66445), 26 (Q 23665), 27 (Q 90277), 28 (Q 90904), 29 (Q 90922), 30 (Q 42152), 31 (HU 63277B), 32, 33 (Q 28971) and 34 (Q 29005), Imperial War Museum, London; 2, 3, 4, 5 and 9, Getty Images; 10, Corbis.

Maps

'Only the dead have seen the end of war'

Plato

About This Book

D URING THE 1960s, forty years after the First World War, two events struck heavy blows against the fragile reputations of the First World War generals, and in particular against that of the British generals. One was the advent of Joan Littlewood's Stratford East musical production *Oh, What a Lovely War*. The second was the publication of Alan Clark's Great War history *The Donkeys*, published by Hutchinson in 1961.

The Donkeys has been in print ever since, and the remark that inspired the title, an alleged exchange between General Ludendorff and an aide, quoted in Field Marshal Falkenhayn's *Memoirs*, that the British soldiers were 'lions led by donkeys', has long since passed into common currency. As for *Oh, What a Lovely War*, the play was subsequently filmed and has been regularly presented by professional and amateur dramatic companies all over the country in the last five decades, playing to packed houses, convinced audiences and general applause.

That these two presentations, the play and the book, have muddied the waters of Great War history to the detriment of the generals is a proven fact. Every Great War historian, academic or popular, knows that however strong and well founded his defence of the First World War generals might be, one TV or local performance of that entertaining musical play puts the generals back in the dock, at least as far as the general public is concerned . . . and so it is for *The Donkeys*, a detailed and damning indictment of the Great War generals' character and competence, written with style and considerable verve.

This present book concentrates on the charges levelled against the generals in *The Donkeys* and arises from the fact that Clark's history is almost entirely concerned with the battles and events of 1915 – just one year in a four-year-long war and a year which, as the military historian Gary Sheffield remarks, 'remains something of a forgotten year as far as the Western Front is concerned'.[1]

This seems to be true, and that alone is somewhat surprising, for 1915 was a very difficult year for the *Entente* powers – France, Britain and Russia – and therefore worthy of much closer attention. As the *Official History* remarks, 'The twelve months following the close of the battles of First Ypres in October and November 1914 brought little but disillusion and disappointment.'[2]

This disillusion and the various disasters that marked out that disappointing year cannot be entirely confined within that single, twelve-month time span. Battles and campaigns do not work like that; they arise from what happened before and contribute, for good or ill, to what follows. On the other hand, the events of 1915 provide a link with the recent past and lead on towards those that followed, while providing experiences that largely relate to that year alone. The chief effect of the 1915 battles was to destroy what was left of the British Regular Army; this army had mustered just eleven divisions in August 1915 and most of these had gone by the end of 1915.

The other effect was on the general public. In August 1914 the British people had rushed to volunteer, many worried that this war would be 'over by Christmas' before they had a chance to take part in it. That rush for glory subsided in 1915, when these eager volunteers, especially those in the Territorial Force, were gradually committed to battles that culminated in the battle of Loos.

Among the deaths of 1915 we must include the death of glory, of any idea that modern war was anything like the popular image of conflict, one where bayonets glint in the sun, generals gallop about on white horses and the skirl of bagpipes fills the air as the infantry go forward. All this was gradually seen to be a complete illusion. When wounded men on stretchers, fresh from the Western Front, carpet the forecourt of London's mainline stations, their bodies caked in mud, any notion of glory swiftly disappears. The notion that war was glorious vanished during the disastrous battles this book will describe.

The cause of those various catastrophes in 1915 lay deeper, not least in the pre-war unwillingness of the British people and government to understand the nature of modern war and make adequate preparations for it, should it ever arise and they opt to engage in it. Nor should it be forgotten that at the start of 1915 the British Army had been engaged in this new and massive war for just five months.

The results of this pre-war failure to understand modern warfare could not be made good in five months and were fully felt during 1915. Added to these errors was the contradictory order given to Field Marshal Sir John French, commander of the British Expeditionary Force (BEF) on his departure to France in August 1914. This order, given in full in the Appendix, directed him to cooperate closely with Britain's French allies but not to hazard his force, which was an entirely independent, British command. Advice on how the field marshal should reconcile these conflicting objectives was lacking – unlike French pressure to conform to French wishes, which was constant.

This book concentrates on the Western Front and the battles fought there in 1915 by the BEF and, at least to a certain extent, by the BEF's comrades-in-arms in the French and Belgian armies. That point made, the Western Front cannot be seen in isolation; the war grew in scale and went on elsewhere. War expanded steadily in 1915, to Italy, Gallipoli and Serbia, to Salonika and Mesopotamia and most notably in Russia. To concentrate on just one theatre of war in 1915, albeit the most important one, without some reference to the others, is to present the narrow view and bias the conclusion.

Nor is it fair to allege that the Allied generals on the Western Front and the 'powers that be' in London and Paris were simply acting like donkeys in 1915. Certainly, the popular impression is that the generals were butting their heads against the Western Front defences as if there was no other way to break through them, while ignoring the possibilities of strategic warfare by attacking elsewhere or developing technical innovations, such as the tank. As we shall see, this impression is totally false; by Christmas 1914, strategic moves and technological improvements were already in hand.

Essentially, the problem for the British generals was time. By the New Year of 1915, they had simply not had the time to make up the pre-war shortages in men, kit and *matériel*, or time to develop either new weapons or a strategic plan. All this would take time, and what could they do in the interim but fight on, doing the best they could in very difficult circumstances?

Doing their best was all the Western Front generals could do in 1915, and the bloody battles of Neuve Chapelle, Second Ypres, Aubers Ridge, Festubert and Loos, five somewhat neglected BEF encounters, are therefore carefully evaluated in this book. These battles saw a gradual escalation in the Western Front fighting, while the second battle of Ypres in the spring of 1915, which is mainly remembered for the German gas attack with which it opened, also saw the end of the professional career of General Horace Smith-Dorrien, one of the better of the First World War generals, a man destroyed by the malice of his senior commander. The character and capabilities of the Allied commanders will be covered in this book, since these personal aspects are closely linked to the battles and the way in which they were fought.

The battles of 1915 enveloped them after the heavy losses in the early campaigns of 1914 and the establishment of the Western Front trench system but before the British generals had the men, the kit or the experience to fight this new kind of war – 'total war', as it came to be called. Any study of that period therefore has to begin by describing the situation in the New Year of 1915, and explaining how this situation came about. The subject of this book is the Western Front in 1915, but that time and place has to be seen in a wider context.

In some ways every year of the First World War was a unique experience and there can be no objection to any author or historian singling out 1915 for special attention or concentrating on its peculiar features. The problem arises when the reader, or the general public, is led to believe that that year was typical of the whole war, or is led to assume that the disasters that occurred during that year went unrecognized or uncorrected. The field commanders are blamed for chronic errors that were not always the fault of the generals and which, in many cases, they were constantly striving to correct.

This is not to say that the generals or politicians of 1915 were entirely blameless for the events of that terrible year; far from it. There were no 'great captains' in the field in 1915 – except in the ever fertile imagination of the French. What we have is a number of general officers striving to get a grip on a war that in almost every aspect was outside their experience and – or so it often appeared – a little beyond their understanding.

Many of the tactical errors should have been foreseen. Many battles, especially the battle of Loos, were fought in conditions or over terrain that virtually ensured failure and great loss of life. The British commanders, Field Marshal French and General Sir Douglas Haig, commander of the First Army, certainly knew this about Loos, and the reasons why they still proceeded with their attack require elucidation. This book is not an attempt to whitewash the commanders or excuse incompetence at any level – and there was plenty of incompetence at every level.

That said, the various tragic events of 1915 should be put in the context of the war as a whole so that we can see what the commanders were trying to achieve at this time, judge whether their strategic decisions were soundly based and examine what other courses of action were open to them . . . at the time. Hindsight is a wonderful gift – historians would be lost without it – but the use of hindsight has to be restricted or objectivity and fair assessment go out of the window. It is also, I think, most important to be fair.

Therefore, before we start on the detail, the background to 1915 can be briefly summarized. Essentially, what the generals of 1915 were trying to do was to make the old methods of war work in an entirely new situation. For several hundred years, certainly since the creation of professional armies in the seventeenth century, the process of fighting a battle had become somewhat standardized. Having reached a point of confrontation, the armies would pound each other's positions with artillery, send in the infantry to force a breach and then exploit any subsequent success with cavalry. Both sides would apply such tactics and the strongest, best-trained force under the most astute general would usually win.

These three elements, artillery, infantry and cavalry, augmented by engineers and, from 1914, by air power, remained the backbone of the military effort in 1915. The generals therefore saw their prime task as a search for a way to use these elements in some combination that would deliver success on the battlefield and victory in this war. What most of them failed to realize was that the kind of warfare they were now engaged in was essentially new.

The hard fact was that the old, proven methods for mounting successful attacks would *never* work on the Western Front. What was needed was new kit, for example the tank, new tactics other than frontal assaults and, above all, new thinking – not least an understanding that global wars had to be fought on a global, strategic basis, employing some form of supreme command, directing the overall effort to a common strategic purpose.

All that would come in time, but that time was not yet, not in 1915. The campaigns of 1915 and the battles they embraced are therefore a particular kind of tragedy, a last attempt to make the old ways work. These battles were fought through a dawning realization that against the defensive combination of barbed wire, deep entrenchments, automatic weapons and artillery that constituted the Western Front, flesh-and-blood soldiers would hurl themselves in vain. You cannot fight flying steel with the bodies of brave men.

Given the inestimable benefit of hindsight we can see all this now, but none of it was quite so obvious in 1915. Both sides had made plenty of mistakes since the guns began firing in August 1914; the evidence of those mistakes still littered the fields around the Marne and the Aisne, along the Belgian frontier and around the town of Ypres; everywhere the bodies and bones of countless thousands of soldiers still lay unburied. All this evidence of the cost of modern war was in plain sight by the start of 1915.

Nineteen fifteen can be seen as a year of striving, of efforts to find some way of breaking the lock that the Western Front had imposed on the tried and tested methods of making war which had delivered victory so often in the past. How that effort was applied and what it led to is the subject of this book.

I

Reflections on the War,
August 1914–January 1915

You will be home before the leaves fall.
Kaiser Wilhelm II, address to the Prussian Guard, August 1914

IN SPITE OF all expectations, the Kaiser's forecast and the hopes of
Europe's embattled populations, this war into which the Continent
had entered so willingly in August was not over by Christmas 1914.
'And so the old year goes out, with rain and wind and sobs,' recorded
Major General Henry Wilson in his diary,[1] before slipping off to dine
in the New Year with the staff of the French Mission. The lesser
orders in the opposing armies were not so lucky; on the front line, a
few miles away, no celebrations saw in the New Year of 1915.

Apart from some social forays into no man's land on Christmas Day,
to exchange gifts and greetings with their German opponents and
bury their dead, the soldiers of the British Expeditionary Force (BEF)
spent the New Year in muddy, waterlogged trenches south of Ypres.
Drenched by rain, frozen by the nightly frosts, hanging on grimly
to their crumbling positions, they waited stoically for the daily rum
ration, the equally welcome deliveries of mail and whatever tribula-
tions the coming months would bring; no end to their current mis-
eries was remotely in sight.

No understanding of the First World War is possible without a firm
grip of the basic misunderstanding with which the European powers
entered into it at this time. Without exception, every nation entered
the war in the firm belief that this sudden and unfortunate conflict
would be short – 'over by Christmas', in the words of the British
public. This war had long been anticipated and war was somehow

welcome and even glorious – at least if the dense crowds cheering the departing units in the streets of Berlin, Paris and London are any yardstick. This general misapprehension that the war would be short and glorious was also widely shared by most public figures, the two notable exceptions being Britain's Secretary of State for War, Field Marshal Lord Kitchener, and the current commander of I Corps in the BEF, Lieutenant General Sir Douglas Haig.

In most parts of the public and political spectrum the military prognosis in the summer of 1914 was favourable. There would be a war, certainly, a brief exchange of gunfire on the frontiers followed by a ceasefire. There would then be a negotiated peace in which the various stresses that had brought the European powers to the battlefield would be resolved and peace restored to a chastened continent. This being so, the important thing for any patriotic young man in August 1914 was to get into the war quickly and so enjoy the excitement of battle before it ended; within days of the outbreak of war the queues outside the recruiting and enlistment offices were both long and impatient. Nor was this belligerent mood confined to the young; Keith Robbins comments that 'Most literate and intelligent men in Europe during the summer of 1914 considered that, in the circumstances, it was rather sensible to go to war.'[2]

The 'circumstances' in question were numerous, and varied from country to country. The French wished to retrieve the 'lost provinces' of Alsace and Lorraine, occupied by Germany since the Franco-Prussian War of 1871. The Germans wished to break the subsequent Franco-Russian alliance and so end the 'encirclement' on their western and eastern frontiers. The Russians wished to protect the interests of Serbia and the Balkan Slavs, now threatened by Austria-Hungary. The Austrians wanted to absorb Serbia into their empire and put an end to insurrection or open revolt in the Balkans. The British wished to maintain or restore the neutrality of Belgium, guaranteed by a general European treaty since 1839 – but were also quietly determined that Germany should not establish a military presence on the Channel coast.

Other nations now in the war, such as Turkey, or about to enter the war, such as Italy, soon had their own agendas, but the underlying cause of this war – the one cause fuelling every circumstance – was fear. Fear of aggression, fear of encirclement, fear of civil insurrection, fear of Germany's growing power and belligerence had gradually led to a general European tension which, many felt, only war could release. As a result, this war in 1914 was not unpopular.

In Britain alone the call to arms produced an immediate and overwhelming response. More than a million men flocked to the colours in the first five months of the war, far more than there were arms to equip, uniforms to clothe, instructors to train or officers to command. These men would be needed later on, to fight the battles of 1916, but by the end of 1914, with the original BEF virtually destroyed in the early battles between Mons and First Ypres, Britain's contribution to the struggle was provided by the remaining units of the Regular Army, recalled from their distant garrisons throughout the empire and, increasingly, by units of the Territorial Force. This current contribution could not be large and was further inhibited by the fact that the arms industry supplying Britain's small army was also small.

By the New Year of 1915, those early hopes of a short war and an agreed peace settlement had seemingly disappeared; the casualty figures alone had seen to that. The British Expeditionary Force that had marched so proudly and willingly to France in August had been destroyed, losing some 89,000 men, killed, wounded and missing, at Mons and Le Cateau, on the Marne and the Aisne, and during the weeks of battle on the Franco-Belgian frontier in October and November that became known as the first battle of Ypres.

These losses, heavy as they were to the small, eleven-division-strong British Regular Army, were a drop in the ocean compared with the losses sustained by the French. Between entering the war on 1 August and 31 December 1914, the French had lost some 300,000 men, an average of 2,000 men killed *per day* – without counting the hundreds of thousands more young men who had been wounded or taken prisoner.[3] Nothing on this scale had been anticipated when the nations went to war in the golden days of the summer of 1914.

Had the French known that the total of their dead in this war would eventually amount to 1.3 million men they might have been more ready to contemplate a peace settlement, but, if anything, the rising casualty list actually stiffened a national resolve. More than a million Frenchmen had been killed or wounded in five months of fighting; surely something worthwhile must come out of such a sacrifice? In any event, after sustaining such heavy losses in so short a time, to abandon the war now was unthinkable.

Losses of a similar, rising dimension had been inflicted on the Germans. The Kaiser had lost hundreds of thousands of men in the first five months of war – some 840,000 casualties, of whom 150,000 had been killed; Germany would lose nearly 2 million men by the time the war ended in defeat four years later.

Nor was this all; at Christmas 1914 the German military and political position may well have seemed precarious. With the failure of the vital Schlieffen Plan at the battle of the Marne in September, the German armies were now fighting a war on two fronts – the very situation the Schlieffen Plan had been designed to avoid – and their original commander, General Helmuth von Moltke, had suffered a nervous breakdown and been relieved of his command. On the other hand, the German armies had enjoyed considerable success on both fronts since the previous August, crushing the Russians at Tannenburg and overrunning Belgium and large areas of northern France. If peace proposals were to be the next game in this war, the Germans would come to the conference table with plenty of cards to play.

With the benefit of hindsight, it is easy to see that the best option open to the combatants at the end of 1914 was a peace conference, but there was a clear, political snag. With Germany holding several strategic cards and plenty of French and Belgian territory, such a conference could not be easily contemplated. Both sides had anticipated a short war with small losses and quick victories, but such a conflict had not materialized.

The war in which they were now engaged was not remotely the kind of war the belligerents had anticipated, a war of movement, cavalry charges, artillery bombardments and infantry assaults, open warfare of a long-familiar kind. That had briefly been the pattern in 1914, when the Franco-British and German armies had fought a war of movement from the Belgian frontier to the Marne. A war of movement would continue in the east, where advances or retreats of hundreds of miles were not uncommon, but in the west the rapid development of the trench system had changed all that. In the west the war had degenerated into a stalemate, with the opposing armies increasingly locked into a trench system which, if still primitive, was proving unbreakable to any frontal assault – and getting stronger by the day.

Nor was this all; the war was growing in size as well as intensity. It was already clear that when modern industrialized nations commit millions of men to battle, no war can be either short or inexpensive, and this war was rapidly spiralling out of control. Total war, with all its costs and uncertainties, was spreading across the world and would continue to spread unless the warring nations accepted that the struggle so gladly entered into would be unacceptably costly, not least in lives, and quickly sought a peaceful solution to their grievances. Sadly, common sense and wars do not fit easily together.

This is especially sad, for a path to the peace conference already existed. It had been marked out by Woodrow Wilson, president of the United States, even before the war began, when Wilson sent his personal emissary, Colonel House, scurrying about the courts and chancelleries of Europe, urging the leaders of Germany and France to settle their differences before it was too late. The snag was that it was already too late when Colonel House's efforts began, and various events in the first few weeks of fighting soon put the colonel's timing out of joint.

When House was pleading with the Kaiser in August, the German armies were surging across Belgium and into France. Their success offered Wilhelm II the entrancing vision of imposing his own harsh terms on the French, possibly in the Hall of Mirrors at Versailles, where his grandfather had been proclaimed Emperor of Germany in 1871. That done, the Kaiser could at last lead a triumphant procession through Paris, a city barred to him since his accession in 1888, in spite of constant hints that an invitation to the *Ville Lumière* was his dearest wish. In light of such a prospect, the colonel's plea for peace was swiftly rejected.

Colonel House met with a similar response from the French a few weeks later when their military star was in brief ascendant. In September 1914, the French government had no difficulty in refusing any negotiated settlement, for in the last weeks the German advance had run out of steam and the enemy armies were now facing defeat on the Marne. From these joint rejections Colonel House learned a hard lesson of international diplomacy: no nation will discuss peace when it thinks it is winning the war.

Colonel House was to try again in early 1915, when American involvement appeared more likely following Germany's introduction of unrestricted submarine warfare for the first time, in the waters round Great Britain and Ireland, and the sinking of the liner *Lusitania*, with great loss of life. Then US government policy and public opinion again swerved in favour of isolation, with President Wilson campaigning for re-election in 1916 as 'The man who kept you out of the war' and telling other, more belligerent politicians such as Theodore Roosevelt that 'there is such a thing as being too proud to fight'. In early 1915, therefore, any hopes of effective US intervention in favour of peace seemed doomed to failure.

In January 1915, three months since the end of the Marne campaign, matters had changed somewhat – and not for the better – for the armies of the Anglo-French *Entente*. Having halted the Germans on the Marne in September, the Franco-British forces had driven the enemy back to the Aisne. There the trench system had first begun to appear as the Germans dug in on the heights of the Chemin des Dames and the Allies, attempting to outflank this position, edged around it to the north and west, constantly attacking and as constantly repulsed. Then followed the so-called 'Race to the Sea' during October and November, the Allied armies attempting to get round the far end of the German line, the Germans shifting ever farther to the north in order to thwart them – and both sides digging in when halted.

And so, from this series of outflanking manoeuvres, the trench system of what came to be called the Western Front gradually came into existence. It was a fairly primitive construction to begin with, but one that grew stronger and deeper all the time as a war of movement gradually gave way to a war of position. Within months the Western Front defences would be increasingly deep and stretch all the way from the North Sea coast to Switzerland.

This trench system offered distinct advantages to the German armies defending it and to their new commander, General Erich von

Falkenhayn. At fifty-three, von Falkenhayn was one of the younger Great War generals, and had taken over the post of Chief of the Imperial General Staff from Helmuth von Moltke on 14 September, just six weeks after Germany entered the war. One advantage was that Falkenhayn's armies could defend the trench system with far fewer men than the French or British armies needed to break it, so freeing German troops for the war of movement against Russia in the east. Falkenhayn was a shrewd soldier and saw no particular need to advance deeper into France at this time; far better to end the Russian campaign while the western armies wasted their men and resources in costly and futile attempts to breach the Western Front.

The recently concluded first battle of Ypres marked the final attempt of both the Allied and German armies to outflank this front before it closed up on the North Sea. Now it had closed, and the advantages arising from that fact rested with the Germans; they occupied much of northern France, including some prime industrial areas, and the cost of evicting them, be it political or military, would be heavy. Writing to Field Marshal French on 2 January 1915, Lord Kitchener, Secretary of State for War, summed up the current situation on the Western Front with his usual precision:

> I suppose we must now recognize that the French Army cannot make a sufficient break through the German lines to bring about a retreat of the German Armies from Northern Belgium. If that is so, then the German lines in France may be looked on as a fortress that cannot be carried by assault and also cannot be completely invested, with the result that the lines may be held by an investing force while operations proceed elsewhere.

The French and British had – albeit narrowly – won the battle of First Ypres in November and so prevented Falkenhayn's attempt to restage the Schlieffen Plan, but that was all. The Western Front trench line had now been established and the two sides now glared at each other across the shell-pitted waste of no man's land, counting their losses, wondering what to do next, their political and military masters brooding on what operations might be launched elsewhere.

The options were not numerous. The armies could sit tight and wear each other down until one side or the other sued for terms, but that might take years. They could appeal for President Wilson's arbitration and talk peace, but on what basis? They could try to find some way to outflank the opposing trench lines or they could attempt to breach them with frontal assaults. All these options were duly considered but every one presented difficulties.

As briefly related, a peace conference was judged impossible, for Germany held all the negotiating cards. Even if the Schlieffen Plan had failed to deliver its promised defeat of the French and Russian armies in six weeks, it had still endowed Germany with vast amounts of foreign territory. German armies now occupied Belgium and Luxembourg and large areas of northern France, including the important industrial and mining centres around Lille, and were digging in to retain them. These possessions created a powerful bargaining chip for any negotiations.

Moreover, Germany's terms for a peaceful settlement were known to be excessive. They included the setting up of German trading and political hegemony over central Europe – '*Mitteleurope*' – the annexation of Belgium, secure possession of Alsace and Lorraine and much other French territory, including the occupation of the French coast as far south as the River Somme, and the ceding to Germany of the French Mediterranean naval base at Toulon. Belgian possessions in the Congo would be used to found a German empire in Africa – *Mittelafrika* – and further demands would surely appear at any sign of weakness among the *Entente*.

The French could never agree to any of this, but what had the *Entente* powers left to bargain with? All that the French and British had to show for five months of total war was a long casualty list, ever expanding military cemeteries and the prospect of further losses as the war continued. Granted, the cost to Germany in terms of lives lost had also been high, but the large German population – 66 million Germans to 37 million French – was able to absorb this. The stark choice – the only apparent option – was to continue to fight and attempt to kill as many German soldiers as possible; perhaps, as German losses mounted, the prospect of victory would gradually grow dim or the steps to a peaceful solution would start to appeal to them – in either case that outcome would take time.

With peace not currently an option, the war would therefore continue. The questions that now arose were 'where' and 'how', but those questions did not permit of easy answers – except to the French. To M. Raymond Poincaré, the French president, to General Joseph Joffre, the French commander-in-chief, and to the French nation, in or out of uniform, the answers were simple. France had been invaded and large parts of her territory now laboured in the grip of the Boches. This was an intolerable situation which must be ended – and ended without delay – with the rapid expulsion of the enemy from the sacred soil of France, whatever the cost. Any attacks elsewhere, any diversion of Allied strength to other fronts, were seen in France as intolerable distractions from this main task.

It was clear to the French that the war must be fought in France and Belgium and prosecuted by a series of strong Franco-British-Belgian offensives. These offensives would break the trench system and drive the Hun back across the Rhine in short order, overwhelmingly defeated. According to the French the only requirement necessary to achieve the prompt arrival of this desirable end was the British commitment of every man and gun the British Empire could provide, all of it preferably operating under French command and control.

For their part, the British were not at all sure that this was the only option, let alone the best one. Besides, even after five months of war they were not remotely ready for the kind of all-out, total, European war they had now got involved in. The BEF – the Old Contemptibles – that had marched to war in August 1914 consisted of just five divisions, four infantry and one cavalry, and was a fine fighting force – up to a point. The snag was that the BEF and indeed the entire British Regular Army of the pre-1914 years had been manned and equipped for campaigns on the fringes of empire, probably and preferably against opponents armed with spears.

The BEF had been formed in the early years of the twentieth century to avoid the sort of chaos that had ensued during the South African War of 1899–1902. During the immediate pre-war years, however, that devious and rabidly Francophile officer, Henry Wilson,

currently a major general and sub-chief of staff to Field Marshal Sir
John French, had laboured mightily to get the BEF committed to the
battle alongside the French in the event of a European war.

Wilson succeeded in that particular aim, but his scheming had
produced two fatal flaws. First, he could not persuade the British
government to equip the British Army for a *European* war in which
the enemy forces would be numbered in millions and enter the fray
equipped with all the necessary impedimenta for such a struggle,
including heavy guns and unlimited quantities of ammunition. The
BEF was a small, *colonial* army, created and designed to protect British
interests, not to pursue French ones.

Unlike the continental powers, Britain had not introduced military conscription in the pre-war years and had failed to expand her
armaments industry. As a result, the British Regular Army of 1914
was small and the arms industry that supported it was also small. Post-
August 1914, this last was the more serious problem. A million men
might rush to the colours but until they had been armed, trained,
organized and equipped, they could play no part in the war. A shortage of factories and machine tools and the stubborn resistance of the
trade unions to 'dilution', the employment of unskilled labour and
women in the arms industry, further inhibited an increase in arms
production – and therefore the expansion of the British armies in
the field.

The second flaw arising from Wilson's scheming was a growing misunderstanding with the French. In those giddy pre-war years, the
French had convinced themselves, or been convinced by '*cher Henri*' –
Henry Wilson – that on the outbreak of war the British would rush to
their aid with every means the nation and empire had available and put
their troops under French command. The French were therefore
considerably put out to discover in 1914 that this was not the case, and
put this lack of instant support down to British perfidy.

This ingrained belief that British resources were not automatically
in the French gift was not because the French had not been told;
time and again since the signing of the *Entente Cordiale* in 1904,
British ministers had told French ministers that the *Entente* was *not* a
military pact and should not be seen as one, but the French, aided

and abetted by Henry Wilson, had ignored those facts they did not care to acknowledge.

Five months into the war, however, it is at least arguable that the French had some right on their side. They were currently fielding the largest army and provided all the logistical elements, such as ports and railways, without which the BEF could not function. At this time it therefore made good sense to let the French call the tune, unless British interests were seen as fatally compromised or the slender BEF resources seemed likely to be squandered in some futile offensive.

The snag was that, with the exception of a few battles, notably at Guise and on the Marne, most of the French battles had been both costly and futile and the British generals were therefore understand-ably wary of putting their men under French control. They preferred to wait, to occupy the line they now held and defer further action until the larger, volunteer, British armies were in the field. The snag with that argument was that these 'New Armies' would not take the field until 1916 and the French could not – and would not – wait that long.

Granted, steps to create strong British and empire forces and get them ready for the fray were already well in hand. The Territorial Force, amounting to some fourteen divisions, had mustered, disposed of those legal restraints that kept territorials from deployment over-seas and was now sending units to the front. Territorial Force units had already fought with distinction at First Ypres and were now com-ing out to France in battalions and brigades – the first territorial division would arrive in the spring of 1915.

The empire was also rallying to the cause. An Indian corps was already in France, the Indian sepoys and Gurkha riflemen suffering ter-ribly from the European winter, while the first Canadian division was already formed up for embarkation. Back in Britain, Lord Kitchener was mustering his New Armies from that early host of eager volun-teers, but creating those assets would take time – and time was the problem. The French were already agitating for a renewal of the Western Front offensives in the spring of 1915 and demanding that the British Army, ready or not, should join them in the struggle.

While these various steps towards more of those costly offensives were being taken in France, some minds in Britain were considering other options. Pressing forward with further offensives with inadequate amounts of artillery and plenty of frontal assaults was always likely to be costly until some way was found to breach the enemy wire and eliminate the plentiful German machine guns covering that wire. In December 1914 a proposal was already on the table for the creation of an armoured fighting vehicle, a tracked machine that could cross muddy ground, crush barbed wire, span trenches and be impervious to machine-gun fire; this machine – the tank – would be developed during 1915 and make its debut at Flers–Courcelette on the Somme in September 1916; developing a new weapon of war and fitting it into the army's order of battle takes time.

If frontal attacks and prolonged offensives on the Western Front were the chosen French option, some means of defeating the trench, wire and machine-gun combination, something like the tank, would clearly be necessary, and the current assets, in men, heavy guns and high-explosive shells, would need to be greatly expanded. But were assaults on the Western Front really the only option available at the start of 1915?

One man, the First Lord of the Admiralty, Winston Churchill, thought not. Though its flanks rested on the Swiss frontier and the North Sea, Churchill believed that the Western Front could be out-flanked by an attack on Turkey, a new enemy which had entered the war on the side of the Central Powers in October 1914. The way to attack Turkey, Churchill declared, was by a naval assault through the narrow waterway of the Dardanelles and so to Constantinople, the Bosporus, the Black Sea and Russia. This assault, if successful, would lead to the capture of Constantinople – now Istanbul – the rapid elimination of Turkey from the war, the acquisition of further allies from the currently neutral Balkan states and an ice-free, year-round route across the Black Sea through which the large, mobile but ill-equipped Russian armies could be supplied.

The Russian armies certainly needed more arms; in early 1915 recruits in Petrograd were being trained with only one rifle for every three men and 2 million trained soldiers that could have been sent to the front were kept in their barracks as they were without rifles. As for artillery ammunition, the entire Russian arms industry could produce only 35,000 shells of all calibres in a month, when the armies could have expended that amount of ammunition in a day – had it been available.[4]

A success in the Dardanelles would outflank the Western Front and enable military *matériel* to reach the Russian armies, which were currently in full retreat before the German and Austro-Hungarian armies. In early January Churchill asked the naval commanders in the Mediterranean and Aegean for an appreciation of a plan to force the Dardanelles by naval units alone – without any commitment by the army or any amphibious landing – an appreciation that would lead in April 1915 to the launching of the Gallipoli campaign . . . and another disastrous failure.

The Russians clearly had to be supported and kept from defeat. Should Russia capitulate, even more German divisions would be sent to the Western Front. Even the French saw the dangers there, though urging, inevitably, that the best way to keep more German divisions from heading to the Eastern Front was to engage the German armies with strong Franco-British offensives in the west.

From this brief overview it will be seen that at the start of 1915 the Allied leaders, civil and military, were neither short of ideas nor unaware of the need for a strategic view of the war – and some new equipment. There is little evidence that any of them were 'donkeys'. What was lacking, in London and Paris and St Petersburg, was any organization capable of undertaking such a strategic view or enforcing some unity of command. There was no Supreme Command, assessing political and military objectives and drawing up plans to implement an overall strategy for victory. The armies of the *Entente* powers – French, British, Russian and Belgian – were, in effect, fighting separate wars.

To give just one example of such diverse aims, the state of affairs in the British cabinet at this time is described in the memoirs of General Sir William Robertson:

It thus came about by the end of 1914 that while the Secretary of State for War was aiming at decisive results on the Western Front, the First Lord of the Admiralty was advocating the seizure of the Dardanelles and Constantinople; the Secretary of State for India and the Indian government were conducting a campaign in Mesopotamia while the Secretary of State for the Colonies was concerned with operations in certain parts of Africa; and the Chancellor of the Exchequer was impressing on his colleagues the strategic advantages to be gained by transferring the main British military effort from the Western Front to the Balkans and Syria. A more deplorable state of affairs can surely never have existed in the conduct of any war.[5]

This picture, while indeed deplorable, does not entirely describe the situation between the French and British commanders on the Western Front. When Field Marshal French took command of the BEF in August 1914, he had received a directive from Lord Kitchener, outlining his responsibilities and the position he should adopt in his relations with the French. This directive – see the Appendix – was, to put it mildly, somewhat ambiguous.

Two points stand out. On the one hand, the field marshal was directed to work closely with the French commanders and meet their requests for cooperation with sympathy. On the other hand, he was to remember that his was an entirely separate command and he was in no circumstances to consider himself under the command of any other general – in other words of General Joffre, the French commander-in-chief. The first part of this directive provided useful ammunition to General Joffre and his close associate, General Ferdinand Foch; the second part they tried to ignore. The combination of these incompatible parts put a great strain on the BEF commander, Field Marshal French, who was not capable of absorbing much strain.

Field Marshal Sir John French was sixty-two when he was selected to command the BEF in France. French had made his name as a cavalry brigade commander in the South African War, and it is more than possible that brigade command – or perhaps, to be charitable, divisional command – was about French's level. 'Over-promotion' is a constant trap for military talents and French's talents were to prove woefully inadequate during his time commanding the BEF. This fact was pointed out to anyone who would listen by the field marshal's most trusted subordinate, Lieutenant General Sir Douglas Haig.

French had made one major political error in early 1914 when, with Henry Wilson, he became involved in the disputes that arose over the 'Curragh Incident', a small-scale mutiny among some cavalry officers stationed in Ireland and opposed to the notion that the army

might be used to force the Ulster Protestants into a united, independent Ireland. French was forced to resign but was recalled to duty on
the outbreak of war and given command of the BEF, where his numerous limitations were soon revealed.

Most of French's failures arose from his character, which has been
described as 'mercurial'. French was volatile, short tempered, very
prone to mood swings, constantly changing his mind, always liable to
agree with the last person he spoke to and putty in the hands of Henry
Wilson and Ferdinand Foch – at least, as we shall see, until the advent
of the battle of Loos.

He could also bear a grudge. His vindictive pursuit and constant
disparagement of his other principal subordinate in the BEF, General
Sir Horace Smith-Dorrien, was shameful, quite uncalled for and
a sore waste of everyone's time. This hatred of Smith-Dorrien dated
back to 1907 when Smith-Dorrien followed French in command at
Aldershot and promptly ordered the cavalry to stop dashing about on
horseback with sword and lance and pay more attention to musketry
and infantry tactics.

French saw this not only as an open criticism of his own methods
but as an attempt to turn his beloved cavalry regiments into mounted
infantry. From that time on, his enmity for Smith-Dorrien knew no
bounds. Criticizing Smith-Dorrien provided the field marshal with a
useful diversion from more serious matters when Smith-Dorrien was
sent out to command II Corps of the BEF.

In his relations with General Joffre, Field Marshal French handled the
situation fairly well, choosing to regard the French commander-in-
chief as the 'Generalissimo' of the Allied armies in France, one whose
instructions and requests – never orders – were to receive the most sym-
pathetic British consideration at all times and be complied with where
possible – unless the field marshal chose to dig in his heels and refuse.

This compromise solution had already led to at least one difficult
moment. In the days immediately before the battle of the Marne
the field marshal had suddenly declared not only that the BEF would
take no part in the forthcoming counter-attack but would actually
withdraw from the Franco-British front to rest and re-equip beyond
the Loire. It took the personal intervention of Lord Kitchener, who

came to France and ordered French to keep the BEF in the line, to resolve that issue.

General Joffre made his enduring reputation during the campaign of 1914. This culminated at the battle of the Marne in September 1914 when the French armies rallied and sent the German armies in full retreat back to the Aisne. During this time Joffre also displayed his other talent, as a great sacker of the slow or incompetent; in the first six weeks of the war he dismissed three army commanders, ten corps commanders and no fewer than thirty-eight divisional commanders for incompetence or because they broke down when confronted with the reality of war; one cannot help wonder how long Sir John French would have survived under Joffre's direct command.

Joffre was, above all, phlegmatic, stubborn, imperturbable and not prone to panic however dire the circumstances. Whether his habitual calm was due to those personal assets or to an inability to grasp how serious the situation actually was is still debatable but, by staying calm when all about him was collapsing into chaos, Joffre saved the French armies from total defeat in 1914 and delivered the most significant victory of the war on the Marne.

Even before the Marne, Joffre found reasons to doubt the resolve of the British, and these doubts continued. In October 1914, Field Marshal French suddenly announced that he intended to withdraw the BEF from their positions on the Aisne and take up a fresh line in the north, near Ypres and closer to the Channel ports. French intimated to Joffre that he would do this however much the French objected, and as a result no obstacles were put in his path. The BEF marched north in time to contest the German attack at Ypres during October and November, and the French began their years of struggle in Artois and along the Chemin des Dames in Champagne.

This constant need to compromise did nothing towards creating the necessary unity of command, but Anglo-French relations were inhibited by many other factors. The first was the character of Field Marshal French. Sir John did not speak French and did not like the French. He owed his post-South African War promotions and his current command of the BEF to the seniority system and the even more obvious incompetence of his colleagues in South Africa. The list of

French's shortcomings included an inability to curb the activities of his wily sub-chief of staff, Major General Henry Wilson, a man who was deeply devoted to Foch and more than willing to press French interests over British ones.

Henry Wilson's influence on French is hard to underestimate – though even French saw through Wilson in the end. Wilson's most obvious characteristic was his Francophilia; to say that Wilson adored France and the French is to severely understate the case. Wilson's second characteristic, which he was at some pains to conceal, was his inbuilt passion for intrigue – or 'mischief', as he called it. Wilson was more of a politician than an army officer, never happier than when shuttling between the British headquarters (GHQ) and Joffre's headquarters at Chantilly (GQG) or dining with General Foch at Cassel or conspiring with his French counterpart, Colonel Victor Huguet, to bend the BEF and its commander to French designs.

Since Wilson spoke fluent French and was known to be on intimate terms with the French General Staff, Sir John and most of the British staff, both those in France and those at the War Office, relied on Wilson for an overview of French intentions and to present British views and arguments to Joffre and Foch. The only man outside this loop was the War Secretary, Lord Kitchener, who also spoke fluent French and felt no need for the intervention of Henry Wilson, a man he publicly endured and privately despised.

When this story opens in early 1915, Wilson was busily engaged in attempts to replace his immediate superior, Major General Sir Archibald Murray, as BEF chief of staff. Obtaining this appointment would place Wilson in the position of puppet master to Sir John French, the more easily to manipulate his weak and indecisive commander. Unfortunately for Wilson, neither Kitchener nor the prime minister, Herbert Asquith, would hear of it – Asquith had not forgotten Wilson's intrigues during the Curragh Incident. Their rejection did not deter Wilson from continuing to press his appointment on Sir John. Writing in his diary in December 1914, Wilson records:

I told him that when he, Kitchener and Asquith thought they had solved the problem by allowing things to stay as they were, they made a great mistake. I analysed the objections to myself as C of S and pointed out that while Kitchener's were a matter of opinion, viz, personal dislike and belief that I was a rather mischievous fellow, Asquith's objections were political, because of Ulster and this war and that here there was a matter of principle.

I said that in my judgement he *must* remove Murray. He *must* beat Asquith on the matter of principle and he *must* offer me the appointment.[6]

In spite of support from Joffre and Foch, Wilson's demands got him nowhere. Murray duly went home but his replacement as chief of staff was Lieutenant General Sir William Robertson, formerly the BEF's quartermaster; Wilson was promoted to lieutenant general and after briefly commanding a corps was sent to Joffre's GQG as chief liaison officer.

It will be seen from all this that the BEF situation at the start of 1915 was far from happy. The BEF had coped well with the situation it had been flung into in August 1914 but had suffered severely in the subsequent campaign and full recovery was still a long way off. This war called for numbers of men and equipment that Britain did not currently possess and it would take years – certainly until 1916 – before the army had either the necessary numbers or the essential equipment – especially heavy artillery. Various options were on the table but other than an immediate commitment to battle in France or Flanders, none of them was likely to appeal to the French.

Herein lay another problem. If unity of command on the Western Front was desirable, as it certainly was, then the post of allied commander would certainly go to a French officer – most probably General Joffre, the hero of the Marne. The British commanders were firmly opposed to any such appointment and for precisely that reason – the Supreme Allied Commander would be French. The French generals may have regarded themselves as the heirs of Napoleon but the British saw little current evidence to support this claim – quite apart from the fact that the Duke of Wellington had defeated the Emperor Napoleon back in 1815. The solution adopted by Field Marshal French, of regarding Joffre as the Allied *generalissimo* and meeting his requests wherever possible, was as far as they were willing to go and probably the best solution in the circumstances.

The '*de haut en bas*' French attitude to the BEF and British military ability in general created another problem. In spite of the stout fight put up by the BEF at First Ypres, in early 1915 the French had come to regard the British Army and its officers as fundamentally useless. The French conceded that the BEF was perhaps employable for defending sections of the line and so freeing French divisions for those costly attacks, but they regarded the BEF as of no particular use as a fighting force, not least because the British seemed unwilling to adopt the French practice of making all-out assaults – the '*offensive à outrance*' – on the enemy line, whatever the resulting casualties.

This is not the place to debate this French contention, which time and some appalling British casualty figures would eventually dispel. The point is that the French held this view of the British Army, and it was an opinion that the British commanders were most anxious to refute. Why this should be, why the British commanders paid the slightest attention to this French attitude, remains a mystery, but one of the underlying reasons for the British assaults on the German lines during 1915 was an attempt to correct this impression.

The points raised in this chapter will at least serve to put the 'donkeys' allegation in context. It will be seen that the situation at the start of 1915 presented the British generals with more problems than opportunities and that the root cause of all these problems was time. If the British wanted to help the French in the coming year in any meaningful way, then the steps to create a suitable force for this war should have been taken long before the war began. To create a large, powerful and well-equipped army suitable for this spreading Continental struggle in five months was simply not possible and no amount of carping from Paris or Chantilly or later historians could or can alter that fact. As the *Official History* points out: 'For the British nation the period was one of grave anxiety but tireless preparation; the forging of material and the raising and training of new forces. The Old Army had been practically annihilated and the New Armies were not ready; the vast material resources required were only in the course of production.'[7]

Nevertheless, something had to be done and done quickly. Doing nothing to prosecute the war on the Western Front was definitely not an option, but again the problem was *time*. The New Armies – or the 'Kitchener Armies' as they also came to be called – could not take the field before 1916. The tank, which was to provide one answer to the defensive combination of wire, trenches and automatic weapons, was not yet even at the prototype stage and, again, would not be ready before 1916 – always assuming it was a viable weapon anyway.

For the next year the options for the Anglo-French alliance rested on either finding some way around the German positions on the Western Front or striking on some combination of force and tactics, some reworking of the old tried and proven methods, that would enable the *Entente* armies to break through the German line. The outcome of the first option led to Gallipoli. The search for the second solution in 1915 would lead to further catastrophes on the Western Front.

2

The British Armies in France

What a year this had been! The prophets were right when they
said that there would be an Armageddon.

Brigadier General Sir Archibald Home, diary entry,

31 December 1914

ON CHRISTMAS DAY, 1914, orders were issued for the formation
of two armies from the sixteen British divisions – eleven
infantry and five cavalry – now comprising the BEF on the Western
Front. This formation would take place on the following day, Boxing
Day, 26 December. The First Army, under General Sir Douglas Haig,
would consist of the I, IV and the Indian Corps. The Second Army,
under General Sir Horace Smith-Dorrien, would contain II Corps,
III Corps and the 27th Division, until more divisions arrived in
February to create a full corps, V Corps, under Lieutenant General
Sir H. C. Plumer. The cavalry divisions were formed into a Cavalry
Corps under Lieutenant General Sir Edmund Allenby and an Indian
Cavalry Corps under Major General Rimington.

More divisions, including the last three Regular Army divisions, the 27th, 28th and 29th, were also forming in the UK and
were due to arrive shortly, as was the 1st Canadian Division, a newly
arrived force of over 25,000 men which had been training in England
since the autumn and would shortly deploy to France. This development, the formation of armies from the original if much-
expanded two BEF corps, indicates that the BEF was becoming
richer in manpower. In the five months since the start of the war no
fewer than 1,186,337 men had enlisted for war service in the UK.

21

Thousands more had enlisted in the empire and colonies, though it would be another year before these new recruits reached the front line.

All this was to the good, but the current problem was not manpower but supply, especially artillery supply . . . and kit. The BEF was still woefully short of artillery, high-explosive shells and trench stores of every kind, from duckboards and sandbags to hand grenades, trench mortars, picks and shovels. Many of these shortages were due to the simple fact that the British Army had not anticipated a trench war, but the artillery problem had its roots in the scale of equipment laid down by the War Office long before the war began.

In 1914 each infantry division had a support scale of just four 60-pounders, the heaviest gun then in service, which allowed about sixty heavy guns for the entire British Regular Army – plus a few more for training establishments and coastal defences. The much larger German Army had some two thousand heavy guns with the field divisions and as many more in frontier fortresses, guns that could quickly be transferred to the front. A significant number of these heavy guns were very heavy indeed and had recently been employed in reducing the defences of Liège and other Belgian fortresses.

As for the French, most of their heavy guns were deployed in fortresses along the Franco-German line. Although many of these, most notably the guns of Verdun and other fortress positions, would gradually be removed from these fixed positions and used by the field armies, the main French artillery piece was the famous '75-mm' – the Soixante-Quinze, a quick-firing field gun, very useful against enemy infantry moving in the open but quite inadequate for reducing entrenched positions and dugouts.

Nor were the British any better endowed with field artillery. As the armies expanded, some two thousand field pieces were ordered, but a year after the war began fewer than half of these, just 803 in all, had yet been delivered. The same story held true for howitzers, of which only 165 out of the 530 ordered had reached the units in the field before the middle of 1915. This last shortfall was particularly serious, for only the plunging fire of howitzers could penetrate narrow trenches and deep dugouts.

So short were the British of plunging-fire weaponry that during 1915 they were forced to borrow some ancient 'Coehorn' mortars, dating from the reign of Louis Philippe in the 1830s; these weapons, known as 'Toby' mortars, were soon to be used in the upcoming battles at Neuve Chapelle and Aubers Ridge.

If the shortage of guns was serious, however, the shortage of artillery ammunition for the guns now in service was little short of disastrous. Here the problem can be related, at least in part, to one of scale. The pre-war 'scale' – the calculated amount of ammunition held by the artillery batteries and regiments, and in reserve – soon proved totally inadequate for the consumption required by a European war. In the early battles of 1914 the BEF artillery expended more ammunition than it had fired in the entire South African War and would have fired more if sufficient shells had been available.

It was also necessary to provide an adequate scale of high-explosive shell for the field artillery, but this need had not been appreciated by the General Staff in the pre-war years. They had concentrated on providing shrapnel ammunition, the kind most useful against mounted Boers in the South African War or infantry in the open, rather than high-explosive shell, which could have been used against troops in trenches.

Nor was it simply a matter of shells. The army had plenty of shells, more than 2 million in base stocks, but these could not be used as none of them had fuses. This shortage of fuses was to continue throughout 1915 and contributed to the 'Shell Shortage' scandal in midsummer. The *Official History* devotes several pages[1] to the problem of arms and ammunition, and these pages reveal just how complex and widespread the problem was.

The Great War was becoming, and remained, an artillery war. In such a war an adequate artillery supply was essential, but at present, if there was enough ammunition, it was of the wrong kind of calibre or without fuses. With two BEF armies going over to the offensive the great need in 1915 was for high-explosive ammunition, to shatter enemy trenches and dugouts, rather than shrapnel shells for use against infantry. There was also the need for a shell that could cut wire, but that had yet to be invented; barbed-wire entanglements were currently subjected to fire from heavy guns and the effectiveness of this fire varied considerably.

These shortages extended to more mundane matters. Trench warfare demanded many kinds of stores: duckboards, to keep the men out of the mud, gumboots for where this method failed and, when it did in winter months, gallons of whale oil to rub on wet and chilled feet in a bid to prevent the prevalent and crippling form of frostbite called trench foot.

On the First Army sector of the BEF front, in the low-lying dreary country south of Ypres, the water table was very high, barely half a metre below the surface in many places. Deep trenches could not be dug here and even shallow ones filled rapidly with water. The only solution was to build up defences from sandbags, but sandbags were also in short supply, as were picks and shovels and barbed wire. For offensive operations, the troops also needed hand grenades, but the British Army did not possess a hand grenade of any kind in 1914 or early 1915. As a result the troops were obliged to improvise such weapons, creating primitive hand grenades by cramming guncotton and nails into jam tins. Another weakness was a shortage of medium machine guns, the Vickers belt-fed MMG, while the new, portable – if heavy – drum-fed Lewis machine gun was only just coming into service.

Nor were the arrangements complete for training the troops in the basics of trench warfare. A handbook on *Drill and Field Training*, produced for the forces in 1915 by the publisher John Murray and based on the army's 1914 infantry training manual, contains no references *whatsoever* to hand grenades or barbed wire; the use of such kit and the problems caused by its absence were simply not addressed – the men had to be trained in trench warfare when they arrived at the front.

Given that these shortages in scale and kind still existed five months after the war began and would continue to exist for another year at least, it is only fair to enquire how the BEF generals were to engage in major offensive operations in 1915. They barely had sufficient kit and stores to maintain their own lines and keep the enemy at bay, but it was certain that when the weather improved, further offensive operations would be undertaken; the nature of the Franco-British alliance would see to that.

The root of the problem can be traced to two harsh pre-war facts. The first has already been touched upon; because the British Army was small, the munitions industry created to supply it was also small and could not be quickly expanded. Before the supply of guns and shells could be increased, factories had to be found or built, machine tools created or installed and workers trained in using them. This last task would not be easy either: the trade unions were anxious to use the war situation to improve the wages and conditions of their members and determined to resist the employment of unskilled or non-union labour; attempts by the employers to alter this situation led to a rising number of industrial disputes and strikes. Shell production actually fell in January 1915 because the munitions workers insisted on having their New Year holiday with the usual post-party absenteeism.

In such circumstances the wisest course for the BEF in 1915 was to hold its line in the forthcoming year and hang on until the necessary assets were available for further offensive action in 1916 – unless peace fortunately intervened in the meantime. That course of action was put out of court by the second fact, the existence of that Anglo-French alliance, the *Entente Cordiale*, which has also been touched on but requires further clarification.

The original 1904 *Entente* was an agreement that Anglo-French disputes would in future be settled by debate rather than war and included various agreements settling current Anglo-French disputes along the North African shore. The French, however, were not happy with these limitations. They wanted to transform the *Entente Cordiale* into a full-scale military alliance and pressed the British government repeatedly to take this further step, aided in this quest by Brigadier General Henry Wilson, Director of Military Operations at the War Office.[2] This French pressure was not simply for a political commitment; it included demands for pre-war steps that the British were extremely reluctant to take, such as national conscription for compulsory military service and the creation of a large, well-equipped army, ready for a European war.

Not wishing to indulge in such a war – or be dragged into one – the British government prevaricated. The outcome of that prevarication was a growing French conviction that the British had somehow agreed to support the French in the field when war came but were quite unwilling to take the necessary prior steps to make that support effective. In spite of the fact that the British had made no promise of direct military support *whatsoever*, when the war came the French were quickly convinced that Britain had let France down.

Britain's reasons for entering the war in 1914 had nothing to do with the *Entente Cordiale*. On 3 August, the British government declared that it had sent an ultimatum to Berlin demanding the withdrawal of German troops from Belgium, because of the 1839 treaty, signed by Britain, France, Prussia and other European powers, guaranteeing Belgian neutrality. This treaty – a 'scrap of paper' to the German government – and the protection of 'poor little Belgium' to the British Parliament and public, was only the official reason. Of more strategic relevance was the British determination that the powerful German Army must not be allowed to establish itself on the Channel coast of France and Belgium, from where it could be conveyed to Britain in a matter of hours, protected by the powerful modern warships of the High Seas Fleet. British self-interest, not French demands or any notional alliance between the two *Entente* powers, sent the BEF to France in August 1914.

The BEF did well in the fighting of 1914 and suffered grievously during it, but this sacrifice did not impress the French, who were making even greater sacrifices. In the early days of the war they became convinced that the British Army and its generals were either reluctant to fight or simply no good at it. The *Official History* confirms this point: 'The failure of the British to accomplish anything in the December battles in Flanders had impressed the French very unfavourably. Until the battle of Neuve Chapelle was fought there is small doubt that they were of the opinion that the BEF might be helpful to hold the line but would be of little use to drive the Germans out of France.'[3]

This conviction had been further strengthened by the failure of the BEF's December attacks on the southern edge of the Ypres salient.

No progress was made and even the British *Official History* describes these attacks as 'half-hearted'.

This impression, that the BEF was reluctant to fight, was one that the British government and the generals were most anxious to correct when they looked ahead to the spring of 1915. That underlying fact should be remembered, for it has a bearing on most of the BEF actions of 1915. Whatever benefit they might offer tactically or strategically should these attacks succeed, or whatever disasters might befall and lead to failure, these actions would still be useful if they demonstrated to the French that the British were totally committed to victory in this European war. It was therefore inevitable that the battles of 1915 would be fought in line with French wishes; the two army commanders, Haig and Smith-Dorrien, would be obliged to support the French attacks, however unprepared and ill equipped their forces might be.

Having previously analysed the limitations of Sir John French, at this point it would be as well to examine the character, expertise and reputation of these general officers and the man currently at the head of the British military establishment, Field Marshal Lord Kitchener, the Secretary of State for War.

For a serving officer to occupy a political post was unusual, but then Herbert Kitchener was a most unusual man. He had been commissioned into the Royal Engineers in 1871, but made his name as a field commander in the wars against the forces of the Mahdi in the Sudan, culminating in the defeat of the Kalifa, the Mahdi's successor, at Khartoum in 1898. From then on Kitchener of Khartoum, 'K of K', was a British icon, famed for his military sagacity and his prowess in the field. This reputation was apparently confirmed during the last stages of the South African War (1899–1902) when forces under Kitchener finally defeated the Boer commandos and brought that costly conflict to a close.

Kitchener then occupied a number of high military positions and consolidated his considerable reputation in India and Egypt. In August 1914 he was hastening back to Egypt when he was hauled off the Dover–Calais ferry and offered the appointment of Secretary of State for War, a post he accepted with considerable reluctance.

One of the most unusual aspects of Kitchener's performance is that it improved as he rose in rank; most commanders are eventually promoted to their level of incompetence, that point where their rank exceeds their ability and – as with Sir John French – their limitations are suddenly and starkly revealed. Not so Kitchener; as he was promoted, his performance improved. He was no better than adequate as a field commander in the Sudan but he performed good service thereafter as a soldier and a diplomat, not least in defusing the potentially disastrous confrontation with a French officer, Captain Marchand, at Fashoda in 1898; their encounter might have precipitated a Franco-British war but in fact paved the way for the *Entente Cordiale*.

In 1914 Kitchener was among the first to realize that this war on which his nation had now embarked would not be short. He also realized what that conclusion must mean – the creation of large armies and a large munitions industry. He was also able to exploit his considerable reputation with the public when calling hundreds of thousands of volunteers to the colours; that famous poster, showing the field marshal over the slogan 'Your King and Country Need You', brought in the men who were mustered into several armies, the New or Kitchener Armies, which took the field in 1916.

This eighteen-month delay in committing these troops to the battle, from the autumn of 1914 to the summer of 1916, was largely due to Kitchener's insistence that these armies should not take the field until they were trained, equipped and fully ready for the field. French demands that the new armies should be committed to the fight, division by division, as they were formed and equipped in 1915 were largely resisted and no pressure from Paris changed Kitchener's mind – to send untrained troops into battle, he said, 'was little short of murder', a fact most clearly demonstrated by the fate of two New Army divisions at Loos.

One man who shared Kitchener's conviction that this would be a long war was the First Army commander, General Sir Douglas Haig. Douglas Haig has long been the vector for all the accusations and myths that have surrounded the Great War generals, and those myths are still current among the general public. More informed authorities, following the lead set by the late John Terraine, have long concluded that Haig, while by no means a military genius, was a perfectly competent officer, whose actions, in the main, were both sensible and understandable in the context of the time. Haig, though not without faults, was certainly no donkey.

Douglas Haig was born in Edinburgh on 19 June 1861 and was just fifty-three and one of the youngest generals in the army when he went to France in August 1914. The Haig family came from ancient Border stock with a seat at Bemersyde near Kelso, though Haig's father came from Fife and was a distiller of whisky; Haig's whisky can still be consumed in British pubs. The Haig family were comfortably off but were not members of the aristocracy or the 'landed gentry'; they were 'in trade', barely a cut above the middle classes.

Like Sir John French, Haig was a cavalry officer. He was commissioned into the 7th Hussars in 1885 at the age of twenty-four. In December 1886 the 7th Hussars went to India, and by July 1888 Haig was a captain and adjutant of the regiment – a fairly rapid promotion. He spent four years as adjutant before becoming a squadron commander in 1892. He then returned to England to sit the Staff College entrance exam, in which, to his considerable surprise and disappointment, he failed to gain enough marks for a competitive vacancy.

He returned to India and devoted himself to his regimental duties until recalled to England for a one-year stint as ADC to the Inspector-General of Cavalry. Haig then joined the staff of Colonel John French, a rising star in the cavalry world, who had recently been tasked with writing a new cavalry drill book. When French went to the Aldershot command, Haig took on the task and the new cavalry drill book, by Colonel French and Captain Haig, duly appeared in 1896.

Haig got most of the credit for this work, and in February 1896 he was nominated for a place on the next staff course, entering the junior division at Camberley. Haig clearly did well at Camberley; the chief instructor, Lieutenant Colonel G. F. R. Henderson, a man not known for tolerating fools, is alleged to have remarked that Haig would one day be the commander-in-chief of the British Army.

Douglas Haig then saw active service, joining Major General Kitchener's 1898 campaign against the dervishes in the Sudan which culminated in the battle of Omdurman. During this campaign Captain Haig served in the Egyptian cavalry as a major – a *bimbashi* – and as chief of staff to the commander of the cavalry at the battles of the Atbara and Omdurman, all useful experience.

Up to this time, Haig's career does not appear to be flourishing academically, although he had passed into the Staff College by nomination. On the other hand, when set an academic task, at Oxford University, the War Office or at Camberley, he appears to have done well – or well enough. At this stage in his career he was doing adequately, but not noted as a rising star.

After the Sudan, however, his career began to pick up. In 1898 Haig became a brevet major, a man marked for promotion, and returned to the UK in November to become brigade major of the 1st Cavalry Brigade at Aldershot, under Major General John French. This acquaintance must have deepened into friendship, for later that year Haig loaned French £2,000 to cover losses French had incurred either from speculating in South African gold shares or from dallying with the ladies, two activities to which Sir John was somewhat prone. This loan enabled French to pay his debts and so remain in the service.

The next call to arms soon took both men to the South African War of 1899–1902, French as commander of the cavalry, Haig as his deputy acting adjutant general (DAAG). They arrived at Capetown on 10 October 1899, the day before the Boers declared war. The war in South Africa was a graveyard of British military reputations in the opening years of the twentieth century, but Haig emerged from the conflict as a substantive lieutenant colonel and French came home famous for the relief of Kimberley. Haig became an area commander for part of the Orange Free State, and was also appointed to command the 17th Lancers. Haig gained useful experience in that three-year debacle but he remained firmly convinced that the shock of the *arme blanche* cavalry charge was still a battle-winning tactic. Like General French, Haig was a stout opponent of the growing use of cavalry regiments as mounted infantry.

Haig returned to England in 1902 in command of the 17th Lancers, relinquishing that post in 1903 to go to India as a colonel, rising on arrival to the rank of local major general. In that rank he took up the post of Inspector General of Cavalry under the Commander-in-Chief India, Lord Kitchener – a man he would meet again in 1914.

In 1906, after three years in India, Haig returned to Britain, but the period had been marked by two significant events. In 1905, after a meeting at Windsor and a whirlwind courtship, he married Dorothy Vivian, a lady-in-waiting to Queen Alexandra and sister of a brother officer, Lord Vivian, who had served in the 17th Lancers during the South African War. Haig was already well connected or he would not have been invited to Windsor by Edward VII, but this marriage took him into a realm well beyond mere social duties. After his accession, King George V took a deep and personal interest in military affairs and expected to be consulted on all matters concerning appointments and promotion. The king's influence was profound, and before long King George was happy to indulge in long conversations with Major General Haig – a man with experience in many aspects of the military establishment – and listen to his comments and advice.

Haig also wrote a book, a worthy if misguided work entitled *Cavalry Studies, Strategical and Tactical.* This book draws on his experience as Inspector General of Cavalry in India and contains much good advice on the handling of cavalry regiments, but it also offers some intriguing insights into what Haig saw as the cavalry's decisive role in a major war.

General Sir James Marshall-Cornwall, otherwise a great supporter of Haig, states that on the basis of this book Haig 'could certainly not be considered among the prophets', and that his faith in the future role of cavalry was 'a pipe dream'.[4] This comment is certainly true. The invention of the magazine rifle and automatic weapons inevitably reduced the role of cavalry to that of mounted rifleman; while the horse continued to provide mobility up to the battlefield and in pursuit, the day of the *arme blanche* cavalry charge, with lance and sabre, was long over.

There were, however, a lot of cavalry diehards about in the opening decades of the twentieth century, and Haig's views were received with respect. On returning to England in 1906 he was appointed a military secretary by Richard Haldane, later Lord Haldane and Secretary of State for War in the pre-war government.

Military secretaries are charged with appointments and promotions and this post gave Haig a position of considerable influence with the king and the army at large.

Haig played a significant part in various developments, including the General Staff concept, the creation of the Territorial Force for home defence and the all-important reorganization of the British Army into an expeditionary force of six infantry divisions and a cavalry division – though not with matters concerning its deployment. Like most people in government or the army, he assumed that the BEF would be sent to some trouble spot in the empire; only a few people, most notably Henry Wilson, foresaw a British commitment in a major European war. His next appointment was as Director of Military Training (DMT) at the War Office, responsible for training areas, methods, schools of instruction and the writing and publication of training manuals.

In 1907 he was appointed Director, Staff Duties, in the General Staff Directorate, remaining there until 1909, when he went to India as Chief of the General Staff to the commander-in-chief. Before taking up this appointment Haig was knighted by King Edward VII at Balmoral. Haig's list of honours was growing – by 1914 they included KCB (Knight Commander of the Bath), KCVO (Knight Commander of the Victorian Order), KCIE (Knight Commander of the Indian Empire) and ADC General.

All but the first of these honours and awards were in the royal gift and had no particular connection with the military world. Haig had not been admitted to the Distinguished Service Order (DSO) or military rank in orders such as the Order of St Michael and St George, which leads one to suppose that his social position was due more to his royal connections than his military reputation or expertise.

Haldane did not forget his useful subordinate. In 1911 he wrote offering Lieutenant General Haig the prestigious Aldershot command, which Haig took over from Horace Smith-Dorrien in March 1912. The officer commanding at Aldershot would automatically take command of I Corps of the BEF should Britain go to war during his appointment, and so it proved. When the Great War broke out in August 1914 that post fell into General Haig's lap.

Haig reached two immediate conclusions about this war: first, that it would not be short; second, that Field Marshal French, the newly appointed commander-in-chief of the BEF, was not the man to command Britain's armies in the field during such a conflict. A far better choice, Haig averred, would be someone . . . well, not unlike himself.

At this point the writer must declare an interest; he is no admirer of Field Marshal Sir John French. This author believes it would have been better for the reputation of the Great War generals and – more importantly – for the lives of the soldiers in 1914 and 1915 if French had been removed from his command in 1914, before the battle of the Marne, when the numerous deficiencies in his abilities were rapidly becoming clear. By comparison Douglas Haig must be regarded as an officer of some intellect and considerable efficiency, a much better choice for commander of the BEF than his shallow and indecisive commander.

Most of the tales told about Douglas Haig are simply not true. He was neither callous nor incompetent, nor stupid. He had studied the military art carefully, had gained wide experience in South Africa and India and was perfectly willing to employ new methods and kit – such as the aeroplane and the tank – as soon as they became available. As we shall see, he was also willing to learn from his mistakes and vary his plans accordingly. He had done very well at First Ypres and was highly regarded by his corps and by his colleagues. On the professional competence issue, Douglas Haig is hard to fault – within the limitations of the time.

There are, however, a number of problems with his character. Underneath his somewhat dour, Border Scots façade, Douglas Haig was an optimist. This aspect of his character is illustrated by his reply to Colonel Repington, the military correspondent of *The Times*, at the end of January, when Repington asked whether it was possible to advance on the British front. Haig's reply was that 'as soon as we are supplied with ample artillery ammunition of high explosive I thought we could walk through the German line at several places'.[5]

Optimism is generally no bad thing in a general, but with Haig it often went too far. Haig tended to believe that one more effort, one more push, one more sacrifice, would carry the day and bring victory in the field – when the evidence often suggested that the attacks should be discontinued. This was not always the case but, as we shall see, the law of diminishing returns applies as much on the battlefield as in the field of economics, and Haig sometimes failed to realize this.

Haig was also something of an intriguer, a flaw he detected and deplored in that arch-intriguer, Major General Henry Wilson, the current sub-chief of staff. Haig's intrigues were subtle, long-term, largely directed against his superior officer, Field Marshal French, and began as soon as war broke out. When King George V asked Haig for his opinion of the field marshal on 11 August, one week into the war, Haig replied that, while he was sure Sir John would do his utmost to carry out his orders, he had grave doubts whether his temper or his military knowledge was 'sufficient for him to discharge properly the difficult duties which would devolve upon him'.

In his diary entry Haig then added his private thoughts. 'In my own heart I know that French is quite unfit for this great Command at a time of crisis in our Nation's History. But I thought it sufficient to tell the King that I had "doubts" about the selection.'[6] Haig continued to express these doubts to anyone who would listen, and the fact that he was entirely right in such assessments does not make his actions more attractive.

One other problem, though one not entirely Haig's fault, was to cause problems later. Douglas Haig was notoriously inarticulate. He could issue clear orders and write detailed and unequivocal letters, but when it came to standing up and stating his plans verbally Haig tended to ramble. This problem was compounded when another gruff, inarticulate soldier, Sir William Robertson, became CIGS at the end of 1915 and the two men were later confronted with the silver-tongued prime minister, David Lloyd George. All too frequently the prime minister could not make head or tail of what these officers were trying to tell him and therefore tended to assume they were being economical with the truth regarding the situation in the field.

Haig is not an easy man to understand. His competence and character are best explored though his actions and will be revealed as this story of 1915 develops. His colleague, Horace Smith-Dorrien, was a much less complex character but an equally competent general. Indeed, it might be that Smith-Dorrien was more competent than Haig, but his talents were unappreciated by Sir John French and his career as an army commander in the Great War was therefore regrettably short.

General Sir Horace Smith-Dorrien was an officer of wide experience, noted both for a ferocious temper and as one of the few British officers to survive the massacre of the 24th Foot at Isandlwana during the Zulu War of 1879. Born in 1858, Smith-Dorrien was now fifty-six and had commanded II Corps with skill and distinction in recent months, especially at Mons and Le Cateau, but also in the various engagements during the first battle of Ypres. Smith-Dorrien's abilities did nothing to endear him to Field Marshal French, who never ceased to denigrate him, not least to his brother officer and I Corps colleague, Douglas Haig.

In a diary entry on 5 February, for example, Haig records French telling him that 'Sir H. Smith-Dorrien is a weak spot and that he ought not to be where he is in command of an Army, but that he could not pass him over at this stage in the campaign'. Haig records telling French that he could not give an opinion about S-D as he did not know enough of the facts, but thought S-D's staff were 'useless'.

Should anything happen to Sir John French, either Smith-Dorrien or Haig would be in line for command of the BEF armies – the only other possible contender was General Sir Ian Hamilton, and he was to lose his chance and much of his reputation at Gallipoli. This being so, it was not in Haig's interest to defend Smith-Dorrien against French's enmity, though there is no evidence that he added to it. The irony is that French was still quite unaware that his main enemy within the BEF in 1914/15 was his trusted confidant, Sir Douglas Haig.

On the day these two BEF armies were formed, the battlefront of the BEF stretched for some 32 kilometres, from St-Eloi on the southern tip of the Ypres salient to Cuinchy on the La Bassée canal. The Second Army would occupy the northern part of this line, with II Corps north of III Corps, while the First Army occupied the ground to the south, again with two corps, the third corps in reserve. The French Eighth Army occupied the Ypres salient, while south of Haig's force the French Tenth Army took up the line towards Arras.

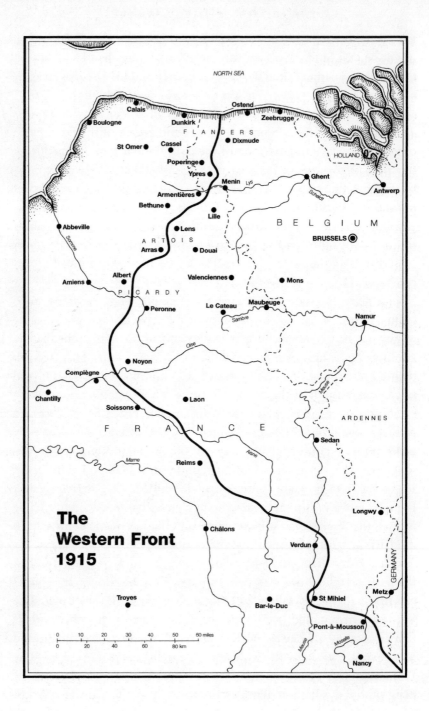

The
**Western Front
1915**

This arrangement sandwiched the BEF between two French armies, and for the moment General Joffre was happy with this arrangement. If he could not persuade Sir John French to accept his authority and obey his direct orders, he could at least confine the BEF to operations that largely depended on French cooperation, if only to cover its flanks.

This is not to say that Joffre ceased making demands on his British ally, mainly that BEF units should take over more of the French line, so enabling the French generals to form reserves for further attacks. In itself this was sensible, for to mount a successful attack a commander needs reserves. The troops making the initial assault would usually be too tired, confused and reduced in numbers to exploit any success; fresh troops are needed and must come forward quickly, to hold any salient or exploit any breakthrough.

This basic fact, and Joffre's demands, reveals a basic Franco-British problem. There is nothing wrong with Joffre's demand; creating strong reserves was necessary for any French success. The problem was that creating and retaining reserves were also essential for any British contribution to that French attack, a contribution Joffre would insist on and French's orders (see the Appendix) urged him to supply. Sir John French could create reserves for his armies and then either support French attacks or launch offensives on his own, or he could take over more of the French line – he could not do both.

Joffre knew all this but he did not care; this was a British problem and they should solve it to his satisfaction by sending out more troops. He had his own requirements, and in early 1915 these demanded that the BEF take over more of the Ypres front and free the French IX Corps for operations in Artois with the Tenth Army. This move, said Joffre, was 'a necessary condition for an offensive by the Tenth Army'. Further demands for the BEF to take over more of the front would be made throughout 1915.

At first sight, Joffre's demands again seem reasonable. Apart from a short section north of Dixmunde, south of the North Sea and held by the Belgians, and that 32 kilometres held by the BEF, at the start of 1915 the remainder of the Western Front was held by the French

Army. Right to the end of the war the French held more of the front than the British, who never held more than 160 kilometres.

On the other hand, if the British front was shorter, it was usually far more active in between offensives. Apart from mounting all-out offensives, the British and empire units were always more aggressive in carrying the war to the enemy and keen to dominate that muddy, shell-torn, corpse-littered stretch of ground between the lines known as no man's land, and they did so with a constant round of local attacks and trench raids. The French, on the other hand, generally adopted a rather sensible policy of 'live and let live' with the enemy and left their part of the line quiet unless an attack was being planned or actually executed.

Such attacks were already being planned in the New Year of 1915. When the year opened the British were contemplating an advance up the Channel coast to seize the ports of Ostend and Zeebrugge. This attack would be supported by naval gunfire from the warships of Admiral Hood's Channel Squadron and aimed at preventing the Germans developing these Belgian ports as submarine bases. The French were not keen on this operation, and in early February the proposal was abandoned.

General Joffre had other plans, notably for a major offensive designed to pinch off a great bulge in the French line known as the Noyon salient, a relic of the German advance in 1914. This salient peaked at Noyon, just 90 kilometres from Paris, and threatened the vital railway lines between Paris and the northern section of the front. If an attack from the north and south against the base of this salient was successful, it would cut the rail communications feeding the troops at the head of the salient from the east, force their withdrawal and perhaps restore open warfare. In Joffre's plan, this major French assault would be supported by a limited British attack north of the La Bassée canal – an attack that will be fully discussed in the next chapter. This Noyon offensive, according to Joffre, would certainly help the Russians and perhaps end the war.

There was another reason for pushing ahead with a major offensive in the west. Pressure was building in Britain for a diversion of strength to another theatre, and this pressure was currently shifting in favour of an attack on the Dardanelles, a move supported by the prime minister and the First Lord of the Admiralty, Winston Churchill. Both Joffre and French were totally opposed to any diversion of strength away from the Western Front, and a strong offensive was one way to bring the focus of attention back to France. Their demands were partially successful; at the end of January 1915, plans for what became the Gallipoli campaign were being pushed ahead in London and Egypt, but otherwise the current preoccupation was with forthcoming operations on the Western Front.

The time for a major attack against the Noyon salient seemed propitious. At the end of 1914 the Germans had started to shift divisions to the Eastern Front; eight infantry and six German cavalry divisions had already been taken from the Western Front and twelve new divisions formed in Germany since the outbreak of war had also gone east to confront the Russians. At the end of First Ypres the Germans had 106 divisions on the Western Front; now they had ninety-eight and none of these was fully up to strength.[7] On the other hand the Germans had the benefit of the Western Front trench system which they were steadily developing, but – Joffre thought – given sufficient artillery and some support from the BEF, even that obstacle could be penetrated.

Three lines of attack on the Noyon salient presented themselves to General Joffre. The first was an attack from Artois to the east, forcing the Germans away from Arras and pushing across the Artois plateau to Douai, eventually cutting the German communications somewhere between Rheims and Arras. Another attack might be mounted from Champagne, this one heading north towards the Ardennes and so cutting the railway lines to the German armies west of Rheims. A final option was to advance from Verdun and Nancy, heading north through the Rhine provinces to cut the German communications across the Rhine to France – and threaten Germany itself. Joffre was evolving a strategic plan, and attempts to implement this strategy were to dominate Franco-British actions for the rest of the year.

General Joffre was not a man to do things by halves. Faced with the choice of three options he opted for all of them. Attacks in Champagne had been going on for months; in the early spring these would continue and expand while the plans to attack in Artois and from Verdun–Nancy were put in hand. The Artois attack would be delivered in cooperation with a major push in Champagne. When those attacks were fully in train, the third attack would be launched from Verdun–Nancy (see map, p. 36). If all went well, the Germans would be obliged to retreat from their current positions. Once on the move they might then be pushed back to the Rhine and beyond; if a war of movement could be restored to the Western Front, who knew what might happen?

Up to a point, Field Marshal French was in full agreement with the French commander on his plans for 1915; like Joffre, he 'strongly deprecated the idea of sending French or British troops to any theatre other than the Western Front'.[8] Until the impossibility of breaking through on the Western Front had been proved, he averred, 'there could be no question of making an attempt elsewhere' – for example at Gallipoli.

This argument did not entirely sway opinions at the War Office, where the regular 29th Division, which French desperately wanted in France, was now marked for a move to the eastern Mediterranean, actually departing on 15 March. It was replaced by a Territorial Force formation, the 46th (North Midland) Division, which arrived in France at the end of February.

Field Marshal French was neither pleased nor impressed with this substitution. Since early February he and Sir Douglas Haig had been contemplating offensive operations at Neuve Chapelle in support of the French attack in Artois.

On 15 February, French asked Haig to draw up plans for an attack on the First Army front at Neuve Chapelle with the low height of Aubers Ridge and beyond as the ultimate objective. On the follow-ing day this plan was given further impetus by a request from Joffre, detailing a proposed attack by the French Tenth Army between Arras and Lens with the object of taking the heights of Vimy Ridge. This attack, said Joffre, would be aided if at the same time the BEF would make an attack just to the north, against Aubers Ridge. Together, these assaults would extend the combined Anglo-French attack front to one of some 112 kilometres.

Before proceeding with this account, it is necessary to refer the reader back to the early part of this chapter in which the state of the BEF in 1915 was described. From this it will be clear that in 1915 Sir John French's force was not equipped for breakthrough offensives and barely equipped for 'bite and hold' attacks, those limited offensives designed only to seize parts of the enemy line.

This sensible course of action was not one of the available options. The French wanted to attack in Artois and Champagne and expected support from the BEF south of the Ypres salient. That commitment was inherent in Franco-British relations, and the notion that the British were unreliable allies was one that Field Marshal French and his superiors were currently most anxious to dispel. Military realities had nothing to do with it; whatever the difficulties, when the French soldiers went forward in the spring of 1915, the BEF would match them stride for stride.

At this point it would therefore be as well to discuss briefly the two main Allied tactics that the armies employed for the rest of the war, operations usually described as the 'bite and hold' and the 'break-through'.

Both of these were designed to cope with the situation created by the existence of the Western Front defences and the end of open warfare. 'Bite and hold' is self-explanatory; after a preliminary bombardment, the Allies would launch an attack that aimed to grab – or bite off – a section of the enemy line. With that much achieved, the artillery would be moved forward and cavalry or infantry rein-forcements would come up to hold this newly acquired territory against the inevitable German counter-attack. If this portion could be held, then it could be used as a base for further 'bite and hold' attacks. According to the theory, so the Allied line would advance and the enemy line be gradually eroded.

There were various snags with 'bite and hold'. The first of these was that – usually – it did not work. The normal result of a 'bite and hold' operation was to create a narrow salient, which the enemy quickly brought under fire and then counter-attacked from three sides. The movement forward of artillery and reinforcements across no man's land was rendered difficult if not impossible by this fire and the shell-torn ground, communications broke down and the attack disintegrated; the usual outcome was a pinching out of the salient with considerable loss to the attacker. There was also the problem created by the inherent design of 'bite and hold' attacks – how many of them would be needed to create a German withdrawal or drive the enemy back to the Rhine?

Breakthrough attacks were much larger and altogether more ambitious. These were on a wider front, employed more units and aimed at a complete breakthrough of the enemy line on a front too wide to be pinched off. After breaching the line the attacker would bring up the cavalry and move forward to either cut the enemy's communications or roll up his defences from the flank; in either case the outcome should be a major enemy defeat, a full-scale retreat and the restoration of open warfare – or so it was hoped.

The problem with this form of attack will be revealed in subsequent chapters, but the main snag was the initial one – that of breaking through the enemy defences. It was tacitly assumed – and the generals were absolutely correct in this assumption – that the only way to breach the enemy line was by using an abundance of artillery and a vast quantity of shells. Given such assets, attacks were to prove that the enemy line could indeed be penetrated – but not without problems thereafter.

The first problem was to balance the extent of the attack front against the availability of artillery. It was accepted that the key to breaching the enemy front was an abundance of artillery, and this must be heavy artillery firing a great quantity of high-explosive shell. In 1915 the problem was twofold; first there was a great shortage of heavy guns and shells, and second, the more the front of the attack was extended, the more the available artillery must be thinned out in order to cover it. The only answer to this conundrum was a super-abundance of artillery and high-explosive shell, but that solution was a long way off in 1915.

Nor was that all. Even assuming the enemy front could be penetrated, there then arose the problem of exploitation – of expanding the breach and pushing forward from it to complete the breakthrough and roll up the enemy line. The attacking forces could rarely manage this – their energies and much of their manpower would have been exhausted or lost in achieving the breach. What was now required was a rapid commitment of reserves – probably the cavalry – and the forward movement of the guns in order to cover further advances in the exploitation phase of the battle.

At this point all manner of problems arose, most notably one of communications. No portable battlefield wireless sets were available in 1915; they would not become available until later in the war when wireless sets could be carried in tanks or aircraft, but they were not light enough to be man-portable. The commanders' only means of communicating with the front-line troops was by field telephones and land lines – and then only when the men were in fixed positions. Hence the need for pre-planned attacks, for the commanders had no reliable means of communicating with their troops once those troops moved beyond the front-line trench.

Other means of communication did exist – visual sightings, runners, flash signals, even carrier pigeons – but all these had limitations. Visual sightings were limited by the sheer scale of the action – the days when an army commander could see the whole battlefield by using his telescope from the back of a horse were long gone – and the battlefield was anyway obscured by smoke and dust. Runners did not live long on a battlefield swept by machine-gun bullets and shellfire, or got lost or delayed.

Visual signals, using lamps or flares, were also inhibited by dust and smoke and rarely proved effective, and the only recorded use of carrier pigeons comes in an apocryphal story which recounts how, after a number of carrier pigeons had been issued to front-line officers before an attack, one such pigeon was retrieved from the divisional pigeon loft bearing the unhelpful if understandable message 'I am fed up carrying this bloody bird all over France'.

The problem of reliable battlefield communications is still in existence in the early years of the twenty-first century and has to be fully grasped if the problems facing the Great War commanders are to be understood. It was not just the problem of communicating orders to the troops. There was also the matter of finding out what was going on at the front, during the attack, under that pall of smoke and dust, so that sensible orders, relevant to a changing situation, could be issued and distributed. The basic rule in battle is to reinforce success, but how is that rule to be followed when the commander has no reliable means of finding out which part of his attack is forging ahead and which part is a total disaster?

Communications apart, the Great War armies faced one insurmountable burden – they had great weight but little mobility. Opportunities for the rapid exploitation of any initial success – and the word 'rapid' is the crucial one – were limited by the fact that the Great War armies relied for their mobility on the feet of the infantry and the hoofs of the cavalry. Load an infantryman with 27 kilograms of kit, plus his rifle and ammunition, and he will not be able to run about for very long – a slow plod over churned-up, muddy ground is the best that can be expected. The cavalry is in little better condition, and both infantry and cavalry, when moving in the open, are vulnerable to enemy fire.

Then there is the matter of the enemy. However much he may have been surprised by the initial bombardment and attack – and that depended on a wide range of factors – his reaction would usually be prompt and vicious. The troops he has in the line will fight back, reserves will be rushed to the scene and heavy guns brought into play to stem the attack and seal off any salient. Unless the attack is executed with surprise, force and speed of exploitation, it is unlikely to succeed.

Then there arises the matter of training one's own troops. The units at the front in 1915 were composed either of a declining number of regular soldiers, trained for open warfare of the small-scale colonial variety, or Territorial Force volunteers who were barely trained at all. The histories and memoirs of the time are full of complaints about the poor state of training among the arriving troops, and the first requirement for any unit reaching the front was to train its men in the new kind of warfare – trench warfare or siege warfare – in which they were now engaged. This involved grasping trench routines, wiring and digging, patrols in no man's land and trench raids, sniping and trench reliefs, plus all the day-to-day chores of living and surviving in a muddy trench a few hundred yards at best from the enemy line.

Useful and necessary as these skills were, they were not the skills required for a successful attack. During attacks the need for 'fire and movement' tactics, field craft and basic infantry skills, the vital import-ance of taking ground, exploiting success while 'mopping up' cap-tured enemy positions, became paramount. These skills and tactics cannot be learned overnight and can only be kept at the desired level by sound training and constant practice. The harsh fact is that the BEF of 1915 was not particularly skilled in either kind of warfare and would need time, training and experience before reaching the neces-sary state(s) of competence.

It will therefore be seen that carrying out an attack – be it 'bite and hold' or an all-out attempt at a 'breakthrough' – could never be easy and was especially difficult at this time when neither the kit nor the competence existed. For these shortfalls the generals are usually blamed, but the fault lies with the politicians of the pre-war years, most of whom were members of the current government, who had failed to provide the army with either the geo-political direction or the necessary funds, manpower and industrial backing to play a swift and decisive part in this new and expanding war. The time lost in the pre-war years now had to be made up; to blame the generals for this situation and label them 'donkeys' for the resulting losses is to ignore the underlying factors.

The points raised above will come into focus shortly, for there was a small snag with Joffre's plans for 1915, one that closely affected the BEF. To increase his forces for these large attacks Joffre required the BEF to take on more of the French-held line, specifically by re-placing the French IX and XX Corps north of Ypres with British for-mations so that one of these corps could join in the Artois attack and the other extend the French front north of the La Bassée canal – a position currently held by I Corps of Haig's army.

Back in January French had agreed, albeit unwillingly, to carry out this relief as soon as he was reinforced by the 1st Canadian Division and the regular 29th Division, both of which were expected in February. Joffre then changed his mind and proposed letting the British retain the front north of the La Bassée canal – and launch an attack from there and from Armentières along the Lys river valley.

The French XX Corps could therefore stay where it was, but IX Corps, said Joffre, was 'absolutely indispensable' to his Artois attack and must be relieved. Deadlock yet again; French could either abandon his attack at Neuve Chapelle or relieve IX Corps – and Joffre wanted him to do both.

On 28 February Haig visited his neighbour, the Tenth Army commander, General de Maud'huy, hoping to complete their arrangements for joint support in the coming offensive. Haig was then informed that unless IX Corps was relieved and sent to him, General de Maud'huy would be unable to offer any support to the British attack going in on his left flank at Neuve Chapelle; the attack of the Tenth Army would be postponed.

'The net result of his information', Haig told Field Marshal French, 'is that our proposed offensive action must be considered an entirely independent operation.' On 7 March Joffre confirmed de Maud'huy's statement, but the BEF went ahead anyway. Three days later, on 10 March 1915, the First Army attacked the German line at Neuve Chapelle.

3

Planning Neuve Chapelle, March 1915

In addition to demonstrating to the Allies the earnest intentions
of the British Government, the battle had also raised the prestige
of the BEF as an efficient instrument of war in the eyes of friend
and foe, as was soon made manifest.

British Official History, 1915, Vol. I, p. 153

T HE SENTENCE ABOVE encapsulates the prime aim of the BEF
offensive at Neuve Chapelle. It reveals that the objective was not
just to take ground south of Ypres, but to convince the French that
the BEF could do more than simply hold a few miles of trench; this
battle would demonstrate to Britain's ally that the British soldier was
capable of aggression.

A battle must be viewed, at least partially, in terms of its objectives
and intentions as well as of its results; victory over the enemy might
not be the entire motivation, though General Haig, the First Army
commander, was in no doubt about his aims – at the least a breakthrough in the enemy line and the capture of a position 2 kilometres
to the east known as Aubers Ridge. This is clear from his diary entry
following a conference with his corps commanders on 5 March, five
days before the battle began:

We are embarking on a serious offensive operation with the object of
breaking the German line. There is no idea of merely taking a trench
here, or a trench there. My object is to surprise the Germans and push
forward to Aubers ridge *with as little delay as possible*, and exploit the
success thus gained by pushing forward mounted troops as quickly as

possible so as to threaten La Bassée from the northeast, in which direction there are no fortifications.

As far as Haig was concerned, the first object of his offensive was to take Aubers Ridge, a small escarpment astride the village of Aubers, leading up to dryer ground above the Lys valley at the eastern edge of the Douai plain. Aubers Ridge had been briefly held by Smith-Dorrien's II Corps in the autumn of 1914 before the big German advance on Ypres had obliged II Corps to withdraw into the muddy swamps of the Lys valley, where the BEF had just spent a most miserable winter. With Aubers Ridge back in British hands, it might be possible to push east on drier ground towards Lille or, as Haig indicates, veer south to roll up the enemy line at La Bassée. The first step towards either aim was to capture the village of Neuve Chapelle, which lay in the centre of the First Army line.

The dreary hamlet of Neuve Chapelle lies off the main La Bassée to Estaires road, on a turning between places then known as the 'Moated Grange', a farmhouse on the road to the hamlet of Fauquissart, and 'Port Arthur', a small salient on the main road between Estaires and La Bassée – a close study of the map on page 49 will be helpful at this point. Places to note include the Bois du Biez, the Smith-Dorrien trench and the 3-metre-wide Layes brook, all of which will feature in the account that follows. For the moment it is necessary to understand the plan and the ground.

The battlefield of Neuve Chapelle is not extensive. It can be walked over completely, if not easily, in half a day, the difficulty being caused by the fences, streams and ditches that criss-cross it and the trench-seamed woods and copses that screen parts of it from view. The entire width of the First Army attack front in March 1915 barely exceeded 2 kilometres, and the depth obtained by the attacking forces was approximately – and briefly – 3,000 metres, at its greatest point. This attack would be mounted by two First Army corps, Lieutenant General Sir Henry Rawlinson's IV Corps and Lieutenant General Sir James Willcocks's Indian Corps. Each corps would initially deploy one division, the Meerut Division of the Indian Corps and the 8th Division of IV Corps.

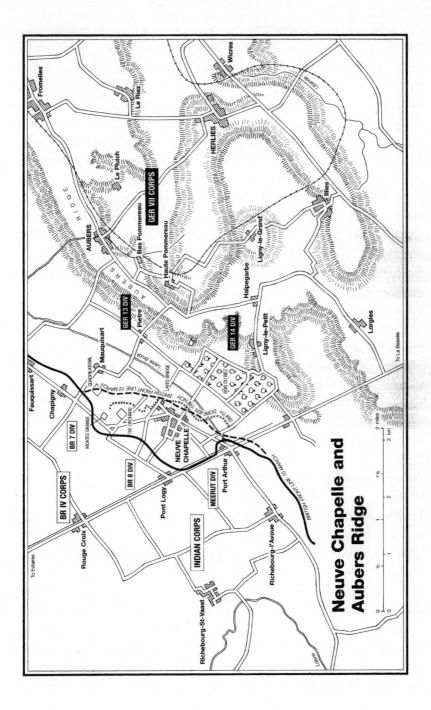

Neuve Chapelle and Aubers Ridge

The attack on 10 March faced a number of physical obstacles: the German defences, trenches and sandbagged emplacements, the wrecked but well-defended village of Neuve Chapelle, the dark thickets of the Bois du Biez wood just east of the La Bassée road, the wide, flooded Layes brook, which runs across the eastern edge of Neuve Chapelle and curves away to the north. Farther south still, the flooded, abandoned trench line known as the Smith-Dorrien trench lay as a relic of the fighting in October 1914. Beyond all this, just to the east, lay the strategic objective of this and all subsequent First Army attacks in this sector during 1915, the 12-metre-high rise called Aubers Ridge.

Aubers Ridge is barely a fold in the landscape – the usual reaction of battlefield tourists today is to exclaim 'Is that *really* Aubers Ridge?' But in the flooded terrain of 1915, a small rise could make a big difference. Taking this ridge would lift the BEF out of the flooded Lys valley to the drier plateau east of the village of Aubers; whatever the political ambitions of the British government vis-à-vis the French, the drier, higher ground beyond Aubers Ridge was something that the British soldiers saw as a position worth fighting for. The plan called for Neuve Chapelle and the ridge to be attacked and taken by two corps of General Sir Douglas Haig's First Army on 10 March, and with the utmost dispatch – the Indian Corps attacking to the south of the village, into the Bois du Biez, IV Corps attacking Neuve Chapelle itself.

At First Ypres, Haig had been a corps commander, acting under the direct orders of Field Marshal Sir John French; four months later he was a full general, commanding a much-enlarged force, now the First Army, and fully responsible for planning and managing its attacks. Though the field marshal was always hovering at his elbow, Haig was quite capable of handling Sir John and the Neuve Chapelle offensive was very much Haig's show.

In the early months of 1915 Haig's First Army occupied the line south of Smith-Dorrien's Second Army in Ypres, with the French Tenth Army on its right flank, across the La Bassée canal. For his opening offensives in 1915 Field Marshal French intended to use his two armies alternately, first putting Smith-Dorrien's Second Army on the defensive at Ypres while using Haig's First Army to strike some telling blows south of Armentières – notably those in support of the main French attacks in Artois and Champagne.

Haig records another reason for this strategy in his diary: that 'he [Field Marshal French] could never be certain of getting satisfactory results from Smith-Dorrien and because my troops were better'.[1]

Both claims are highly debatable. The first is simply an unattractive repetition of the snide remarks commonly made about Smith-Dorrien by Field Marshal French, and the second is without supporting evidence; there was no appreciable difference between the soldiers of the First and Second Armies. Smith-Dorrien's troops were well commanded and did what was demanded of them, often in very difficult circumstances.

As related, the battle at Neuve Chapelle was originally supposed to be part of an Anglo-French offensive on Vimy Ridge and not a discrete British affair. In mid-February, however, Joffre began his costly attacks in Champagne; these attacks gradually drained his forces – losses in the Champagne offensive eventually amounted to 40,000 men – and the French commitment to an attack in March on Vimy Ridge by the Tenth Army was abandoned at the end of February, an action that could be attributed to – or blamed on – the British refusal to relieve IX Corps at Ypres and take on more of the front.

The fact that the French had abandoned any intention of attacking in Artois or making a bid for Vimy Ridge, and bearing in mind the chronic British shortage of heavy guns and artillery ammunition, should have led to cancellation of the Neuve Chapelle attack. This it might well have been, had not those other factors – such as the need to demonstrate British commitment to the common struggle – already been in existence.

Like Lord Kitchener, Field Marshal French was most anxious to disabuse his French ally of any notion that the British Army was useful only for holding a defensive line. This being so, and in spite of the fact that the Neuve Chapelle attack had been based on the promise of French support and made in conjunction with the Tenth Army, the field marshal ordered Haig to proceed with his plans and attack at Neuve Chapelle as soon as possible. In practice this meant as soon as the ground was dry enough to permit the attacking troops to entrench, having taken their objectives – there would be no time to build sandbagged defences and after a winter of rain the water table was barely half a metre below the surface.

Haig's Operation Order No. 9, for Neuve Chapelle, dated 8 March 1915, laid out his plan for the attack in some detail. The aim was to force the enemy's lines at Neuve Chapelle and drive his forces back from the line Aubers–Ligny-le-Grand, so cutting off the German troops holding the line between La Bassée and Neuve Chapelle. This British attack enjoyed the advantage of superior numbers, for the German Sixth Army line at Neuve Chapelle was thinly held.

Following the transfer of units to the Eastern Front, the Sixth Army, nominally of eight corps, had only three and a half corps to confront the six corps of the BEF along their 36 kilometres of front and only VII Corps, of two divisions, held the line between the La Bassée canal and the Bois Grenier. The 13th Division front ran from Neuve Chapelle to the Bois Grenier, and the 14th Division occupied the front from Neuve Chapelle to the La Bassée canal. Neither division was up to full strength, for in early March they had to transfer one regiment (brigade) each to the newly formed 50th Division on the Champagne front. These divisions therefore contained only nine battalions, and even with the help of the 11th Jäger Battalion had been obliged to thin out their line. The net result was that two weak German divisions were facing the six divisions of Haig's First Army – some 20,000 men to oppose over 85,000.

At Neuve Chapelle, three battalions of the 16th Infantry Regiment (14th Division) opposed the Indian Corps, the Jäger Battalion held the centre and the 13th Infantry Regiment (13th Division) carried the line north from the British 8th Division front into that of the 7th Division. In the early stages of the coming battle, six German companies – one and a half battalions – with two companies in reserve would oppose fifteen British battalions. In terms of numbers, the odds were all in Haig's favour. Haig was therefore able to tell his men on the eve of the battle that he was 'sending 48 battalions to attack a locality held by three German battalions'.

This assessment was quite correct but did not allow for the German heavy guns, or a flat terrain around Neuve Chapelle, ideal for the deployment and use of machine guns, or the enemy's ability to rapidly move up reinforcements. In short, First Army's superiority was in infantry, and that superiority would be brief. Unless that infantry could get forward quickly and dig in to fend off the inevitable counter-attack, it would be fully exposed to enemy artillery and automatic fire and then confronted by German reserves hurried up from the rear.

The Intelligence Department at GHQ estimated that the enemy could put another 4,000 infantry in the line at Neuve Chapelle within twelve hours of the battle starting and a further 16,000 by the evening of the second day.[2] As in many Great War battles, the success of the assault therefore depended on the *rapid exploitation* of any breach in the enemy line. The problem, yet again, was time.

The first assault would be made by Lieutenant General Rawlinson's IV Corps and Lieutenant General Sir James Willcocks's Indian Corps, the 8th Division of the former corps attacking from the west, and the Meerut Division of the Indian Corps attacking from the south. The reserve for this attack consisted of the Cavalry Corps and the Indian Cavalry Corps, a total of five divisions, and the 46th (North Midlands) Division (TF). This reserve, the GHQ Reserve, was kept under the direct command of Sir John French and could not be moved without his permission. This was a problem for the First Army commander since any attack needed reserves on hand.

Haig solved this problem by redeploying his I Corps, which was not directly involved in this attack, and by using new units that were now coming out to France. I Corps took over the 2-kilometre front occupied by the right-hand brigade of the Indian Corps and the strong 1st Canadian Division – mustering some 24,000 men – which had arrived at the end of February, took on the frontage of the 7th Division, south of Bois Grenier. The net result of this deployment was to shorten the Indian Corps front to just over 3 kilometres and that of IV Corps to 5 kilometres, thickening their fronts and enabling each division to put one brigade into reserve for exploitation. It also meant that the Neuve Chapelle attack could be carried out without calling for the release of units from the GHQ Reserve.

Haig was relying on surprise to carry the day and stated that his intention was 'to surprise the Germans, carry them right off their legs and push forward at once to the Haute Pommereau–Aubers Ridge line'. In the face of the general view held about Haig's abilities, his actions and orders in the days before the battle are interesting – and fly in the face of received opinion that he was a donkey.

Haig's planning for Neuve Chapelle began on Sunday, 6 February, when he met General Rawlinson, told him of an intention to put in an attack at Neuve Chapelle and ordered him to prepare plans for an operation in about ten days' time. Three days later Haig is examining the ground before the Bois du Biez and concludes that the terrain is still too wet for an attack but might be expected to dry out as spring arrives. He also required information on the German defences in the Bois du Biez and sent off a request for more heavy guns. For the moment, until the ground became drier and he had more guns, the attack must be postponed . . . but the planning and consultations went ahead.

On 10 February, Haig had a meeting to discuss artillery preparation for Neuve Chapelle with Major General Fredrick Mercer, his Major General Royal Artillery (MGRA). The problem confronting them was simple to define but hard to solve; how much shelling would be required to smash the enemy defences and did the First Army have enough guns and high-explosive ammunition to carry this task out? In addition to solving that problem, how long would it take to do it?

Mercer initially proposed a four-day bombardment of the German wire and lines about Neuve Chapelle but, anxious to achieve surprise, Haig suggested compressing all this fire – and the available shells – into one crushing three-hour bombardment before the infantry assault. This need to make maximum use of the available ammunition was confirmed the next day when a signal to Haig from GHQ carped about the amount of ammunition currently being expended by First Army.

The problem of artillery ammunition continued and is revealed in Henry Wilson's diary entry for 10 February: 'The figures are exceedingly bad. In no case have we more than 800 rounds per gun in this country and probably not more than 40 of these are H.E. Nor is our output at home of any real use, for in the case of the 18-pdr which is the most favourable, we are only getting 12 rounds a gun a day, of which 4 are H.E. Now this is a scandalous state of affairs.'[3]

On 16 February Haig had a meeting with Major Hugh Trenchard, the officer commanding the Royal Flying Corps (RFC) wing attached to First Army. Trenchard, the 'Father of the RAF', was to do great things in this war and went on to command the newly formed Royal Air Force after the war. The subject of this meeting in 1915 was the use of RFC aircraft for reconnaissance, artillery spotting and post-attack communications. Haig's interest in these tasks does much to dispel the 'donkey' allegation; even in the planning for Neuve Chapelle Haig was attempting to solve old or current problems using new methods – and in 1915 the RFC was very new indeed. The various uses of this new arm were still being explored; their success depended on an open-minded approach by commanders such as Haig and a willingness to experiment and take risks by the pilots and observers of the RFC, who were presented with three specific tasks for Neuve Chapelle.

First of all, Haig wanted the RFC to examine and photograph the enemy defences and trench lines on the attack front. This task was duly carried out, at considerable risk, with the result that for the first time in war an attacking commander had a complete and up-to-date set of aerial photographs, which Haig used to brief his subordinates at a corps commanders' conference on 22 February. 'Thanks to the wonderful map of the enemy trenches which we now have as the result of this reconnaissance, it was now possible to make our plans very carefully beforehand.'[4]

There was then the problem of artillery spotting, the need to range the guns on enemy positions and batteries without alerting the enemy to the fact that this ranging was a preliminary to an all-out infantry attack. Using aircraft speeded up the ranging process, and as there was a great shortage of observation points in this flat country made spotting the fall of shot both faster and more accurate. Though a portable wireless set for the infantry was still a distant dream, wireless sets could be carried in spotter aircraft and, using Morse, the observers could pass ranging corrections to the Royal Artillery batteries on the ground.

The RFC's next task would be to note and report on the movement of troops and the position of the attacking units after the battle began. The problem of battlefield communication was not yet solved but it had at least been appreciated, and steps were being taken to alleviate the situation. Seven months into this war and technical innovations were being implemented as quickly as they were discovered; there is little evidence that the generals were hidebound, or rejecting the inherent possibilities of new inventions, or turning a blind eye to the difficulties before them.

Haig was also keeping a close eye on the tactical planning at divisional level and was not always happy with what he found. On the day after his corps commanders' conference, Haig visited IV Corps HQ and was annoyed to discover that the staff had passed the tactical problems of Neuve Chapelle to the commanders of the 7th and 8th Divisions. Haig told Brigadier Alistair Dallas, the Brigadier, General Staff (BGGS), that IV Corps should not ask for suggestions but order the divisional commanders to submit their attack plans forthwith . . . and if they could not do so, they should be sacked. In the event, one man sacked was Brigadier General Dallas.

The IV Corps plan for the attack duly arrived from General Rawlinson on 28 February. Later that day Haig had a meeting with Rawlinson and the Commander Royal Artillery (CRA) for the 8th Division, Brigadier General Arthur Holland, to discuss the artillery arrangements, which Haig rightly regarded as crucial. The problem was how to estimate the amount of fire necessary to reduce a position and, rather than underestimate the task, Haig decided to request more heavy guns, notably two batteries of siege artillery currently in line from the UK.

Haig found Rawlinson's overall plan fairly satisfactory but somewhat lacking in energy. The objective, Haig explained again, was not to take Neuve Chapelle. What Haig wanted was a new line well to the east, running from Illies to Herlies and on the La Bassée road to Lille – and then for the First Army to break the enemy front. IV Corps should therefore plan to advance *rapidly* to this line, without any intermediate stops.

The schemes of the 7th and 8th Divisions also struck Haig as indicating only a limited advance, which was not his intention at all. When Rawlinson and the commander of the 8th Division, Major General Francis Davies, proposed stopping the first day's advance on the eastern side of Neuve Chapelle, Haig rejected this suggestion with a flat 'no'. Every advantage must be taken of surprise and the initial heavy bombardment – no planned delay was acceptable.

A similar lack of grip seemed to exist in the Indian Corps, where, on 3 March, just one week before the attack, the corps commander and the GOC of the Meerut Division, Major General Anderson, were found to be in England on leave. Their plan also called for a two-phase attack on the Bois du Biez, which Haig promptly rejected, though finding other parts of their plan well worked out.

The need to restate the objectives of the offensive time and again to his subordinate commanders reveals another problem for General Haig – the difficulty of getting people to grasp the prime purpose of this attack. From the start he had made it clear that he wanted a 'break-through'; there is no mention in his orders or in the notes of his consultations of a limited attack to capture 'a trench here or a trench there'. And then, when Haig examines the plans laid out by his corps and divisional commanders, he discovers that they have either overlooked this point completely or chosen to ignore it; they are planning a series of 'bite and hold' attacks, aiming to seize only a limited portion of the enemy line and pause to regroup before moving on again.

These subordinate commanders were not donkeys either. General Haig may have proposed and planned this attack but they had to carry it out and their plans reflected the difficulties they saw in doing so. Essentially, they wanted to advance in a series of bounds, drawing up their administrative tail – supplies of ammunition, food and reinforcements – and relaying the guns on further objectives before moving on again. These are perfectly sensible proposals but they overlooked one crucial element – the enemy.

The enemy would react swiftly to this attack, especially after his defences had been penetrated. Artillery fire would be concentrated on the breach, any surviving troops would be ordered to hang on and delay the British advance as long as possible, and reserves would be rushed up to seal off any penetration. The problem, again, was one of time.

The time available for the First Army to exploit any breach in the German line was limited – perhaps a day, perhaps only a few hours. Haig was trying to offer his assaulting troops as much time as possible, with the use of surprise and as much artillery fire as he could muster to support their advance – but if they frittered that time away by halting after a limited advance, those assets would quickly disappear and the prime object of the operation would be lost. The corps and divisional commanders were therefore directed to study their orders and redraft their plans.

Discussions over the artillery bombardment still continued. General Mercer had been consulting the battery commanders and returned with a proposal that the initial bombardment should be reduced to thirty minutes. Haig brooded over this suggestion – which offered the advantage of surprise – but still wanted some estimate of how long the artillery commanders thought it would take to effectively demolish the enemy defences on the attack front. Was half an hour of fire sufficient if it left some wire uncut and some machine guns in action? When the weight of shot had been calculated against the task in hand, Haig might reach a decision. General Mercer went off for further consultations with his artillery commanders and returned with a minor adjustment.

The opening attack would be supported by a short but intense thirty-five-minute bombardment by the corps and divisional artillery. The available artillery totalled 530 guns of various calibres; over half of these were 18-pounder field guns, tasked for wire cutting and firing shrapnel, and not heavy guns and howitzers firing high explosives to demolish trenches and sandbagged positions. Those houses and farmyards on or behind the German front line had probably been turned into strongpoints.

There was, moreover, a small but critical omission in the artillery plan. Haig had been promised all the guns that the BEF could spare from other essential tasks, and these duly arrived. The promised support also included those two batteries of heavy guns, 6-inch howitzers of the 7th Siege Brigade (59th and 81st Siege Batteries, RA) brought out especially from the UK. These might have been a valuable addition to Haig's firepower but the guns did not leave England until 5 March and did not arrive at Estaires, 5 kilometres north of the BEF line, until 9 March, the day before the attack; they still had to be moved forward, dug in and ranged on their targets – and there was less than a day to do so.

These heavy guns were tasked to bombard 400 metres of German trenches on the left-hand edge of the British assault, where the 23rd Brigade of the 8th Division, IV Corps, would attack. Unable to range on this position, the artillery support here was totally inadequate, so this delay, says the *Official History*, 'was to have unfortunate results'[5] – as we shall see.

Field Marshal French had also taken some steps to minimize the chronic effects of the artillery shortage across his entire command. The divisional artillery had been taken from direct divisional control and placed in 'zones' all along the front. This was sensible, for divisions were always being moved between corps and their artillery would otherwise have had to constantly relay and register their guns on fresh targets. Now they provided gunfire support for a section of the front, whatever division was holding or attacking in that sector. French's second decision was to organize the heavy guns, those of 8-inch calibre and over, into Heavy Artillery Reserve (HAR) groups, from which they were allocated by GHQ to any army that had particular need of them.

But even these moves, however useful, could not make up for the basic fact that the BEF was very short of artillery, especially heavy artillery, and chronically short of shells, especially high-explosive shells. This last shortage was especially serious, for any phase of the advance, including those subsequent to the initial assault, depended on prior artillery preparation and the reduction of fixed defences. Haig's plan for Neuve Chapelle allowed for the fact that he had only enough artillery ammunition for three days of support; after that the attack must be called off.

In the artillery plan for the coming attack, the bombardment would start suddenly at 0730 hours. It would lift to reach beyond the enemy trenches at 0805 hours, when the British and Indian infantry assaulted the German front-line trenches before Neuve Chapelle and the Bois du Biez. The 'barrage' – the term adopted here for the first time – would then pound Neuve Chapelle for a further half-hour. That done and the enemy duly dismayed, the infantry would advance on the village at 0835 hours. While this was going on, the other units of First Army would act or 'demonstrate' on their front with rifle or artillery fire to indicate a pending attack and so prevent the Germans diverting reinforcements towards Neuve Chapelle. When the Neuve Chapelle position had been taken the troops would then press on, without delay, to Aubers Ridge.

As the above account illustrates, Haig made careful preparations for his attack and these arrangements cannot be seriously faulted. In battle things will go wrong – that 'no plan survives the first shot' is a tried and trusted military maxim. That maxim is no excuse for having a faulty plan in the first place or for leaving to chance any aspect of the attack that can be covered or catered for beforehand. Taking Haig's plan apart reveals few flaws and many attempts to cater for known difficulties – the communications problem and the problems of artillery observation in particular. It is fair to say that when the troops advanced to the attack at Neuve Chapelle, they were as well prepared as possible and working to a sensible, realistic plan, and Haig deserves full credit for this. It now remained to rest the troops and watch the weather before the order to launch the attack was given.

The infantry brigades charged with the initial assault – the Garhwal Brigade from the Meerut Division of the Indian Corps and 23rd and 25th Brigades from the 8th Division of IV Corps – were withdrawn from the line on 2 March for rest and field training, a reminder that trench warfare and open warfare were two very different skills.

This training included a careful briefing of every officer and man on what was to happen and what their units were to do. Supplies of ammunition, food and water were dumped close to the front and the guns duly registered the German front line.

The night of 9/10 March was wet, with steady rain and occasional snow flurries, but these cleared away after midnight and the order went out for the attack to proceed as planned. The three assault brigades duly came forward, stopping on the way for a hot meal and entering the forward trenches by 0430 hours. The front-line troops had already been active, opening gaps in the British wire, removing any obstacles likely to impede a rapid advance and digging a number of shallow jumping-off trenches for the assault troops.

The order to start the attack came from First Army HQ at 0630 hours, and at 0730 hours on 10 March 1915 the artillery of both corps opened fire on the German trenches before Neuve Chapelle. Ninety 18-pounders concentrated their fire on the German wire and the remainder, including howitzers, poured fire on the German parapets, at the rate of 100 shells a minute. This was observed fire on previously registered targets, except on the left of the 23rd Brigade, where the newly arrived siege batteries were charged with reducing the enemy line as best they could. So the opening barrage began, and thirty-five minutes later three brigades of British and Indian infantry went over the top and began to plod across the muddy fields towards the enemy line.

4

The Battle of Neuve Chapelle,
10–12 March 1915

The battle of Neuve Chapelle was the first planned British offensive. It demonstrated that a break-in was possible, under certain conditions.

British Official History, 1915, Vol. I, p. 151

THE OPENING STAGES of the attack went very well. There is no indication that the enemy were anticipating this assault, total surprise was achieved, and the initial bombardment, if short, had been heavy and accurate and had done its work well, levelling many parts of the German defences. The wire had been cut or tossed aside, trenches and breastworks had been destroyed. Those of the enemy who had not been killed or badly wounded by this fire had either fled or were too shocked to offer much resistance when the barrage lifted beyond Neuve Chapelle and the infantry went forward. All this was to the good, but an examination of the progress made by the various brigades, even at this early stage, shows the start of a growing problem.

The Indian Corps attack had quickly met misfortune. The Garhwal Brigade had sent four battalions forward on a 600-metre front to spearhead the advance north and west of Port Arthur. Unfortunately, two of the leading companies of the 1/39th Garhwal Rifles mistook their direction and came against a portion of the German line that lay outside the artillery zone. The wire here was uncut, the defence alert and the enemy greeted the Garhwalis with heavy fire. Although the Garhwalis pressed on through the wire and took the German front trench, they lost all six of their British officers and a considerable number of men in the process. Though holding this position, they were unable to continue the advance.

The other three battalions enjoyed better luck. The artillery had done its work and within twenty minutes of the order to move forward the Indians had crossed the 200-metre-wide no man's land, captured the German front-line and support trenches and reached the trench of the Smith-Dorrien line. This was found to be full of water so the Indians – Gurkhas, Garhwalis and men of the 2nd Leicestershire Regiment – dug in some 50 metres to the rear, with the 2nd Leicesters digging in along the line of the Layes brook. Unfortunately, no attempt was made to push forward beyond these obstacles in readiness for a further advance.

Nor was this all. That misdirection by the 1/39th Garhwalis had created a gap some 250 metres wide between that battalion and the 2nd Leicesters on their left. In the German trench spanning that gap about half a company of German soldiers from the 16th Infantry Regiment still held out and were now improving their defences and clearly determined to fight on. This information was passed back to Brigade and the 1st Seaforth Highlanders were ordered forward to deal with this situation, but that would take time.

In IV Corps, the 25th and 23rd Brigades of the 8th Division were doing well. The 25th Brigade, in its first action, advanced across no man's land to the left of the Indian Corps, passed the shattered wire and took the German first-line trench, all with little loss. The leading battalions – the 2nd Royal Berkshire and the 2nd Lincolnshire – then moved on to occupy the support trench about 200 metres west of Neuve Chapelle. The *Official History* comments that, 'As in the case of the three battalions of the Garhwal Brigade, they had demonstrated that a break in was possible, and without severe losses.'[1] So far, so good indeed; having arrived in the German support line at 0820 hours these battalions waited there while the artillery pounded the shocked defenders of Neuve Chapelle.

The bombardment lifted from the village at 0835 hours and the infantry advanced, clearing Neuve Chapelle by 0850 hours and then passing on to the country beyond, joining the Indian units on the Layes brook and the Smith-Dorrien line. By 0940 hours the 25th Brigade had reached its initial objectives and saw little sign of the enemy to their front. The CO of the 2nd Rifle Brigade therefore asked Brigade whether he should continue to advance but was informed that the 23rd Brigade on their left had been held up and for the moment no further advance was possible. This being so, the 25th Brigade dug in. Apart from the 1st Royal Irish Rifles, which had been enfiladed by machine-gun fire from the hamlet of Mauquissart on the Piètre road, casualties in the 25th Brigade had been light.

Not so in the 23rd Brigade. Their advance had been led by two battalions, the 2nd Scottish Rifles and the 2nd Middlesex, with the 2nd Devonshires in support, and the 2nd West Yorkshire in brigade reserve. The opposition to this brigade was small, consisting of two companies of the 11th Jäger Battalion. The artillery support for this 23rd Brigade included those two batteries of siege guns, which arrived only the previous day and had not been able to register their targets on the German line. Their bombardment therefore failed to either cut the wire or demolish the enemy emplacements, and the defenders here were fully alert.

As soon as they left their trenches, the 2nd Middlesex were met with heavy and accurate fire from the rifles and machine guns of the Jäger Battalion. The two leading companies were wiped out and the advance here was halted at 0830 hours while attempts were made to bring the guns back for another bombardment of the German line.

Matters had not gone much better for the Scottish Rifles on the right. They too met stubborn resistance to their front and enfilade fire from the Jäger Battalion currently punishing the Middlesex. The colonel of the Scottish Rifles was killed and seven other battalion officers became casualties; by 1000 hours the advance of the 23rd Brigade had been stopped and the men went to ground, attempting to shelter in shell holes.

Nor were the Germans simply enduring these infantry attacks. At 1000 hours, the VII Corps commander, General von Claer, ordered the 14th Division to reoccupy Neuve Chapelle[2] and detailed both infantry battalions and artillery, including heavy artillery, for this purpose. A request for more troops also went back to Sixth Army. This rapid reaction by the Germans contrasts with the delays that constantly inhibited the British and Indian attacks throughout the first day.

Even so, the first assault had gone well. The enemy line had been broken on a front of some 1,600 metres, Neuve Chapelle had been taken and both corps now had a line along the Smith-Dorrien trench east of the village. The current snags were that the Germans still held strong positions on either flank and were rushing up reserves, gathered in from divisions on their flanks. One other fact was already apparent; any advance depended on the prior preparation of the enemy position by shellfire. Where this had been provided Haig's attack had gone well; where, for any reason, the infantry had not been supported by artillery, the advance had been costly.

The next problem, however, was caused by a tactical error. Having advanced to the line of the Smith-Dorrien trench, the British attack halted and the men either occupied German positions or attempted to dig in where they were. This was a mistake, and the very one Haig had been most anxious to avoid; granted, there were gaps in the British line that needed closing and some mopping up of German resistance seemed called for, but this delay wasted some of that vital time given by the initial surprise and enabled the Germans to regroup. The leading battalions had carried out their orders, however; they had broken through the enemy front and support lines. Any further advance depended on the reserves.

While this attack had been in progress the reserve brigades of both divisions – the Dehra Dun Brigade from the Meerut Division and the 24th Infantry Brigade of the 8th Division – were coming forward and forming up in the former British front line. The assault brigades were ordered to consolidate and hold the ground gained while the reserve brigades took over the advance. The main concern now was the heavy machine-gun fire coming from those still-untaken enemy strongpoints on the flanks and an increasing weight of fire from German artillery positioned behind Aubers Ridge; this was now falling on Neuve Chapelle and the ground leading on to Aubers.

Delays were to dominate the attack at Neuve Chapelle and these delays were largely caused by failures in communication. At 0900 hours, hearing that the German line had been breached, Haig asked Field Marshal French to move at least one cavalry brigade forward so that if – or rather when – the enemy front collapsed, he would be able to harass the retreating Germans and prevent them digging in again.

Nothing happened for two hours. Then, at 1115 hours, Field Marshal French ordered the 5th Cavalry Brigade to move to Estaires, 5 kilometres north-west of Neuve Chapelle. There they would be in a good position to edge forward after the rest of IV Corps and the Indian Corps had advanced on Aubers Ridge . . . but again, nothing happened for several hours; neither the cavalry nor the reserve infantry brigades moved forward.

The crux of the problem was the difficulty of getting accurate information from the front-line units. General Rawlinson did not intend to move the rest of his corps forward until the situation on his front was clear, and throughout the morning he continued to believe that the German positions on his front were still untaken and a further advance unwise. Attempts were still being made to close the gap left by the 1/39th Garhwalis, and Rawlinson had come to believe that any advance on his left flank would be inhibited by German fire from a position known as The Orchard, a few hundred metres south-east of the Moated Grange, between the inner flanks of the 8th and 7th Divisions. The Orchard was stormed just after noon and found to be unoccupied – but this belief had caused further delay. With his 23rd and 25th Brigades now on their objectives, at 1330 hours General Davies ordered the 24th Brigade to prepare for a further advance.

Time, that precious time, was seeping away. General Rawlinson did not order the 7th Division to advance until 1315 hours, and it was not until 1400 hours, five hours after the German positions and strongpoints around Neuve Chapelle had been taken, that an advance towards Aubers Ridge actually began – only to stop again shortly afterwards, thanks to some confusion between IV Corps and the Indian Corps.

A delay had already occurred on the Indian Corps front, where General Willcocks was still encountering resistance from the German salient at Port Arthur, resistance that held the advance up until 1300 hours. At 1415 hours General Willcocks was also waiting for news of the IV Corps move before ordering his advance, for the two corps commanders were determined that their forces should advance on Aubers Ridge together; making this happen was rather more difficult.

At 1335 hours, Rawlinson telephoned Willcocks and said that the 7th Division was ready to advance and would move at 1400 hours. Willcocks replied that the Meerut Division was not yet ready to move, so Rawlinson decided to delay his advance until the Indians were ready. This information was passed to a worried General Haig at 1445 hours, but a few minutes later, much to Haig's relief, General Willcocks declared that his division *was* ready. Both corps then prepared to set out, the Indians to clear the Bois du Biez, IV Corps for Aubers Ridge.

The damage had been done, however. The initial attack had gone in at 0805 hours – it was now 1500 hours and the second phase of what should have been a continuous advance had only just begun. This seven-hour delay after the initial breakthrough allowed the Germans to muster some local reserves and dig in on a good position near the crest of Aubers Ridge, from where a heavy cross-fire from rifles and machine guns could rake any troops advancing from Neuve Chapelle.

It takes time to get a division moving, and the advance on Aubers Ridge did not actually begin until 1730 hours when two battalions of the 7th Division moved forward; other battalions from both corps did not move until 1800 hours, when it was already starting to get dark, and none got very far among the ditches and fences in open country or in among the thickets of the Bois du Biez.

The troops advancing across the open country between Neuve Chapelle and Aubers were soon under heavy fire and brought to a halt, and the Indian Corps, having advanced into the Bois du Biez, quickly encountered stiff resistance. By nightfall on 10 March, the attack at Neuve Chapelle had clearly stalled.

The reasons for this halt have already been described but are worth summarizing. The success of the Neuve Chapelle attack depended on surprise, artillery and rapid exploitation. Only one of these – surprise – had been fully delivered, and that advantage had now been squandered by delays, largely caused by communication problems. It now seemed more than likely that the advantage would pass to the Germans, who could be relied on to take full advantage of the exposed British position and punish any further advance.

To do this they were hurriedly improving and occupying the second-line position they had marked out on the ground in February. This ran about a kilometre behind their front line and when completed would have run from Mauquissart south across the Layes brook bridge and along the western edge of the Bois du Biez. Strongpoints along this line had been completed, including those at Mauquissart, the bridge and a group of ruined cottages on the eastern side of the Layes brook. All these would cause problems, and study of the map on page 49 will again be helpful.

This position and other positions had to be manned. On the first day the majority of the Germans defending Neuve Chapelle – about 1,400 men – had been lost, but fresh forces were being fed in from the flanks or rushed up by train from Lille and beyond; any British problems on the first day could only increase thereafter.

All that said, General Haig was not entirely displeased with the first day's work. Losses had not been heavy, at least by Western Front standards. The 25th Brigade had lost 781 officers and men, the 23rd Brigade 1,241 of all ranks. The Meerut Division had lost around a thousand officers and men, mostly from the Garhwal Brigade.

Some setbacks were only to be expected, and the First Army had advanced about 1,200 metres on a 4-kilometre front, pushed back the original German salient and taken Neuve Chapelle and the trench lines beyond it. They were now poised to advance on Aubers Ridge, and what should have been done today might still be done tomorrow. To help exploit this attack, Haig had ordered the 2nd Cavalry Division to follow the 5th Cavalry Brigade to Estaires, but Sir John French quickly cancelled this order. This division and the rest of the Cavalry Corps – containing a further two divisions – and the 46th Infantry Division stayed in their billets, miles from the battle.

During the night of 10/11 March, both sides were bringing up reinforcements and preparing to renew the struggle at dawn. The Germans brought up more machine guns, dug deeper trenches on their second line and reinforced the strongpoints. They also sent up a fresh formation, the 14th Bavarian Reserve Brigade from the 6th Bavarian Reserve Division, then based east of Lille, tasked to counter-attack and retake Neuve Chapelle at dawn. Fortunately for the British defending the village, this brigade was delayed, but other German units, including four infantry battalions, were being moved up by rail to seal this sudden breach in the line at Neuve Chapelle. The net result was that a line held by fewer than four German battalions on the morning of 10 March was held by sixteen battalions on the morning of 11 March.

Haig's orders for 11 March were to continue the attack. IV Corps was to press on towards Aubers Ridge, while the Indian Corps supported this attack with an advance through the Bois du Biez. This advance was to commence at 0700 hours and, said Haig, 'was to be pressed vigorously as from information received it appears the enemy before us is in no great strength'.

This 'information received' was increasingly out of date. RFC reconnaissance aircraft had seen German units marching towards Neuve Chapelle on the previous afternoon but had not sighted any troop trains. Haig had therefore assumed that any German reinforcements arriving overnight were battalions culled from local divisions already in the front line and therefore not numerous. In fact, the Germans were rushing troops forward from Artois and Ypres and their line at Aubers Ridge was growing stronger by the hour.

Haig's orders, issued at 2330 hours on 10 March, were for the advance to start again at 0700 hours and 'be pressed vigorously at all points'. Meanwhile, farther south, I Corps was to continue with supporting attacks with the object of capturing German trenches as far south as the La Bassée canal. The IV Corps attack would be supported by an artillery bombardment of Aubers Ridge, concentrating on the positions between Aubers and La Cliqueterie Farm, south of Aubers village, where the IV Corps line met that of the Indian Corps.

The main problem faced by the artillery that night might now be explained. To hit a target accurately, guns and batteries must be 'registered' on to it; that is, the gun sights must record the actual range and deflection from the battery position to the target. This has to be done by firing 'ranging shots' and then adjusting the gun sights – and therefore the shells – on to the enemy position, originally calculated by observation or from a map. Registering the guns takes time and depends entirely on the artillery observer being able to note the fall of shot around the enemy position and his ability to pass back corrections to the gun position.

Registration was not easy on 11 March; the enemy positions were either new or had previously been beyond the range of the British guns before 10 March, so fresh registration was now required. There was no time to do this on 10 March, it could not be done in the dark and the daylight on 11 March proved misty, concealing the ground from RFC observers – and there was also the chronic communications problem. As a result, when the infantry moved out at 0700 hours, most of the British artillery had not been able to range on the new German line and the infantry were greeted with a storm of machine-gun and artillery fire.

By daylight the German VII Corps had mustered their battalions to screen Aubers Ridge, all ready to stem the British advance. It should have been obvious to Haig and his corps commanders that with surprise lost and the enemy strength and defences improving, the task before the troops on the second day would be much harder than on the first day, and so it proved.

Visibility remained limited, making artillery registration on the fresh German trenches and artillery positions difficult, though the advancing British infantry quickly came under fire from German artillery and machine guns, firing shrapnel shells blindly into no man's land. In the 7th Division, the 20th Brigade lost heavily from this fire, while the men of the 21st Brigade were forced to halt and dig shallow holes in the muddy ground as shells and machine-gun fire raked their lines. Losses started to soar, the battalion commanders reporting back that unless the enemy positions could be reduced by shelling, a further advance was impossible.

In the 8th Division, the 24th Brigade was unable to move forward more than a few metres in the face of machine-gun fire. The German bombardment on the area of Neuve Chapelle was so heavy that all the telephone lines back to the artillery batteries were cut, and runners from the advancing battalions of the 7th and 8th Divisions were unable to move across the open ground to let the brigade commanders know what was going on. Fresh telephone lines had been run forward overnight but the German artillery fire that began just after dawn soon cut these and runners did not survive for long on this open ground. The *Official History* records that 'all telephone communications between the brigade headquarters and the battalions had broken down and messengers were unable to move across the open to the front trenches'.[3]

One effect of this communications breakdown was that messages ordering the guns to bring their fire back and pound the German defences were never delivered. The infantry therefore remained pinned down in the open while the supporting artillery barrage moved steadily away from them, anticipating an advance that was not taking place.

The same situation affected the Indian Corps, which met heavy resistance at the very start of the attack. This was compounded by a confusion over orders. The commander of the Dehra Dun Brigade (Lahore Division) had become convinced that he should not advance until the 25th Brigade of the 8th Division arrived on their flank at Neuve Chapelle. The 25th Brigade had actually been placed in divisional reserve so, as the *Official History* remarks, the Dehra Dun Brigade 'waited in vain for its arrival on their left'.[4]

The Jullundur Brigade had moved up and taken cover in and around Neuve Chapelle but otherwise the Indian Corps did not move at all that day. As communications broke down all along the front under the rain of shells and the sweep of machine-gun fire, so the second day's attacks petered out. The *Official History* provides one explanation for this dire situation: 'The breaking of all communications with the front line battalions by the German artillery bombardment and the time – *two or three hours* – taken by runners to get back with reports, made it difficult for the corps and divisional commanders to take any action during the morning.'

This delay played into the hands of the Germans, who had now managed to establish their second defence line in front of Aubers. Haig and his corps commanders were not yet aware of this, but even had they known the situation, the impossibility of contacting the front-line units, now isolated by German fire, would have prevented the mounting of another attack. The only order that went forward was the first one – that the attack 'must be pressed home vigorously'. This the leading brigades and battalions of both corps were already trying to do, supported by artillery that had not been able to register its guns on the new enemy line and therefore failed to hit it.

As a result, casualties were mounting swiftly. Realizing this, some battalion commanders were already ordering their men to stop advancing and dig in where they were. At 1450 hours, one commanding officer, Lieutenant Colonel Pritchard of the 1st Worcesters (24 Brigade, 8th Division), called off his attack entirely, telling his brigade commander bluntly that: 'It is a mere waste of life, impossible to go to 20 yards, much less 200 yards. The enemy trenches have not been touched by artillery.'

One can only admire Colonel Pritchard's courage in defying his superiors and calling off this attack, though he was entirely right to do so. The 24th Brigade had already suffered severe casualties, the 2nd Battalion, The Northamptonshire Regiment, having been reduced to twelve officers and 320 other ranks while the Sherwood Foresters had lost over three hundred men, more than a third of its strength. None of the battalions had made much progress towards Aubers Ridge. The same story was true for the Indian Corps, for which the word 'survivors' is frequently called into play to describe the remaining men in several battalions.

Another word that accurately describes the situation at Neuve Chapelle on the afternoon of 11 March is 'shambles'. The British attack had been halted. Communications had completely broken down, all the way from battalion up to corps, the artillery had still not been able to register on the new German positions, and the infantry were pinned down in the open and taking heavy losses; chaos was reigning at every level. The need to coordinate a viable plan for the second day of this battle had been thwarted by the fact that the commanders were unable to communicate with the assaulting battalions or to direct the artillery on to the German defences before Aubers.

The first day of this battle had gone roughly according to plan with no more than the usual upsets inevitable in any battle; on the second day the attack had quickly fallen apart. The action on the second day saw the advancing British and Indian infantry met with machine-gun and artillery fire from positions that had to be reduced by artillery before they could be overcome by any infantry attack . . . and delivering such fire was impossible.

Here again, the Official History recognizes this fact: 'It was clear that until the new German position could be prepared for assault by an effective bombardment, the prospects of a successful advance by the infantry were negligible.'[5] General Haig had now appreciated this. On the evening of 11 March, following a visit to the front line, he ordered the guns to be brought up closer to the front and ranged on the enemy trenches, intending to renew the attack towards Aubers Ridge at 1030 hours on the following morning. What perhaps he did not contemplate was what the enemy might be doing.

The usual answer to an attack is a counter-attack. Such a counter-attack was currently being prepared as the Germans brought six fresh battalions of Saxon and Bavarian troops into the line on the night of 11/12 March and prepared to push the British back on a front between Mauquissart and the Bois du Biez. With other units arriving from the flanking units, by dawn on the 12th the Germans had ten battalions in the front line before Aubers Ridge, a force estimated at some 16,000 men, poised to attack with the bayonet and without any prolonged artillery preparation. This attack was delivered at 0500 hours, after a violent half-hour's bombardment. The Germans were relying on surprise and initially they were lucky; mist again shrouded the battle-field and the German infantry were within 55 metres of the British line before they were detected.

Even so, this German counter-attack failed, with heavy losses. As had happened with the British and Indians on the previous day, the German infantry wilted before the rifle and machine-gun fire of the British and Indian soldiers. This German attack at least disproves the popular allegation that sending in waves of infantry to take well-defended positions was a tactic peculiar to the British generals – the donkeys.

The German attack left over four hundred dead before the trench of the 1st Sherwood Foresters alone, though the losses were not all on one side; the Sherwood Foresters had already lost half their officers – sixteen – and 342 men. Another 200 Germans lay before the trench lines of the Garhwal Rifles and another hundred before the trenches occupied by the 2nd Green Howards. The few survivors of the German attack on the 2nd Northamptonshires retired to their trenches, as the *Official History* puts it, 'pursued by bullets and losing heavily'.[6]

By 0730 hours the enemy's counter-attack had been heavily defeated, but poor communications between divisional and brigade HQs and the front-line battalions meant that this repulse was not followed up; no attempt was made to advance and overrun the German defences and so another opportunity to regain the initiative was lost. General Haig was determined to stick to his original plan for a set-piece attack towards Aubers Ridge; he would not be diverted from this aim by any local success.

The problem with continuing the attack centred on the artillery. Visibility was restricted, for the mist that had concealed the German advance at dawn still concealed the German positions a few hours later. The British artillery observers were therefore reduced to 'firing off the map', with no idea where their shells were actually falling and no information from which to correct the fall of shot. The British attack was due to go in at 1030 hours after a half-hour bombardment of the enemy line, but at 0920 hours General Rawlinson reported that certain German strongpoints on his front had not yet been subdued. Haig therefore put back the attack until 1120 hours to allow time for the mist to clear and the artillery to engage the German line accurately. There was then a further delay, and the assault finally went in at 1230 hours – and was soon in trouble.

In 8th Division's sector, the 25th Brigade lost heavily in the first half-hour; the artillery barrage had not been accurate so the wire before the German strongpoint on the Layes bridge was still uncut and covered by the fire of at least fifteen machine guns. Brigadier General Lowry Cole therefore halted the attack and told his divisional commander, Major General Davies, that it was pointless to attack again until dark. The other assault brigade, Brigadier Carter's 24th Brigade, had not fully reorganized after repulsing the German counter-attack and did not attack at all, while the last brigade in the division, the 23rd Brigade, remained in divisional reserve on the Armentières road.

On the 7th Division front, all the runners had been killed, so the message postponing the attack did not reach the leading battalions. The two leading battalions, 2nd Scots Guards and 2nd Border Regiment, therefore advanced at 1030 hours without any artillery support and were quickly brought to a halt by machine-gun fire from a German position known as the Quadrilateral, west of Mauquissart, after advancing only 90 metres. The order delaying the advance until 1230 hours was held up as they lay pinned down in the open under artillery fire.

Fortunately, the 7th Division artillery then took a hand, and their guns were accurate. While these guns pounded the German defences, the Guards and the Border infantry crept forward and finally advanced on the Quadrilateral with the bayonet, taking some four hundred prisoners. Once again, though, communications between the front line and divisional HQ broke down, and this led to further confusion as to the extent and location of the 7th Division in this advance towards Aubers Ridge. In fact, by 1310 hours the 7th Division advance had stopped on the line of the Mauquissart road, north of Neuve Chapelle.

The advance of the Indian Corps began at 1300 hours, half an hour after the attack by IV Corps. After half an hour of artillery fire on the German positions, the two leading formations, the Sirhind and Jullundur Brigades of the Lahore Division, pushed towards the Bois du Biez. They quickly encountered heavy machine-gun fire from the Layes bridge redoubt, and by 1345 hours, barely half an hour after advancing, these brigades had been brought to a halt.

Confusion was now starting to grip the staff at Haig's HQ, where messages recounting the repulse of the German counter-attack that morning were only now being absorbed, giving Haig's staff the erroneous impression that matters were now going well. The notion that the 7th Division had actually succeeded in breaking through the German defences along the Mauquissart road north of Neuve Chapelle had taken hold, and at 1506 hours Haig sent an order to his troops for a further attack: 'Information indicates that enemy on our front are much demoralized. Indian Corps and IV Corps will push through barrage of fire regardless of loss, using reserves if required.'

Why General Haig thought that the Germans were 'demoralized' is difficult to say, but a degree of self-delusion seems probable; there is an understandable, if dangerous, tendency for battlefield commanders to believe good news and reject any evidence countering that impression. The order to attack 'regardless of loss' was both unwise and unworkable – if casualties are too high an attack cannot be sustained – but these statements indicate that, probably frustrated by the delays in communication, Haig wished to take advantage of this 'promising situation' when – at least according to reports from 7th Division HQ – there was a gap in the German line.

These communication delays and the garbled nature of much of the information delivered were largely due to the state of communications in 1915 and technical deficits, which were not Haig's fault. In 1915, battlefield communications were primitive, aerial observation by RFC patrols was inhibited by mist and shell smoke hanging over the battlefield, and runners did not live long on ground swept by machine-gun fire.

For the last two days Haig had been trying to push his men forward quickly and so retain the initiative, only to be thwarted by a constant succession of delays. The information reaching him now seemed to indicate a breach in the enemy line, and if that was so a rapid advance all along the line was the right thing to attempt, but it must be made quickly, before the enemy regrouped following the failure of their morning counter-attack.

Haig therefore asked Field Marshal French to send the cavalry forward, and told the infantry divisions to prepare for a general advance. Unfortunately, thanks to the mist and the chronic lack of accurate information, this intention was based on a false premise; the new German line before Aubers Ridge had not been breached at all.

Owing to the inevitable delays in passing orders forward, the attacks went in late, as dusk was falling. It was not until 1700 hours that the Ferozepore Brigade, the reserve unit for the Lahore Division, advanced on the Bois du Biez, while further delays in organizing artillery support held up the advance of the Sirhind and Jullundur Brigades of the same division. This last brigade had already suffered nearly nine hundred casualties during the attacks that day, about half of its rifle strength, and was in no state for further action. Any advance by the Ferozepore Brigade was inhibited by fire from that strongpoint on the Layes bridge, east of Neuve Chapelle.

Inevitably, the time for this fresh attack was put back, first to 2030 hours and then to 2230 hours. Brigadier General R. G. Egerton, commanding the Ferozepore Brigade, then telephoned his divisional commander, General Willcocks, and stated that in his opinion an attack over unreconnoitred ground and in the dark was unlikely to succeed. General Willcocks agreed with this opinion – and cancelled the attack entirely.

Similar events were taking place on the IV Corps front. The corps artillery was growing short of ammunition and did not fire on the Mauquissart road line, believing that it was already in British hands. The 25th Brigade attacked as ordered at 1745 hours, only to report back within minutes that the attack had failed. Every man who attempted to advance had been shot down, though the brigade commander, Lowry Cole, declared that he was willing to try again under cover of darkness.

The other 8th Division formations, the 23rd and 24th Brigades, put in a confused night attack at 0130 hours on the night of 12/13 March, after more delay caused by difficulties in rounding up the battalion commanders for briefing. Once again the result was chaos and loss; the companies that did attack ran into barbed wire and machine-gun fire and the assault was quickly cancelled. The rest of the night was spent by the brigade and battalion commanders trying to find out what was going on, a task made more difficult by the fact that after three days and nights without rest, the men went to sleep whenever they stopped, and were hard to find on the corpse-littered battle-ground. The IV Corps commander, General Rawlinson, realized that after three days of battle his troops were exhausted and would need rest and reorganization before they could be used again.

General Haig was coming to the same conclusion. It was now clear that the German positions before Aubers Ridge had not been breached and that the enemy had managed to construct a new line and were reinforcing it by the hour. At 2240 hours on 12 March Haig ordered that all attacks should now be cancelled; the troops should dig in and hold the positions they now occupied. This order took some time to reach the forward troops, with the result that local attacks were still being put in hours after the battle of Neuve Chapelle had been called off.

During 13 March, Haig and his commanders had the opportunity to look around and see what had been accomplished in three days of costly fighting. At its widest point, astride Neuve Chapelle, the British line had been pushed west for perhaps 1,000 metres, eliminating the former German salient. Neuve Chapelle was now in British hands and the British front line now ran from just south of the crossroads at Port Arthur, north and west to cut the Layes brook and the Smith-Dorrien line, embracing the Moated Grange and cutting the Mauquissart road. The shallow German salient had been pushed back but the Bois du Biez and Aubers Ridge, that dry and much-desired objective, still lay in German hands.

In return for these slender gains, the First Army had lost 583 officers and 12,309 other ranks. The heaviest casualties fell in the 8th Division, which lost 4,814 officers and men, more than twice the total of the 7th Division's losses, 2,791 men, or the Meerut Division's 2,353. German losses were estimated at around 12,000, including 1,657 German prisoners. Put together, the total losses, German, British and Indian, in the three days of fighting for an insignificant objective, came to some 25,000 men.

The *Official History* account of Neuve Chapelle was not published until 1927 and therefore enjoys the benefits of hindsight, not least in pointing out that given sufficient artillery support a breakthrough was possible. This appears to be true, but a breakthrough is only the start of the battle and arguably not the most important part. If the breakthrough is to offer any advantage it must be exploited and the objective of the breakthrough achieved.

In this case the objectives were to impress the French and gain the higher ground of Aubers Ridge. The second objective was not achieved and evidence to support achievement of the first objective is somewhat scanty – even assuming that impressing the French was a worthwhile aim in the first place, let alone at the cost of 12,892 casualties. If the loss of over 80,000 British soldiers between Mons and First Ypres in 1914 had not convinced the French that the British soldiers were suited for war, it is hard to see how the sacrifice of another 12,000 men would change their minds.

The *Official History* thought otherwise, however, claiming that the battle at Neuve Chapelle enhanced the reputation of the British Army in France and demonstrated the offensive capability of British troops. It also, allegedly, impressed the enemy, for this was the first time the German front line had been broken. All in all, though, it is hard to avoid the conclusion that Neuve Chapelle was a costly failure.

As a result, after the battle there was a certain amount of buck-passing among the commanders. On 16 March, Rawlinson sent a message to Haig, complaining about the conduct of Major General Davies, commander of the 8th Division, who, said Rawlinson, had failed to push on quickly after taking Neuve Chapelle on the morning of 10 March. Haig supported this allegation and proposed to Field Marshal French that Davies be relieved of his command and sent back to the UK.

Later that day, however, another letter arrived from Rawlinson, including one from Davies, the latter pointing out that Rawlinson himself had postponed the advance from Neuve Chapelle until 1530 hours. In his letter, Rawlinson now took full responsibility, and Haig duly wrote to French, cancelling the request for Davies's dismissal. The truth is, said Haig, that Rawlinson 'was trying to put the blame on him for the delay. Rawlinson is unsatisfactory in this respect, loyalty to his subordinates'.[7]

The reasons for failure at Neuve Chapelle should be analysed and the first point worth making is that this was, as the *Official History* points out, 'the first planned British offensive' of the war. The battles of 1914, even First Ypres, had been scrambled affairs, forced on the BEF by the need to stem the enemy advances. Clearly, the British commanders still had a lot to learn about the set-piece battle, but the initial plan for the attack is hard to fault. Surprise was achieved and the initial objectives were taken; only then did matters go awry. Unlike their French and German opposite numbers trained in mass armies in peacetime, many of the British formation commanders, from Haig down, were commanding at that level in battle for the first time, and had not had the benefit of doing so on peacetime exercises, so were at the bottom of a steep learning curve.

The main problem was delay, largely caused by communication difficulties. These led to constant hold-ups and provided the enemy with enough time to reorganize, prepare a new line and bring up reserves. As the *Official History* points out: 'Given that the front of attack was wide enough to make it impossible for small local reserves to deal with the situation, success was shown to be a time problem.'[8]

The battlefield commanders cannot be held responsible for the state of battlefield communications in 1915. These were a problem – and would remain a problem until the battalions and brigades were equipped with wireless sets. Communication problems caused difficulties between the commanders and the sub-units and between the artillery observers and the guns, and this led to confusion and a lack of the necessary artillery support, which the commanders were most anxious to supply.

The delays greatly helped the Germans, who were able to bring up reserves and seal off the breach, but the tenacity of some German front-line units, notably the men holding the Layes brook strongpoint, should not be overlooked; they showed how a few men armed with automatic weapons could hold up a far stronger force attempting to move in the open.

One point emerges clearly, the one anticipated before the attack began; success depended on artillery support. That support was never sufficient; there were either not enough guns, or not enough guns of the right calibre, or the guns had not registered on the right targets.

They also used unexpected amounts of ammunition. Taking the 18-pounder guns as an example, in three days of battle they fired an average of 245 shells, which was one sixth of all the 18-pounder ammunition available for the entire BEF and represented seventeen days' full-scale production of 18-pounder shells from the munitions factories in the UK. On 13 March, the day after the battle, Field Marshal French claimed that a shortage of artillery ammunition was one of the reasons for calling off the attack, the other being the exhaustion of the troops.

Neuve Chapelle was an attempt to make the old, traditional methods of warfare work. Unfortunately, while these methods did not lead to victory, they worked well enough to encourage the British commanders to try such methods again, not realizing that the old ways – artillery bombardment followed by an infantry advance and cavalry exploitation – would never work against the dire defensive combination of wire and trenches manned by resolute opponents equipped with automatic weapons. Perhaps further losses would be necessary to drive this harsh fact home, and these would soon appear. But then, on 22 April, while Haig was still hankering for the higher, drier ground of Aubers Ridge, the Germans struck hard at the Second Army along the salient at Ypres.

5

Gas! The Start of Second Ypres, 22–23 April 1915

Apart from the usual disabilities of a salient, the situation of the Allies at Ypres was distinctly weak; they possessed superior numbers but were very inferior in heavy guns and means of artillery observation.

British Official History, 1915, Vol. II, p. 162

THE SECOND BATTLE of Ypres, which began on 22 April 1915, is the most memorable Western Front battle of 1915. There are two reasons for this significance. First, at Second Ypres it was the Germans, not the Franco-British armies, who did the attacking. Second, the German attack was marked by a massive discharge of chlorine gas, so introducing a new element to the existing horrors of total war.

Gas had previously been regarded as a forbidden weapon, its use declared 'contrary to the laws and usages of war'. The use of gas, both poison and asphyxiating, had been prohibited on these grounds by Article 23(A) of the 1907 Hague Convention respecting the Laws and Customs of War on Land. This prohibition built on a previous agreement to ban the use of gas drawn up at The Hague in 1899. The very existence of these prohibitions indicates that the use of gas had been at least contemplated before the turn of the century and in the context of total war, *circa* 1914, it is hardly surprising that gas was soon brought into play. Even so, its use at the battle of Ypres in April 1915 took the Franco-British armies completely by surprise and without any equipment available to mitigate its effects.

This neglect was an error, for signs that the Germans were preparing to use gas had been increasing in the days before the first gas cloud rolled over the French lines. Reports of the Germans using gas on the Eastern Front had been made early in 1915, and on 15 April, a report warning of a pending German gas attack on the Western Front was sent on to French's GHQ by Second Army.

This report had been sent to Smith-Dorrien's HQ by the British liaison officer at the headquarters of General Putz, who commanded the Détachement de Belgique, a formation consisting of two French divisions, the 45th Algerian and the 87th Territorial, both currently tasked with holding the northern edge of the Ypres salient from Langemarck to the Belgian border. The report originated with a Belgian source described as 'a reliable agent', as well as from the interrogation of a German prisoner captured near Langemarck.

Reliable or not, no action seems to have been taken on this report, perhaps because the night attack allegedly due on 15/16 April failed to materialize and General Putz sent this information to Second Army with the comment that he did not believe it. The report deserved closer attention, for the details supplied by the German prisoner were quite specific – for example, that the gas would be released from tubes deployed at 40-metre intervals along the German line at Ypres rather than from shells – and he carried a primitive form of gas mask in his pocket. A lack of Allied liaison may have caused this neglect, for on 30 March the bulletin of the French Tenth Army had contained a report claiming that the enemy intended to use gas along the front at Zillebeke. No one, apparently, put these two pieces of intelligence together.

On 16 April another report, probably from a spy behind the German lines, reported that the Germans in Ghent had manufactured 20,000 'mouth protectors' which, when soaked in some suitable liquid, would provide some protection against asphyxiating gas. This report was sent to GHQ and on to Second Army and then to General Plumer's V Corps. General Plumer duly circulated this information to his divisional commanders with the dismissive comment that he sent it 'for what it is worth'.

Then came an interesting development. On 17 April the Germans circulated a radio report alleging that on the previous day the British had employed gas in bombs and shells at Ypres. This report was a typical German trick, another example of the enemy 'getting their retaliation in first', a common political ploy. In August 1914, for example, as the war opened, the Germans had alleged that the French had violated Belgian territory and that French aircraft had crossed the German frontier. Neither accusation was true, but the allegation was being used for propaganda purposes and to justify German violations. Had anyone taken the time or trouble to analyse it, this German claim on the British use of gas might have provided further proof that the Germans were preparing to use it. In the event, none of this intelligence was used and the German gas attack at Ypres on 22 April came as a complete surprise.

The battle of Second Ypres lasted from 22 April to 25 May. As with many of these Great War engagements, this period has been broken down into a series of specific 'battles', starting with the battle of Gravenstafel Ridge at the end of April and ending with the battle of Bellewaarde Ridge at the end of May, with several other 'battles' around the salient in between. All these battles took place in or on the edge of the Ypres salient, and any understanding of these battles – a better word is 'operations' – should begin with a study of the ground.

The Ypres salient has often been described as resembling a saucer. This is a fair description, up to a point, for to the east of the town of Ypres a ridge some 70 metres high forms the saucer rim. This ridge runs raggedly round the edge of the salient, from Langemarck in the north, round and due east through Poelcappelle and then south to Passchendaele on the eastern edge. The ridge then continues south to Polygon Wood, where it turns west and forms a southern boundary through Sanctuary Wood to Hill 60. The dip in the centre of this saucer contains the old cloth town of Ypres and the western boundary from Hill 60 north to Boesinghe and Steenstraat is formed by the Ypres canal. Study of the Ypres map on page 86 will be essential at this point, and time should be taken to locate as many of the points in and around the salient as possible. It is worth pointing out that while many salients were created during the Great War there was only one known as 'the salient' – at Ypres.

The salient also resembles a bicycle wheel, if the spokes are imagined as the various ridges and valleys running in from the rim towards Ypres. The ridges carry roads such as the Menin road and the Zillebeke road, while the valleys contain drainage ditches and streams known locally as 'beeks' – the Steenbeek, for example.

Before 22 April, the Belgian and French armies – the latter consisting only of the two-division-strong Détachement de Belgique under General Putz – held a line that ran from the North Sea to Steenstraat on the canal and then on to just south of Langemarck, where General Horace Smith-Dorrien's Second Army took over. The Second Army held the line under the eastern face of the salient ridge, all the way south past Broodseinde into Polygon Wood and across the Menin Road to Hill 60. For the last 5 kilometres of this line, the Second Army lay south of the ridge – a study of the map on page 86 will again be helpful.

At the beginning of April, Field Marshal French had given in to Joffre's constant demands and taken on another 8 kilometres of front at Ypres, from the Menin Road at Gheluvelt to the Poelcappelle road beyond Zonnebeke. After this move the BEF front ran for 48 kilometres north of Cuinchy to the Menin Road, a continuous line with no French units intervening. Within the salient, the Second Army's line was held by Plumer's V Corps, with the 1st Canadian Division linking up on its left flank with the French 45th Algerian Division. South of the Canadians the line was held by the 28th, 27th, 5th and 3rd Divisions, which manned the front as far south as Wytschaete. Altogether, the Second Army occupied a front of some 16 kilometres.

Field Marshal French's arguments with the French did not fully divert him from that other preoccupation, his long-standing vendetta against General Smith-Dorrien. On 12 March, during the battle of Neuve Chapelle, French had ordered Smith-Dorrien to mount a diversionary local attack at Wytschaete on the southern edge of the Ypres salient; the failure of this attack provided French with yet another opportunity to denigrate his subordinate. On the following day, writes Henry Wilson, 'I went out to Cassel to pick up Foch and we went on to the Schaffenberg to see Sir John. He was up there to pitch into Smith-Dorrien for his attack yesterday had failed; but my sympathies were with Smith-Dorrien who had not sufficient time to prepare, nor guns nor ammunition nor infantry, to carry it out. His attack in front of Wytschaete, therefore failed.'[1]

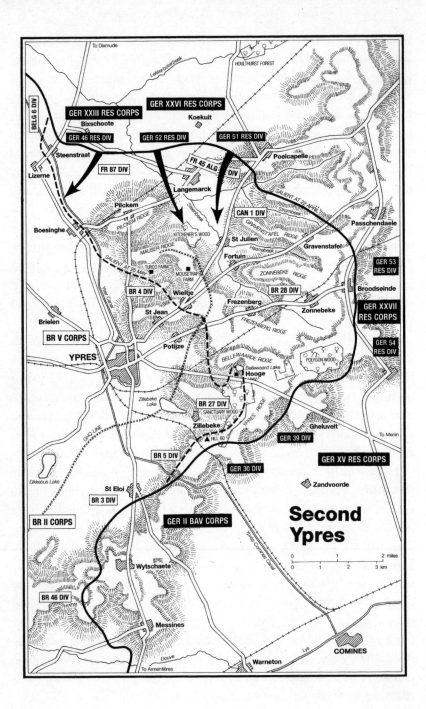

So too had Douglas Haig's attack on the same day, and with more serious losses, but French did not 'pitch into' the First Army commander.

When V Corps took over the French line they found it well wired but otherwise in a deplorable condition, consisting in the main of low, sandbagged breastworks and shallow fire and support trenches. Fortunately, the French had also started to construct another position west of the main front line, a trench running from the Zillebeke lake towards Mauser Ridge, effectively straddling the 'nose' of the salient east of Ypres. This line, known to the BEF as the 'GHQ Line', ran 3 kilometres behind the front line at Zillebeke, widening to 5 kilometres behind that line at Mauser Ridge. This GHQ Line was well constructed, a series of dugouts and strongpoints, 500 or 600 metres apart, each designed for a platoon garrison of around thirty men, with good fields of fire and a strong barbed-wire hedge, 2 metres wide, on the eastern side.

Should the main line be breached, the GHQ Line would provide a good fallback or second-line position, but the main salient ridge was the only truly tenable position east of Ypres. The salient ridge was not high but, like Hill 60, it offered the troops who held it the precious and priceless advantage of observation. He who held the ridge had the troops and guns and roads inside the salient at his mercy, under shellfire by day and night, with every movement observed.

Important as the ridge was, however, some other features would become important during the battle of Second Ypres, not least the valleys and ridges that run into the salient from the outer rim. These are also shown on the map opposite, on which Mauser Ridge, the Gravenstafel Ridge, the Frezenberg Ridge and Pilckem Ridge are particularly important. As elsewhere along the current BEF front, the water table in the salient – if not within the ridge – was very high; men digging trenches within the salient struck water at less than a metre.

Finally, there are some particular points to note, places like Hill 60 at the southern end of the salient, a hill – actually a low mound 60 metres above sea level, hence the name – formed from spoil extracted from the nearby railway cutting, and now a useful observation post. The

Germans had captured Hill 60 in December, and when the regular 28th Division took over the line in February, their first task was to retake this valuable position. The subsequent actions here might therefore be briefly described.

Attempts to retake Hill 60, mostly by mining, were still in hand when the 28th Division was taken out of the line in April and replaced by the 5th Division, which directed the 13th Infantry Brigade to retake the Hill with a ground attack supported by the explosion of mines. These mines duly exploded at 1905 hours on 17 April; troops of the 1st Royal West Kents attacked and were on the hilltop in a matter of minutes. Other units of the 13th Brigade followed and proceeded to dig in, but holding the hill was to prove much harder than taking it.

Heavy shellfire from howitzers descended on the hill, including shells containing tear gas, and several hours of bombardment were followed by infantry attacks lasting from midnight until dawn. These attacks continued throughout the following day, the day after that . . . and the day after that . . . and so onwards. Hill 60 became a charnel house, a shell-pocked heap of raw earth littered with corpses and dismembered bodies. Fighting for this position continued without pause and was still raging when the main gas attack began farther north on 22 April.

The German units hemming in the salient at this time came from four corps of the Duke Albrecht von Württemberg's Fourth Army, the VIIth, the XIXth, the II Bavarian and the XXVII Reserve, together mustering eleven and a half divisions. These corps were well supplied with artillery; over two hundred guns were in the line, many of them heavy and some, notably one of 17-inch and another of 15-inch calibre, very heavy. Even without the use of gas, the Germans at Ypres would be able to launch a devastating attack at any portion of the BEF line.

It appears, however, from the orders of the German Supreme Command, that the prime purpose of the attack on 22 April 1915 was not to gain ground but to try out the effects of gas. Von Falkenhayn selected Ypres, at the northern end of the Western Front, in order to take advantage of the northerly winds that prevailed there in the early spring. The gas was to be discharged from cylinders positioned in the German front-line trenches and a strong wind was required to carry the 'heavier-than-air' gas across no man's land into the Allied trenches. As we shall see, this method of spreading the gas proved unreliable. Before long the enemy had switched to the use of gas shells, which could drench the Allied positions with gas without it seeping back into the German trenches or asphyxiating the wounded in no man's land. The area chosen for the first use of gas stood at the junction between General Putz's detachment and the 1st Canadian Division of the BEF, a formation that should now be introduced.

The 1st Canadian Division was raised in Canada soon after the out-break of war, and after training in Britain disembarked at St-Nazaire on 15 February 1915, before being sent to join Smith-Dorrien's Second Army in the Ypres salient.

The 1st Canadian Division was typical of many dominion units at this time, in that it contained a large number of British-born soldiers. According to the Canadian historian Daniel Dancocks, of the 30,617 soldiers in the 1st Division – the 1st Division was a very large forma-tion – almost twenty thousand were British-born, many of them being recent migrants to the dominion. Empire ties were strong at this time, so their motivation is understandable; the 'Old Country' needed soldiers and they were responding to her call.

A considerable number of the men in the 1st Canadian Division had previously served in the British Army. Indeed, in one regiment, the Princess Patricia's Canadian Light Infantry (PPCLI), prior mili-tary experience was a qualification for enlistment; no fewer than 1,049 recruits out of the 1,089 enlisted in the PPCLI had formerly served in the British Army.

This division was the first formation of what became the Canadian Corps, effectively the Field Army of the Dominion of Canada and one of the great fighting contingents of the First World War. The Canadians' first commander, Lieutenant General Edwin Alderson, was a British officer, an efficient trainer of troops and a wise choice for this command. Alderson had served with Canadians in the South African War of 1899–1902 and the Canadians liked and trusted him. His brigadiers were all Canadian and their number included Arthur

Currie, a territorial officer who would became one of the Great War's most noted battlefield commanders.

Currie is worth noting not simply because he was a great soldier but because he illustrates the nature and character of such rare individuals. Learning to soldier is fairly easy but becoming a 'good soldier', with all that term implies, requires some natural aptitude. Soldiering is to some extent an art and like other arts you have to have a feeling for it. Anyone can learn how to paint, but that will not make him or her Rembrandt. Anyone can learn to play the piano, but they will not usually play like Paderewski, however much they practise. With soldiering, as with the arts, there comes a point where you either 'have it' or you don't; whatever the quality is, you probably have to be born with it and Arthur Currie 'had it' to his fingertips.

Arthur Currie was not a professional soldier. Before the war he had been a territorial officer in Victoria, British Columbia, where he made a thin living as a self-employed 'realtor' – an estate agent – and devoted his spare time to soldiering. When the war broke out in August 1914, Currie was a lieutenant colonel in command of a local militia battalion, the 50th Gordon Highlanders of Canada, and making a very good job of it. He was also concealing a crime.

Currie had been speculating heavily in gold shares, but the expected rewards had not appeared; by the summer of 1914 Arthur Currie was on the verge of bankruptcy. He therefore decided to bridge the gap in his finances by peculation, stealing 11,000 Canadian dollars from the regimental funds to gain time. His finances still did not improve and Currie could not repay the money. He had hoped for a command that would keep him occupied until he could put the money back, but his theft of the funds was already known to one of his officers, Major Garnet Hughes, the son of Sam Hughes, Canada's Minister of Militia and a powerful man in Canadian politics.

Fortunately, Major Hughes was also fully aware of Currie's military abilities. He wrote to his father in praise of Colonel Currie with the result that Sam Hughes offered Currie promotion to brigadier and command of the 2nd Infantry Brigade in the 1st Canadian Division. Currie duly sailed for Europe with the money unpaid and the fear of discovery constantly preying on his mind. 'It was', he said later, 'the first thought that struck me when I woke in the morning and the last thought in my mind when I turned in at night.'

Unknown to Currie, his theft of the regimental funds had already been discovered by the authorities. Before sailing for Britain, Currie had written to a close friend, Arthur Matson, recounting what he had done and stating that he only needed time to pay the money back. Matson wrote to the Canadian prime minister, Sir Robert Borden, enclosing Currie's letter and begging the premier to delay any investigation – and allow Currie the necessary time. Fortunately, Borden had met Currie and had formed a high opinion of his abilities; the premier therefore declined to act when other letters arrived in his office, demanding that Currie be arrested for theft and put on trial.

The missing money was not finally repaid until September 1917 and the theft was to dog Currie's reputation for the rest of his life, but this affair does give some idea of Currie's basic character. He was a gambler, willing to take risks. He had a steady nerve and was not easily distracted from the task in hand. He was by no means a donkey. He also had the ability to attract the attention and approval of his superiors and subordinates; all these assets were to prove useful in France as the Canadian Division prepared for war.

Arthur Currie did not look much like a soldier. In 1914 he was thirty-eight years old, stood over 1.8 metres tall and weighed an imposing 113 kilograms. Unfortunately he was pear shaped, with no discernible waist and several chins, his belly bulging over his belt and straining at the buttons. Currie failed to impress at first sight, but people soon came to like and respect him. 'His sincerity and forcefulness was [sic] marked, he was good-natured, natural, cheerful, imperturbable,' wrote Colonel Birchall Wood, a British officer attached to the Canadian headquarters.

Since the other two brigadiers were not noted for any outstanding qualities, Arthur Currie was quickly recognized as the finest subordinate commander in the 1st Canadian Division. 'Currie is out and out the best of the Brigadiers,' said his new commanding officer, Lieutenant General Alderson, and great things were expected from Currie when the Canadian Division reached the front.

As was customary with new units, the Canadians were introduced to the front line via brief attachments to experienced British formations. On 1 March 1915 the Canadian Division went to Rawlinson's IV Corps in Douglas Haig's First Army and took over a section of the line. They then took a small part in the battle at Neuve Chapelle, aiming harassing fire on the German line; only then was it discovered that their 303-calibre Ross rifles, manufactured in Canada, tended to jam when used for rapid fire or when coated with mud.

The Ross rifle was clearly inferior to the British Short Magazine Lee-Enfield (SMLE) and should have been quickly replaced, but, as previously noted, SMLE rifles were still in very short supply. This defect had not been made good when the Canadians went north to join Plumer's V Corps in Second Army, and the Canadians were still equipped with this inadequate personal weapon when the Germans launched the second battle of Ypres, using gas and artillery to tear a breach in the Allied line.

April 22 1915 was recorded as a quiet day with very little shelling after a brief bombardment of Ypres by the German artillery during the morning. At 1700 hours, however, the German guns started up again, with shells falling on the wrecked town, on the villages within the salient and most notably at the junction of the Franco-Canadian line, north-east of Ypres. French field guns, mostly 75-mms, began to reply, but then those looking towards Langemarck saw a curious, greenish-yellow cloud billowing out of the German trenches and starting to seep across no man's land towards the French line.

The first people to appreciate what this cloud consisted of were two Canadian medical officers, a Colonel Naismith and Captain Scrimger. They were riding behind the divisional lines when they saw this strange cloud away to the north and got their first acrid whiff of chlorine. Realizing this meant a gas attack, they quickly worked out a temporary and unusual solution.

Word was rushed to the Canadian trenches, advising the troops that to combat the effect of this gas they should urinate on a handkerchief, fold it into a pad and keep it over their noses and mouths while the gas persisted. Uric acid causes chlorine gas to crystallize, and this hastily adopted measure worked, enabling at least some of the

Canadian infantry to hold their ground when it spread into their lines. The French colonial troops on their left flank were not so fortunate.

This gas cloud seemed to be joining up as it flowed slowly south and west, and the sound of rifle fire indicated that enemy infantry was coming forward behind it. The 'swimming pool' smell of chlorine was soon being noticed miles behind the British front, but real concern began when swarms of French soldiers, in some chaos and without any apparent leadership, were observed running to the rear. These men were Algerians from the 45th Division, and while their language could not be understood, their streaming eyes, choking and general desperation made the problem abundantly clear.

They had been gassed and, having no means to combat this new terror, had promptly taken to their heels. Any resistance to the German infantry advance was now being provided by the '75s' of the French artillery, but at 1900 hours these guns too suddenly fell silent. Except for a battalion of Zouaves and another of Tirailleurs in position next to the Canadians, the 45th Division had broken – and a great gap had been created in the Allied line on the northern side of the salient.

Brigadier General R. W. Turner of the 3rd Canadian Infantry Brigade, the Second Army formation next to the Algerian 45th Division, quickly appreciated the seriousness of this attack. Turner had two battalions in the line and ordered his reserve battalion, the 14th, into the line to cover the village of St-Julien, well inside the existing front line and halfway towards the GHQ Line. This falling-back manoeuvre, known as 'refusing a flank', was made just in time to stop the Germans advancing behind the gas cloud north of St-Julien, but the Canadian position was still in danger on the flanks . . . and if the Canadians yielded, the entire Ypres position was in danger.

Fortunately, support was coming. At 1910 hours, Currie's 2nd Brigade had been called forward, and gradually the exact position on the Canadian front became clear. Their original line, facing the eastern ridge, still held. The 'bent-back' 'refused flank' at St-Julien was also holding and being shored up by the gradual arrival of more battalions. This is not to say that the position north-east of Ypres was not extremely serious. A large gap, some 8 kilometres wide, now lay open between the Canadians and the Belgian Army on the canal at Steenstraat, and the Germans had penetrated the French line for a distance of some 5 kilometres. The French were withdrawing in haste across the Yser canal, and only the hesitation of the German infantry, reluctant to advance into their own gas cloud, prevented a deeper penetration.

This penetration reached its deepest point at Mauser Ridge, a position 6 kilometres north of Ypres, outflanking the GHQ Line and just to the west of the Bois des Cuisiniers – a thicket known to the BEF as Kitchener's Wood. Once the BEF line had been stabilized, it would be necessary to retake Mauser Ridge and clear Kitchener's Wood, which offered the enemy clear and unobserved access to the eastern edge of Mauser Ridge.

Second Army HQ first learned of the German breakthrough at 1945 hours, when Smith-Dorrien was informed that the French were yielding ground on their north flank and that the 3rd Canadian Brigade was in trouble. Further confirmation came in from General Putz, informing Second Army that a gap estimated at 3 kilometres wide had opened between his force and the Canadians and that his right flank now stood at Pilckem, a village north of Mauser Ridge. Putz's line was actually some distance east of Pilckem and much closer to Ypres, but the danger to that town was immediately obvious to Smith-Dorrien. If the Germans attacked again and broke through, Ypres would certainly fall.

Smith-Dorrien therefore placed his army reserve, the 1st Canadian Brigade, at the disposal of General Plumer, who used it to help General Alderson reinforce his line. Other reserves were also sent forward, and both divisions on the right of the Canadians, the 27th and the 28th, moved troops towards the threatened flank. As a result, during the night of 22/23 April most of the Second Army around Ypres was on the move, either heading into the salient or sending out patrols to locate the precise position of the German line.

Early on the morning of 23 April, four battalions, the 2nd Buffs, the 3rd Middlesex, the 5th King's Own and the 1st Yorks and Lancs, were formed into a separate unit, the 'Geddes Force' or 'Geddes Detachment', under Lieutenant Colonel A. D. Geddes of the Buffs, and tasked to support the Canadian brigades.

The night of 22/23 April saw considerable jockeying for position. The gap in the line between the Canadian left and the canal was held only at three points with wide gaps, ranging in width from 1 to 3 kilometres, in between. Even when these gaps were closed the new defences often consisted of little more than a few strands of wire and a platoon with a single machine gun.

The Germans may have realized this, for at 2100 hours they put in another strong attack against a French regiment that had stayed in the line, the 1st Tirailleurs, on the immediate right of the Canadians. The Tirailleurs first gave way, then rallied and, with Canadian assistance, held the German attack along their 'refused flank' on the Poelcappelle road. Having beaten off the German attack, their original positions were reoccupied.

General Smith-Dorrien was in an unenviable position. Even though his front had either held or was being re-established, this front was on a new line well inside the north-east corner of the salient – and who knew what would happen the next day, when the Germans were sure to renew their attack?

At 2100 hours Smith-Dorrien informed French and GHQ that the situation in the salient was 'rather grave' and that the only solution was for General Foch to order an immediate counter-attack to restore the situation. Three hours later, at 2359 hours, Smith-Dorrien was able to tell GHQ that General Quinquandon, commander of the 45th Division, was preparing to do just that at 0430 hours – and that the Second Army had now managed to form a new flank facing north. This being so, the troops on that northern flank would assist in the French attack.

The task of supporting the 45th Division attack was given to the Canadians. Meanwhile, the Cavalry Corps and the 50th Division moved up from GHQ Reserve, and although more German attacks came in after midnight against the 27th and 28th Division line, these were held without difficulty. The main problem overnight was the heavy and persistent German artillery bombardment of Ypres and the road and canal leading north towards Boesinghe. Meanwhile, there is time to consider the proposed night attack of the French 45th Division towards Pilckem. The declared aim was to restore the French line, but it provides an excellent and tragic example of what was to follow between the Allies in the next few days.

At around 2000 hours on 22 April, a French officer from the 45th Division arrived at Canadian Divisional Headquarters and asked General Alderson for support during this attack. General Alderson quickly complied and sent an order to the 3rd Canadian Brigade at 2035 hours, commanding Brigadier General Turner to mount an attack against Kitchener's Wood in support of the French attack, as soon as reinforcements arrived from the 1st Canadian Brigade. These reinforcements arrived soon after midnight, and shortly afterwards Brigadier Turner sent the 10th and 16th Canadian Battalions forward against Kitchener's Wood.

The result was a shambles. The Canadian advance in full moonlight was promptly greeted with machine-gun fire, which killed the commanding officer of the 10th Battalion. Even so, in spite of losses the attack at first proved highly successful. The Canadians overran the German positions in the wood and discovered some British guns from the 2nd London Heavy Battery, which had been abandoned when the Germans took Mauser Ridge. Having taken the wood, the Canadians then tried to dig in, but the enemy reaction was quick and strong. Plunging artillery fire fell on the wood and quickly reduced the two battalions to a total strength of some ten officers and four hundred men.

Matters did not improve as the night wore on. The French Division's attack, expected at 0430 hours, failed to materialize, and no news arrived of any French advance. When the 2nd Battalion arrived in support from the 1st Canadian Brigade, it was quickly reduced to a handful of men. A cascade of shells detonated in the trees of Kitchener's Wood and the ground beneath them was soon a charnel house of shell splinters and body fragments . . . and there was *still* no sign of any French attack.

At 0130 hours Lieutenant Colonel Geddes had been ordered to push 'Geddes Force' forward and get in touch with the Canadian battalions and, if possible, with the French. The remnants of the three Canadian battalions had now withdrawn to the southern edge of the wood from which their line was later prolonged towards St-Julien by the arrival of the 3rd Battalion from the 1st Brigade. All the artillery batteries of the Canadian Division were also 'stood to' ready to provide fire when daylight arrived, and more infantry from the 14th and 15th Canadian Battalions, plus a company of the Buffs and some of the Tirailleurs, were in the line about St-Julien and digging in.

By dawn on 23 April the situation around St-Julien was as follows. Brigadier Turner and Lieutenant Colonel Geddes had a total of ten infantry battalions, now variously reduced in strength, covering the ground from the old Canadian position on the ridge south-west of Poelcappelle to the east bank of the Yser canal. Another force of three battalions from General Snow's 27th Division was in reserve. The front-line battalions were not all in good order; several had been decimated by shellfire in Kitchener's Wood or while marching up to the line . . . and there was still no sign of the French.

To discover what had happened to the promised French counter-attack by General Quinquandon's division is a difficult task. The first point to appreciate is that when the 45th and 87th Divisions fell back before the gas attack they went back as far as the Ypres canal and then crossed it on to the west bank. There they took up position on the bank of the canal, roughly along the line of the Ypres–Boesinghe–Lizerne road, overlooking a wide expanse of abandoned ground to the west – another look at the map on page 86 will prove useful at this point.

This line along the canal was one the French were most anxious to retain, and that desire took priority over any proposed counter-attack towards Pilckem, which now lay well behind the new German line. It therefore appears that at midnight – 2359 hours on 22 April, four hours after the French request for BEF support during their counter-attack – General Foch told General Putz that his priorities were as follows. First, hold the line he now occupied. Second, prepare this as the point of departure for a counter-attack to recover the ground lost east of the canal. Third, to mount that counter-attack – for which General Foch promised Putz the assistance of another division, the 153rd from XX Corps of the Tenth Army. On the basis of those priorities, General Putz duly called off his attack until the 153rd Division arrived – but he did not think to inform General Alderson of that cancellation, so leaving the Canadians to attack alone.

It was clearly necessary to drive the Germans back as quickly as possible, for the salient had now been reduced to a shallow pocket, 8 kilometres deep and less than 8 kilometres wide, all of it fully exposed to the enemy artillery. The next attempt to retrieve the position north of Ypres began soon after dawn on 23 April with an attack towards Kitchener's Wood and Mauser Ridge by the Geddes Force and the 1st Canadian Brigade.

Colonel Geddes had just two and a half battalions available, but these formed up by the ruins of Wieltje, just west of the GHQ Line. Soon after daybreak they advanced on Mauser Ridge, being greeted at once by another storm of machine-gun fire, which soon brought them to a halt. The Canadians, advancing towards the valley below Mauser Ridge – later known as Colne Valley – were also raked with fire, but the Geddes Force and the Canadians did manage to form a rough line below the ridge – and there they stopped. It should be mentioned that the 90th Brigade of the French 45th Division was also in action at this time. At 0700 hours, this brigade advanced on the east bank of the canal until it too was stopped by fire from the higher ground to its front.

A survey of the situation about noon on 23 April revealed that there were five British and twelve Canadian battalions, supported by half the guns of the Canadian Division, spanning the gap east of the canal and confronted by forty-two German battalions, backed by a quantity of guns, many of them heavy, plus the additional advantage of higher ground – and gas.

In spite of these advantages, the enemy made no serious attempt to advance that day, but continued to shell the BEF lines with a mixture of high explosive and gas. RFC reconnaissance reported that the enemy was now well dug in along a line from Langemarck to Pilckem and, this being so, any advance could be made only when V Corps received reinforcements – and more artillery. The first of these reinforcements, the 13th Infantry Brigade, was transferred to V Corps at 0930 hours, later that day eight more battalions from the 27th and 28th Divisions were also made available.

On the morning of 23 April, Sir John French made a visit to Foch's HQ at Cassel, where he was assured that the French had every intention of retaking their original line and that reinforcements dedicated to that task were even now on their way. The field marshal agreed to cooperate in any French counter-attack later that day, but added that if the old line was not established within a short time he reserved the right to abandon the present exposed position and pull back behind Ypres. On returning to his headquarters, French duly placed the 50th (Northumbrian) Division at Smith-Dorrien's disposal; all then waited to see what the French would do.

The French did nothing. By early afternoon even those battalions of the 90th Brigade that had crossed to the east bank of the canal that morning had been withdrawn. It was now abundantly clear to General Smith-Dorrien and Plumer that if the attack ordered by Field Marshal French was to take place it must go in soon, with or without the French, as the more time the Germans were given to prepare their new positions the harder it would be to dislodge them. Since the French were not yet moving or showing any signs of moving, the only alternative was for V Corps to attack alone.

At 1440 hours Smith-Dorrien ordered V Corps to make a general advance to the north on a line between the canal and Kitchener's Wood, in the general direction of Pilckem. The axis of advance would be the Ypres–Pilckem road with the Geddes Force moving east of it, the 13th Brigade keeping to the west of it and the 3rd Canadian Brigade in reserve; Brigadier Wanless O'Gowan of the 13th Brigade would command this operation.

This advance was due to start at 1500 hours, but then the French intervened, General Putz declaring that the 45th Division would indeed mount an attack on the east bank in support of the British attack; as a result the attack was postponed until 1615 hours. During this delay, Brigadier O'Gowan went forward to examine the ground and found that there were no troops covering the 5 kilometres between the canal and the Pilckem road . . . and where were the French, who had promised to join in this British and Canadian advance?

The *Official History* is very bitter about the subsequent attack of the Geddes Force and the 13th Brigade at 1625 hours, stating that 'the attack on which the Second Army was committed at the request of the French never had any prospect of success'.[2] This was largely due to the ground, which was very open and without any cover, so allowing the Germans on Mauser Ridge, 500 metres away, a clear view of the British advance.

As a result, 'directly the leading line of Geddes and O'Gowan men rose from the ground, the enemy opened with heavy gun and rifle fire'. The French were not entirely absent; as the 13th Brigade advanced, some four hundred Zouaves rose from cover on the east bank of the canal and joined the attack briefly before withdrawing again; their appearance was the only sign of French support that afternoon.

The attack of the 13th Brigade and the Geddes Force was pressed home with great resolution, these units joined in their advance by the survivors of the British and Canadian battalions that had attacked across this ground earlier in the day. The attack continued for two and a half hours until 1900 hours, when all movement came to an end below Mauser Ridge, the survivors clinging to hastily scraped positions in Colne Valley or the ground beyond.

The *Official History's* conclusion on this attack was that 'it certainly had the effect of stopping the enemy's advance but the price paid had been very heavy and actually no ground was gained that could not have been secured, probably without any casualties, by a simple advance after dark'.

The veracity of this last comment seems doubtful, but the casualties were indeed horrific. The 1st Yorks and Lancs had lost 424 men, the East Yorks lost 383 men, the 1st Canadian Battalion eighteen officers and 436 men; total casualties were well in excess of two thousand men, in an engagement that lasted less than four hours. Readers will have noticed the heavy casualties among commanding officers in these close-fought engagements, and so it was again here; the commanding officers of the 1st Yorks and Lancs, the 1st Canadian Battalion and the 3rd Middlesex were all killed in front of Mauser Ridge.

This engagement at Second Ypres, from the opening attack on 22 April until 23 April, is recorded in the *Official History* as the battle of Gravenstafel Ridge. When this battle ended, the right flank of V Corps still held their line along the Ypres salient ridge, facing east. On the left flank, facing north, however, the line had been bent back as far as the canal. This line was thinly held, even though reinforcements, most notably the 10th Infantry Brigade of the 4th Division, were now coming up. Reinforcements were needed urgently, for the cost of forming and holding this new line had already been heavy, but it is important to stress that the salient line had not been broken; it had been bent certainly, but it had now been re-formed, though the new line enclosed a much-reduced position.

The situation had been caused by the collapse of the two French divisions on the left of V Corps. This was hardly surprising, given the shock and losses caused by the unexpected use of poison gas and the Algerian troops, which deserve much sympathy. The failure of Foch and Joffre to send reinforcements up to retake the lost ground, however, had put a great burden on the BEF. The German advance had forced a dent in the BEF line, exposing V Corps' left flank and posing a real threat to Second Army. It was therefore necessary to restore this line, and if the French were unable or unwilling to do so, Plumer's troops must take the task on. The battles at Second Ypres would therefore continue, and began again with great fury on the following day.

6

The Fall of Smith-Dorrien, April 1915

Chief directs you to hand over forthwith to General Plumer the command of all troops engaged in the present operations about Ypres.

> Message from GHQ to General Horace Smith-Dorrien,
> GOC, Second Army, 27 April 1915

WHEN THE GEDDES Force and the 13th Infantry Brigade were repulsed from Mauser Ridge on 23 April, the battle of Second Ypres still had a month to run, but the pattern of the battle was already becoming clear. Whatever strategic advantages the Germans had hoped to obtain by the use of gas, this second battle at Ypres was now being fought for local advantages, specifically the possession of Ypres and whatever that might lead to in the future. Any attempt to regain the lost ground by the Second Army depended entirely on strong support from the French; unless that ground could be reoccupied, the salient either could not be held or could only be retained at great cost.

Gas was still being employed. Later, in its more dreadful forms, with phosgene and mustard gas added to the chemical repertoire, gas would feature in all the battles launched by both sides until the end of the war. That said, heavy artillery was to dominate this second battle for Ypres, as it would all the other Great War battles, in which 60 per cent of the casualties were caused by shellfire. Here, indeed, was the crux of the current BEF problem; the Germans had more heavy guns, and where gas and infantry attacks failed to dislodge the British and Canadian soldiers, they could blast them out of their lines with heavy artillery.

This the Germans were very eager to do. For the German Army, the capture of Ypres could be the stepping-stone to further advances and a rolling-up of the Franco-British line. It was no great distance from Ypres to the Channel coast, and no major physical obstacles stood in the way beyond the Yser canal west of Ypres. If the Allied front could be broken here, the Belgian Army and the floods unleashed north of Dixmunde would be outflanked and a new German front could be established facing south, with one flank resting on the Channel coast.

For the Allies, the possession of Ypres was considered essential for several reasons, not least to prevent the Germans gaining the strategic and tactical advantages listed in the previous paragraph. The Yser canal was an obvious defence line and the town itself a useful bastion, but the Allied reasons for retaining Ypres went beyond purely military and geographic considerations. The struggle for Ypres had now achieved a political and emotional dimension; it had become a place the *Entente* armies were determined to hang on to . . . whatever the cost.

By the spring of 1915, Ypres had become a symbol of the *Entente's* determination to fight the enemy to the end. Shattered though it was, this was the last Belgian town free of German troops, and a great deal of blood had already been expended to ensure its retention, not least by the British. The old BEF that went to France in August 1914 had been expended in defence of the town during the first battle of Ypres in October and November 1914. With the Belgians and French fighting at their side, the BEF had continued to hold the town and the surrounding salient throughout the harsh winter of 1914/15, and to give it up now was simply not an option. That grim decision meant that it would be necessary to retake the salient ridge; without the ridge, possession of Ypres was judged impossible.

In purely practical terms, Ypres was too costly for any strategic or political advantages offered by its retention. Granted, if it fell by assault the Germans might well be able to pursue the defeated Allies back to the coast, but a staged withdrawal to some well-prepared defence line, somewhere without the burden of the Ypres ridge and the advantage that slight height offered the German artillery observers, was certainly possible. The *Entente* never seriously considered such a withdrawal;

the battle for Ypres went on until the end of the war, during which time it became a graveyard for the BEF and especially for the soldiers of the Second Army.

The first engagement of Second Ypres, the brief, bloody battle for Mauser Ridge, which for some reason came to be called the battle of Gravenstafel Ridge, ended on 23 April and was followed at once by the battle of St-Julien. This battle lasted from 24 to 30 April and was marked by another gas attack, this time against the Canadians, further assaults, a proposal to at least consider abandoning part of the salient, and the dismissal of General Horace Smith-Dorrien on 27 April. This last blow was the culmination of Field Marshal French's long and vindictive campaign against the Second Army commander.

By the morning of 24 April the BEF position in the salient appeared to be crumbling. The former, roughly circular network of opposing trenches surrounding the town had been flattened along the northern and eastern rim, driven in by the gas attack and the German advances of the two previous days. If the Germans were to push forward again along this outer sector, it was hard to see where they could be held. This thought had clearly occurred to the Germans as they came forward again with another gas attack on the Canadian sector, aimed at the village of St-Julien, which lies in the centre of the northern front. Study of the map on page 86 will be helpful here.

This move began with a gas attack on the Canadian Division, or to be exact on the Canadian battalions holding the apex of the line north of St-Julien. It started at 0400 hours on 23 April, when a cloud of gas was launched on a front of 1 kilometre, accompanied by an artillery bombardment by heavy guns and mortars; this was followed with an infantry attack by four brigades. Although the gas forced a number to fall back, many more of the Canadians, again draping their faces with primitive gas masks made from towels or cotton bandoliers, stayed in position to greet the enemy with rifle fire. The gas, the artillery fire and the subsequent infantry advance all bore heavily on the position of Brigadier Currie's 2nd Canadian Brigade at Fortuin, just south of St-Julien.

Currie's men held their trenches with considerable resolution and the enemy assault on the positions held by the 8th and 5th Battalions was driven off with loss. Elsewhere the defenders found that their Ross rifles quickly jammed with mud; the 15th Battalion suffered just such a fate, losing a quantity of men and all the officers; a narrow breach was forced in the line here, enabling the enemy to get behind the Canadians defending St-Julien.

The Canadians held their front for three hours and inflicted heavy losses on the advancing enemy until around 0700 hours, when the 13th Battalion of the 3rd Brigade, having lost half its strength, was forced back from its position near Kitchener's Wood. This created another gap in the line, more than a kilometre wide, and the remnants of the 3rd Canadian Brigade fell back on St-Julien. News of this break was relayed back to V Corps, and during the morning General Plumer sent more troops forward, including the 10th and 150th Infantry Brigades.

These reinforcements and the stout Canadian resistance were not enough to stem the assault; German pressure continued to mount. At 1200 hours the Germans took St-Julien, advancing in the face of field guns firing at them over open sights, and they were now behind or in enfilade of Currie's 2nd Brigade. The Canadians hung on where they could, often in scattered companies or even platoons, but their main elements were now falling back. Brigadier General Turner's 3rd Brigade had withdrawn to the GHQ Line by 1530 hours and the 1st Brigade were about to join them. Only Currie's 2nd Brigade was still – just – holding its original position around St-Julien.

This position was now untenable. The withdrawal of the other brigades had left wide gaps, not least one between the GHQ Line and the Gravenstafel Ridge, and the problem was not helped by the fact that all communications had broken down. The weight of the defence now rested on Brigadier Currie, who was unable to find out what was going on or what had happened to the reinforcements he had been calling for all morning.

Finally, at around 1500 hours, Currie came to a radical decision. He would leave his headquarters and go to the rear himself, find those reinforcements and bring them forward. In reaching this decision, Currie again reveals that risk-taking element in his character. For a commander to leave his headquarters in the middle of a battle was not only highly unusual – it was much frowned upon by the High

Command. They – the divisional and corps and army commanders – believed that they must always know where a subordinate was, even if they could not communicate with him – and that was at his head-quarters, not roving about the line.

Currie was well aware of this policy but believed he had no choice. Without support his brigade could not hold their position much long-er, and if his appeals were not being answered, perhaps that was because they were not being received? This being so, he set off alone over the shell-swept ground behind his lines and eventually found his way to the headquarters of the British 150th Brigade, which had just come up.

Unfortunately, in spite of Currie's appeal, the 150th Brigade's com-mander, Brigadier General Bush, refused to order his men forward. He was waiting for orders from his direct superior, Major General Snow of the 27th Division, and would not move without them. Currie duly proceeded to Snow's headquarters, to pursue his mission there, and got a very dusty answer. Not only did General Snow refuse to help, he informed Currie that, had it been in his power, he would have had Currie shot for abandoning his headquarters.[1] This bleak threat should be balanced by the fact that Snow then sent some of his battalions to bolster the Canadian line.

At this point, mid-afternoon on 24 April, two days into the battle, it would be as well to take another look at the situation north of Ypres. The French had been pushed back from their position on the salient ridge and were now occupying and fighting along the line of the Yser canal, except for the 90th Brigade under Colonel Mordacq, which was on a line east of the canal, linking up with the British still hanging on below Mauser Ridge. This line continued in a somewhat jagged fashion, across the northern edge of the shrunken salient, until it reached the former front line east of Gravenstafel.

The line thus formed was tenuous, for the Canadian Division, which held most of it, was faced with two grave problems. First, com-munications between the V Corps commander, General Plumer, General Alderson of the Canadians and General Snow of the 27th Div-ision were virtually non-existent. Nor was Alderson in contact with his brigadiers, who were therefore fighting separate battles, either

Men of the London Rifle Brigade at 'Plugstreet (Ploegsteert) Wood', south of Messines, Belgium, in what could be an administrative area in the support line

Henry Wilson as a field marshal

Haig as a general, taken some time in 1916

Field Marshal Lord Kitchener, Secretary of State for War

General Sir Horace Smith-Dorrien

Right: Robertson and Foch taken after the war, when Roberston was a full general and Foch a marshal of France. In 1915 Robertson was chief of staff to Field Marshal French, C-in-C BEF, and Foch commanded the French Northern Army Group

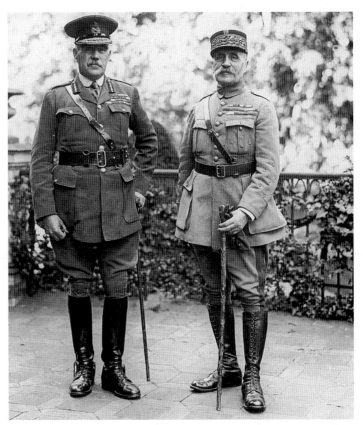

Below: General Joffre after decorating a French soldier

Field Marshal French inspecting troops of the Motor Cycle Machine-Gun Corps in late 1915 or even later. By this time machine guns had been centralized for more efficient use

Trenchard as a major general commanding the Royal Flying Corps (RFC) in France. In early 1915 he commanded the RFC Wing with Haig's 1st Army. He was promoted to command the RFC in August 1915

'Colonel' House, a Texas Democrat, who acted as Woodrow Wilson's emissary in Europe in 1915 and 1916. His title was purely honorary, given to him by a Texas governor whose election campaign he managed

Above: Sir Douglas Haig with a guard of honour provided by The Artists' Rifles, a TA Battalion

Right: Woodrow Wilson, President of the United States, being greeted by the Mayor of Dover after the war

A firing trench along the Messines–Wulverghem road, looking towards Messines, March 1915. At this stage trench systems were not nearly as elaborate as they became later, because the British did not believe the stalemate would last very long

If the ground was too wet to dig, sandbag sangars had to be built. These are in the British front line at Neuve Chapelle on 10 March 1915. The German shells are falling behind the line to hinder the move forward of reinforcements

Transport on the Neuve Chapelle road, March 1915

Far from a chateau: Brigade Headquarters, 21st Infantry Brigade, 7th Division, commanded by Brigadier General Watts during the Battle of Neuve Chapelle, 10–14 March 1915. The headquarters had been burrowed into a haystack, very likely waiting to move forward if the attack were to prove successful

Right: Neuve Chapelle: a German machine-gun post that inflicted heavy casualties on the 1st Cameronians (Scottish Rifles), photographed after its capture

Below: All that was left of a battalion of Gordon Highlanders after the Battle of Neuve Chapelle: about 180 men

engaging the enemy to their front or beating off repeated attacks with little help or reinforcement. To give just one example of the general chaos, at 1600 hours Alderson still believed that the 3rd Canadian Brigade was holding its previous position, while the brigade commander, General Turner, thought that Alderson knew and approved of his withdrawal to the GHQ Line.

Matters were little better farther up the command chain. Field Marshal French had spent the morning working up his resentment against General Smith-Dorrien, urging the Second Army commander to retake the line north of St-Julien and assuring him that 'The Germans are numerically inferior to us as far as we can judge. In fact there can be little doubt about it.'

One can only wonder where the field marshal was getting his information from – though that morning visit to Foch's HQ at Cassel leaves room for speculation. At that meeting Foch had told French that the 153rd Infantry Division was now detraining at Cassel, and he also promised to launch an attack on 25 April, using another infantry division, the 18th Division, which would arrive at Poperinghe that day. 'It is important', added Foch, 'that the British have strong reserves near Elverdkinghe, Ypres and Wieltje. Starting from these four points and eastward of them we will take a vigorous offensive against the front at Steenstraat, Pilckem, Langemarck and east of these places.' After the French prevarications of the last two days, it all sounded very promising.

This information on the number and state of the German units was quite wrong. In addition to gas and an abundance of artillery, the Germans now had no fewer than sixty-two battalions deployed along the northern edge of the salient. The BEF had fifty-two battalions, many of them much reduced by gas and shellfire and all of them weary.

Field Marshal French either did not know this or he believed that Smith-Dorrien was exaggerating the difficulties. The field marshal did understand that the Germans must be pushed back, however, whatever the cost, however meagre Smith-Dorrien's resources. There must therefore be another assault on Mauser Ridge, this time by the 10th Infantry Brigade of the 4th Division, recently arrived from Vlamertinghe. Commanded by Brigadier General Hull, the 10th Brigade and whatever other battalions could be scraped together, a total of fifteen battalions in various strengths, would push the Germans off Mauser Ridge. This attack was set for just before dawn – 0330 hours – on 25 April, and was yet another disaster.

The reasons for this new catastrophe are almost too numerous to describe. To begin with, Hull and his staff had just arrived in the Ypres salient and had no idea of the ground. He could not brief his battalion commanders on the plan for this attack, as they were out in the dark, busy trying to find the start line and get their men in position. Then there was a problem with the artillery support. At 0330 hours it would still be dark and the gunners could not see where their fire was falling. The attack was therefore put back to 0530 hours – which enabled the gunners to observe their fall of shot, but enabled the German riflemen and machine gunners to see the advance of Hull's men on Mauser Ridge.

Nor was this all; news that their plea for a delay had been met and the attack postponed for two hours did not reach the gunners of the 27th and 28th Divisional artillery, who therefore opened fire on time and blazed away into the darkness until they had shot off all their ammunition. The supporting artillery fire therefore stopped just before the 10th Brigade went forward, and the infantry advanced without any artillery support.

The result will by now be familiar. The attack on the German line between Kitchener's Wood and St-Julien failed and the losses were terrible. The dead lay before St-Julien: 'mown down like corn by the machine-guns, they remained lying in rows where they had fallen'. Total losses came to seventy-three officers and 2,236 other ranks, and not a metre of ground was retaken. The 10th Brigade was held before St-Julien and stayed there, sustaining further losses, until the order came to withdraw into the much-reduced salient on 4 May.

The *Official History*, a work not given to harsh criticism, delivers a severe verdict on this futile attack: 'They were called upon to attempt the impossible. Without adequate artillery preparation, and support, over ground unknown and unreconnoitred, they were sent to turn an enemy well provided with machine-guns out of a position which had ready made cover in houses and a wood and splendid artillery observation from higher ground behind it.'[2]

This repulse took place on Sunday, 25 April, on the same day that the British and ANZAC forces landed on the Gallipoli peninsula in Turkey, to begin that longer but equally unavailing struggle in the east. The losses in the Canadian Division for the first three days of this battle came to over 5,400 men, and Smith-Dorrien's message to General Alderson, praising the Canadian troops in France, sums up the results of this sacrifice: 'With less gallant and determined troops, the disaster which occurred outside the line they were holding might have been converted into a serious defeat for our troops.'

That message was dated 6 May. By that date General Sir Horace Smith-Dorrien had been removed from the command of Second Army and was back in England, his career in ruins. His dismissal was a blow to Second Army and the BEF, for it deprived the former of a popular and successful commander and the entire BEF of a man who, being senior to Douglas Haig, might well have succeeded to the overall command when Sir John French was removed . . . and this effect itself needs some explanation.

By the evening of 25 April, the situation at Ypres was as follows. On the western flank, German attacks against the French line seemed to have halted, but there was no sign of that long-promised counter-attack on the east bank by the French divisions, as promised by Foch. A similar inertia seemed to be gripping the BEF headquarters; no orders were issued that day other than one putting the Indian Cavalry Corps on stand-by to move. At Smith-Dorrien's HQ, the staff were still trying to find out what was happening around the perimeter and so fix the current state of the German attack. As for the BEF troops in the line, they were fully occupied hanging on where they were.

According to later information, the attack by the German XXIII Reserve Corps against the French east of the canal had been stopped, though not before the left wing of that corps had reached the canal. In the centre, the right wing of this corps was pushing forward with local attacks.

These seemed to be proceeding slowly, though each advance was accompanied by gas and a heavy bombardment, nibbling away at the BEF line. In short, the enemy was slowly gaining ground and infantry counter-attacks unsupported by artillery were not enough to stop him. What was needed now and had been needed for the past three days was a powerful Anglo-French counter-attack from within the salient, to restore the original line.

The French, in spite of frequent promises, showed no inclination to either start such an offensive or join in one started by the British. This put the Second Army commander in a difficult position, unable to get forward or pull back, his existing positions under constant pressure and his units being gradually reduced.

The choice was stark; either the French came forward and assisted in a major counter-attack to restore the line or the British must evacuate the salient in good order before they were pushed out of it. In an attempt to get some guidance on this point, on the evening of 25 April, Smith-Dorrien motored back to Field Marshal French's HQ at Hazebrouck to explain the situation and get the field marshal's orders.

The field marshal's reply was not particularly helpful. The main Second Army priority at the moment, said French, was to quieten down the situation at Ypres and restore a state of calm so that the upcoming First Army offensive at Aubers Ridge should proceed unhindered. This may have been a desirable outcome for the field marshal but it required the cooperation of the German Army commanders, who clearly hoped that their attack at Ypres, if continued, would make any Anglo-French offensive elsewhere impossible. As a summation of the situation confronting the Second Army it is little short of cretinous.

French's orders regarding the situation within the salient were also unhelpful. If possible, he told Smith-Dorrien, he did not wish to lose any more ground . . . but unless the French recaptured the ground lost it might well be impossible for the Second Army to stay where it was – a point of which Smith-Dorrien was all too aware. Therefore, said Sir John, since the French had got the BEF into this pickle, it was up to them to get it out.

This was another comment that might have been better directed at General Foch, not least because Smith-Dorrien was getting very little change out of General Putz, who had just put the promised two-division attack of 25 April back to 26 April. Sir John directed

Smith-Dorrien to join in this attack with the Lahore Division from the Indian Corps, which had arrived that day south-west of Ypres.

Orders for the Lahore Division were issued at 0215 hours on 26 April and the division duly attacked at 1400 hours, pushing north towards Langemarck on a 1-kilometre front, their advance supported by a forty-minute bombardment by the V Corps artillery. Some hours before this advance began Second Army received a message from GHQ, assuring the commanders that the enemy must by now be tired if not exhausted and, having lost plenty of men in the last few days, could not be numerous.

In spite of this hopeful message, readers will not be surprised to learn that the British and Indian infantry of the Lahore Division met with heavy fire on advancing, fire that destroyed whole platoons and littered the ground with heaps of dead. 'The British and Indian infantry was never able to close with the enemy,' says the *Official History*, 'and the fighting resolved itself into valiant but vain attempts to advance against well-placed machine-guns and superior artillery that had observation over nearly every inch of ground.'[3]

This advance of a few hundred metres cost the Lahore Division 1,857 officers and men. In the six battalions committed to the first attack, two of the commanding officers were killed and three were wounded. Losses in the 149th Northumberland Brigade, supporting this attack, were even more grievous – forty-two officers and 1,912 men, over two-thirds of the force committed.

The French did advance alongside the Indians, at least for a while. At 1400 hours their 18th and 153rd Divisions left their support trenches and went forward, but this advance then stopped until 1500 hours to enable the French artillery to register on the enemy line. Before it could be resumed, gas was released and drifted across the French and Indian attack fronts; discouraged by this, but after making some efforts to get forward, the French fell back. A renewal of their assault at 1900 hours also failed to develop, and the attacks of 26 April gradually petered out with further losses.

On 27 April this continued absence of French support inspired Smith-Dorrien to write a long letter to Lieutenant General Sir William Robertson, the BEF chief of staff. This letter begins: 'In order to put the situation before the Commander-in-Chief, I propose to enter into a certain amount of detail.'

Smith-Dorrien actually put in a great amount of detail, much of which has already been covered; only certain parts, some excerpts from the letter, will be repeated here. Smith-Dorrien continues:

I told Colonel Montgomery [BEF staff] the night before last, after seeing General Putz's orders, that as he was only putting in a small proportion of his troops, and those at different points to the actual attack, I did not anticipate any great results. You know what happened – the French right, instead of gaining ground, lost it and the left of the Lahore Division did the same . . .

The enemy's losses are very heavy. Artillery observing officers claim to have mown them down again and again during the day. At times the fighting has been very heavy and our casualties are by no means slight.

From General Putz's orders for today, he is sending one brigade across the river east of Brielen to carry forward the troops on the east of the canal in the direction of Pilckem and he assured me that this brigade was going to be pushed in with great vigour.

It was not until afterwards that I noticed that, to form his own reserve, he is withdrawing two battalions from the east of the canal and another two battalions from the front line in the same part to be used on that bank of the river, so the net result of his orders is to send over six fresh battalions to the fighting line and to withdraw four which have recently been employed.

I have lately received General Joppe's orders. He is the General commanding the attack towards Pilckem on the east of the canal and I was horrified to see that he, instead of using the whole of this brigade across the canal for the offensive, is leaving one regiment back at Brielen and only putting the other regiment across the canal to attack – so the net result of these latter orders with regard to the troops on the east bank of the canal for the fresh offensive is the addition of one battalion.

Smith-Dorrien continues:

I want the Chief to know this as I do not think he must expect that the French are going to do anything very great – in fact, although I have ordered the Lahore Division to co-operate when the French attack begins at 1.15 pm, I am pretty sure that our line tonight will not be in advance of where it is at the moment . . . I am doubtful if it is worth losing any more men to regain this French ground unless the French do something really big.

He then draws some conclusions from this sorry state of affairs:

Now if you look at the map, you will see that the line the French and ourselves are now on allows the Germans to approach so close with their guns that the area east of Ypres will be very difficult to hold, chiefly because the roads approaching it from the west are swept by shellfire, were all day yesterday and are again today.

   If the French are not going to make a big push, the only line we can hold permanently and have a fair chance of keeping supplied would be the GHQ Line, passing just east of Wieltje and Potijze, with a curved switch [line] which is being prepared . . . through Hooge and Sanctuary Wood, to join our present line about 1000 yards north-east of Hill 60. This of course means surrendering a great deal of trench line but any intermediate line short of that will be extremely difficult to hold, owing to the loss of the ridge to the east of Zonnebeke which any withdrawal must entail.

   I think it right to put these views before the Chief, but at the same time make it clear that although I am preparing for the worst I do not think we have arrived at the time when it is necessary to adopt these measures. In any case a withdrawal to that line in one fell swoop would be almost impossible on account of the enormous amount of guns and paraphernalia which will have to be withdrawn first . . . I intend tonight, if nothing special happens, to re-organize the new front and to withdraw superfluous troops west of Ypres.

Smith-Dorrien concludes: 'It is very difficult to put a subject like this in a letter without appearing pessimistic – I am not in the least but as an Army Commander I have of course to provide for every eventuality and I think it right to let the Chief know what is running in my mind.'

   This letter went off during the morning of 27 April and is an accurate and honest summary of the situation, leading to the conclusion that unless the French moved at least a partial evacuation of the salient was inevitable. Field Marshal French's reply came via telephone at 1415 hours:

> Chief does not regard situation nearly so unfavourable as your letter represents. He thinks you have an abundance of troops and especially notes the large reserves you have. He wishes you to act vigorously with the full means available in co-operating with and assisting the French attack having due regard to his previous instructions that the combined attack should be simultaneous. The French possession of Lizerne and the general situation on the canal seems to remove anxiety as to your left flank. Letter follows by Staff Officer.

The 'letter by Staff Officer', timed at 1635 hours, stripped Smith-Dorrien of his command in the salient: 'Chief directs you to hand over forthwith to General Plumer the command of all troops engaged in the present operations about Ypres. You should lend General Plumer your Brigadier General, General Staff, and such other officers of your Staff as he may require. General Plumer should send all reports direct to GHQ from which he will receive his orders. Acknowledge.'

For the moment Smith-Dorrien remained nominally in command of Second Army; that part of it in the salient now became known as 'Plumer's Force', with the residue, II Corps, still under Smith-Dorrien's command.

The irony of all this is that when the French attack that day failed – as Smith-Dorrien had predicted – GHQ's order to Plumer later that day stated:

> With reference to the failure of the French attack today . . . the Chief wishes you to consolidate the line you now hold so as to render it more secure against attack.
>
> You are also requested to prepare a line east of Ypres joining up with the line now held north and south of that place, ready for occupation if and when it becomes advisable to withdraw from the present salient. It should be such as to avoid any withdrawal from Hill 60.

In other words, within hours of sacking Smith-Dorrien for even proposing withdrawal to a smaller salient, French is instructing Plumer to prepare for exactly just such an eventuality. The *Official History* remarks: 'he [Plumer] was in fact ordered to carry out what had been recently proposed by General Smith-Dorrien'.[4]

Matters then went farther. At 1000 hours on the following day, 28 April, General Plumer was instructed in writing that 'in all probability it will be necessary tonight to commence measures for the withdrawal from the Salient to a more westerly line'.

Having sent this order to Plumer, French then went to Cassel and confronted General Foch. Foch, inevitably, was horrified that French was taking steps to contract the salient, and 'protested vehemently against any thought of withdrawal'. Equally inevitably, French weakened and agreed to delay the withdrawal until the result of French attacks promised for 29 April was known. Even so, he directed Plumer to send out of the salient all the troops and equipment not currently required – another earlier proposal from Smith-Dorrien.

Foch then put his protest in a formal letter, writing to Sir John French and listing the arguments against withdrawal. In his reply, French acknowledged the dangers of withdrawing but pointed out that there were only two solutions to the current situation; either the British withdrew or the French retook the ground they had originally lost and so re-established the line on the salient ridge, a position that the Germans were determined to dominate.

On 1 May the Germans made a determined attempt to take Hill 60, then held by the 1st Battalion, The Dorsetshire Regiment, of the 15th Infantry Brigade. The German trenches were within 100 metres of the Dorsets' line, but the attack was preceded by an artillery bombardment and the release of gas before the German infantry rushed forward.

Supported by the 1st Devons, the Dorsets were able to beat this attack off, but at a cost that indicates the terrible effect of gas; ninety men died from direct gas poisoning in the trenches and of the 207 brought back to the aid stations, forty-six died soon after arrival and another twelve died later, drowning in the fluid that gathered in their lungs.

The French attack on 29 April failed, as did another attack on 30 April; two days later French ordered Plumer's Force to withdraw from the salient rim. The withdrawal took two nights between 1 and 3 May without any major interference from the enemy, though infantry patrols and shelling by gas and high explosives continued. This was followed by a major thrust against Hill 60 on 5 May. This new BEF line retained Hill 60 but the withdrawal meant abandoning an area about 8 kilometres wide, varying in depth from 2 kilometres near Hooge to 5 kilometres at Frezenberg, and shifted the German guns that much nearer Ypres.

On the following day, 6 May, General Smith-Dorrien wrote to Field Marshal French and, citing the 'general lack of trust' he had noticed from the commander-in-chief in recent months, suggested that for the good of the cause he should give up the command of Second Army. This letter did not receive even the courtesy of a reply from Field Marshal French, simply a curt GHQ missive, ordering him to hand over the command of Second Army to Plumer and go back to England.

So, after eight months in command of the BEF, French had succeeded in at least one of his aims: he had dismissed and destroyed his much-detested subordinate, Horace Smith-Dorrien. Various reasons have been put forward to account for French's ingrained antipathy, and the official historian, Brigadier Edmonds, later alleged that 'Smith-Dorrien was removed by French because he stood in Haig's way of the Commander-in-Chiefship'. Since, however, French's dislike of Smith-Dorrien was well known in the British Army long before 1914, this seems unlikely.

When offering Smith-Dorrien command of II Corps in August 1914, Lord Kitchener warned him of French's ingrained dislike and that his tenure under French's command might be uncomfortable, but no general officer could resist a field command at such a time. In his subsequent memoir, *1914* – a work described by the historian Sir John Fortescue as 'one of the most unfortunate books ever written' – French devotes a great deal of space to maligning and libelling his former subordinate. The truth of the matter is that Sir John was a man who knew how to bear a grudge and, nursing that grudge, he pursued Smith-Dorrien relentlessly until he succeeded in removing him from command.

On his return from France Smith-Dorrien was sent to East Africa, but ill health forced him back to the UK, his career over. In 1925, he rushed across Europe to act as a pall-bearer at French's funeral, and he died as a result of a road accident in 1930.

If there is any crumb of comfort to be drawn from this sorry tale it is that Smith-Dorrien's replacement, General Sir Herbert Plumer, was also a very fine general, noted for his meticulous planning and for taking great care of his men. Plumer was to command the Second Army in the salient for the next two years, and score some significant successes in the process; had he been in overall command during the Passchendaele offensive in 1917, it is arguable that matters in that dire affair might have been very different.

The new line occupied by the Second Army was considerably smaller than the one they had held on 22 April. The French portion of the line ran south from the Yser canal at Steenstraat, passing just east of Boesinghe, then edging east to the southern side of Mauser Ridge, just over a kilometre east of the canal. Here the BEF took over the line, continuing south and east, across the GHQ Line to Hooge, then south to Sanctuary Wood, Hill 60 and Armentières, and the completion of the withdrawal on 30 April brought to an end the 'battle of St-Julien'.

Since it forced the BEF to withdraw from their previous positions, this battle can be judged a German victory, but one that fell some way short of the original objectives. The use of gas had produced a great gap in the Franco-British line, but the enemy had done little to exploit this success; as with the British at Neuve Chapelle, the main failure had come during the exploitation phase. Striking at the junction of the French and British positions was sound tactics, but here again the follow-up was marked by indecision; had the German commander concentrated his forces against the BEF at St-Julien or against the French along the canal, much more might have been achieved.

As for the BEF, those successive and costly counter-attacks by the Geddes Force, Hull's Brigade and the Canadians, certainly weigh the argument in support of the 'donkeys' allegation – that callous stupidity or sheer bloody-mindedness resulted in the loss of many brave men in attacks that went in without any chance of success. The problem with the allegation arises when some alternative action has to be suggested. If retaining the salient ridge was considered essential – and it clearly was essential, as subsequent events will show – then the field marshal had no option but to hold off the enemy until the French mounted a counter-attack strong enough to re-form the line.

At the time it was hard for the French or BEF commanders to realize that, once pushed back into a low-lying pocket, surrounded on three sides by German artillery, supporting the French was bound to be both difficult and costly. As we have seen, the problem was that the French, preoccupied with the Artois offensive, were unable or unwilling to commit the necessary forces to ensure a successful counter-attack at Ypres and so, in the end, the Second Army had to withdraw.

Military arguments tend to take a circular course, however, and so it is here; if the withdrawal was necessary, did the BEF withdraw far enough? Many authorities, at the time and since, have maintained that if the BEF had to withdraw from the salient ridge, they should have withdrawn from the salient entirely and formed up along the Yser canal, in line with the French. There is little doubt that the subsequent retention of the reduced salient was an expensive business, most costly in lives. The battle of St-Julien also illustrates the necessity for a unified Allied command. Without it the opportunities for 'buck-passing' are too strong to ignore, and the chance to develop some workable strategy greatly reduced.

As at Gallipoli later, the withdrawal was the most successful part of the St-Julien battle, at least from the BEF standpoint. The BEF divisions – the 4th, 27th and 28th – the Canadian Division having been moved into reserve on 25 April – slipped away with so little fuss that at dawn on 4 May the German artillery continued to shell their now unoccupied trenches, and it was not until early afternoon that the German infantry began to advance towards them. By nightfall, however, the enemy had begun to entrench on a new line varying from 200 to 600 metres in front of the new BEF position.

Though bickering along this new line started at once, with shelling, sniping, the release of gas and the clash of patrols in no man's land, the next major engagement during Second Ypres was the battle of Frezenberg Ridge, which took place between 8 and 13 May, and quickly developed into yet another hard-fought struggle.

Frezenberg was a village on the old salient ridge, and the Frezenberg Ridge, which runs off the main ridge, carries the road from Zonnebeke into Ypres. The German aim was to press west into Ypres along the high ground of the Frezenberg Ridge, and the commander of the Fourth Army, General Duke Albrecht von Württemberg, had assembled three corps astride this road, confronting the 27th and 28th Divisions.

The BEF line here was not particularly strong and was dominated by German guns positioned behind the Gravenstafel Ridge and Zonnebeke, where the ridges offered the enemy excellent observation over the BEF line. This BEF line had not yet been fully prepared; the trenches were shallow and without overhead cover or dugouts, and the communication trenches, linking the front line to the rear, had yet to be dug. The conclusion in the *Official History*, that 'the position, though defensible, was a framework on which much still required to be done',[5] seems entirely accurate.

There was also a shortage of artillery support. The barrels of many of the BEF's guns were worn out and therefore tended to either drop shells short or send them wildly off course, but they remained in service as guns of any kind were still in short supply. The only heavy guns available for the entire V Corps in the salient were six 60-pounders and twelve 4.7-inch howitzers. Two 5-inch howitzer batteries of the 50th Division came up on 8 May but the number of guns available was totally inadequate either to support the divisions in the line or quell the amount of fire the enemy could bring against them.

Anticipating a German attack from an increase in shelling and patrol activity, General Plumer's orders to his troops for 8 May were simple; they were to hold their line and contain the enemy for as long as possible but were on no account to create the need for him to ask for assistance from Haig's First Army, which was to launch its offensive at Aubers Ridge on the following day.

The German bombardment duly began at 0530 hours on 8 May with especially heavy concentrations falling on the positions of the 83rd Brigade of the 28th Division on the forward slopes of the Frezenberg Ridge. This bombardment continued and spread. By 0700 hours the entire 28th Division line was under heavy fire, and by

0830 hours the shallow trenches had been pounded into mounds of earth. Even so, when the barrage lifted to shell the support trenches and the roads to the west, the British infantry were still able to greet the advancing enemy with fire, but not to prevent a German break-through on the 83rd Brigade front.

By the end of the day the three battalions in this brigade had suffered terrible casualties; the 1st King's Own Yorkshire Light Infantry lost two-thirds of its strength while the 3rd Monmouthshire could muster only four officers and 130 men and the 2nd King's Own just four officers and ninety-four men. Two reserve battalions, sent up to re-inforce the line, could muster only 550 men between them.

On the right of the 83rd Brigade, the 80th Brigade holding Hooge Wood and the Bellewaarde Ridge had also been heavily shelled but, by pushing signallers, cooks and clerks into the line, had been able to stave off the subsequent infantry attacks and by nightfall had driven the enemy back. On the left flank of the 83rd Brigade, however, matters went seriously awry.

The line here was held by the 84th Brigade. Their positions were in view of the Zonnebeke ridge and fully exposed to shelling, and when the 83rd Brigade was finally forced back, their right flank became exposed. It was soon apparent that this position could not be held for long and strong infantry attacks in the afternoon gradually reduced the position, again with great loss to the defending battalions; the 2nd Cheshire was reduced to 100 men under two second lieutenants, the only officers left standing, while the 1st Suffolks lost their commanding officer and eleven other officers and had only one officer and twenty-nine men left to man their portion of the line. On the following day, 9 May, the entire 84th Brigade of six battalions could muster only 1,400 men.

These losses did not prevent the 4th Division mounting a counter-attack in the early afternoon of 8 May. At 1440 hours the 85th Brigade and some scratch battalions found from the other brigades put in an attack astride the railway line north of Hooge in an attempt to recover some of the lost ground. This attack was kept up until 2000 hours but was eventually repulsed, again with heavy losses in the battalions con-cerned. The 1st Yorks and Lancaster, which had gone into this attack with 950 officers and men, was reduced to eighty-three men under a sergeant. The 2nd East Yorks could muster just three officers and 200 men by nightfall, the 2nd East Surreys eight officers and 300 men . . . other battalions suffered losses on a similar scale.

Such losses could not be sustained. It should have been clear that until the BEF had sufficient heavy guns to counter the German artillery fire, any men sent forward or left in exposed positions were, quite literally, 'cannon fodder' and destined for slaughter. Nevertheless, the same problem remained; unless this position could be held, even the reduced salient was untenable. It was therefore decided that two battalions of the 10th Brigade, the 1st Warwicks and the 2nd Dublin Fusiliers, should put in one last attack across the German line and attempt to take the enemy in flank.

This attack did not go in until after dark on 8 May and did not go very far, but it succeeded in driving the enemy back from their positions east of Wieltje and also from Frezenberg – according to German accounts, this last and desperate advance by two battalions obliged the German XXVI and XXVII Corps to abandon their positions and put the entire Fourth Army on the defensive. Whether this is entirely true remains debatable, but the enemy made no further attacks at Frezenberg for the next five days.

The end result of this terrible day was that the BEF lost only a small amount of ground and succeeded in both blunting the enemy attack and putting him on the defensive. On the other hand, BEF losses had again been heavy. No fewer than eleven battalion commanders had been killed or wounded that day and a high proportion of the battalion officers and senior NCOs had also been lost.

The French attack in Artois duly opened on 10 May, as did the supporting BEF First Army attack on Aubers Ridge. This did not bring an end to German pressure at Ypres, where the enemy concentrated his fire on the lines of the 27th Division astride the Menin road and commenced a new offensive, the battle of Bellewaarde Ridge. The much-reduced infantry of the 28th Division were now withdrawn from the line and replaced by the troopers of the combined 1st and 3rd Cavalry Divisions. Since the start of Second Ypres on 22 April, the 28th Division had lost more than 15,000 men. Since most of these came from the rifle battalions, this meant that the 28th Division had been effectively wiped out. Even with the addition of numerous re-inforcements, the division could muster fewer than 200 officers and 8,000 men in mid-May and needed a long rest while reinforcements were absorbed.

General Plumer's worries were, however, not restricted to man-power; that chronic problem, a shortage of artillery ammunition, was appearing again. The 4.5-inch howitzers had no shells at all and the BEF, when indenting for more, was then ordered to find 2,000 rounds of 4.5-inch ammunition and 20,000 rounds of 18-pounder ammuni-tion, for immediate dispatch to the Dardanelles. The field marshal's protests were overruled and the ammunition was duly dispatched, but the promise that it would be replaced from stocks in the UK was not met until the middle of the month. Nor was this all. Many units were well under establishment for machine guns and the rifle ammunition in reserve was down to ninety-three rounds per man – and rifles were in such short supply that battalions were arriving without them.

On 13 May the Germans put in yet another strong attack on the Frezenberg position, their artillery concentrating on the BEF line between Hooge and the Ypres–St-Julien road. The pattern of this attack followed the previous model; heavy artillery fire and gas, fol-lowed by infantry assaults. These penetrated the cavalry lines at several points and the enemy then began to clear the BEF trenches using grenades. Generally, though, the cavalry, 4th Division and 27th, all of which became involved that day, managed to hold their lines and defy eviction by the enemy. By the end of the day – which also marked the end of the week-long struggle for Frezenberg – the Germans had driven V Corps off the Frezenberg Ridge and taken over a slice of ter-ritory perhaps a kilometre deep, but that was all. The greatest German success was in the losses they had caused to the British infantry; the six days of the battle of Frezenberg Ridge had cost V Corps 456 offi-cers and 8,835 men.

Although the usual daily attrition continued there was then a pause. This lasted until 24 May, when it was briefly broken by the last engagement of Second Ypres, the two-day battle of Bellewaarde Ridge. The most significant development around Ypres during this pause came on 15 May, when the French finally succeeded in driving the Germans from the west bank of the canal at Steenstraat.

The fight for the Bellewaarde Ridge began at 0245 hours on the morning of 24 May when a heavy bombardment, a gas discharge mixed with high explosives and tear gas shells, fell across the entire V Corps front. This then ran north for 8 kilometres from Hill 60 to a junction with the French at Turco Farm, just south of Mauser Ridge. On many parts of this front the two lines of trenches were so close together that the hiss of gas released from cylinders could be clearly heard in the BEF trenches. This left the V Corps soldiers with little time to put on their respirators, but although the German infantry swept in close behind the gas cloud, in most places they were beaten back with short-range rifle and machine-gun fire.

At several places, however, notably astride Bellewaarde Lake, north of Hooge, held by the 28th Division, and at Mouse Trap Farm, north of Wieltje, where the 4th Division held the left of the V Corps line, the enemy attack, forcefully delivered, did break the British line, causing severe losses, especially at Mouse Trap Farm, where the 2nd Royal Irish and the 2nd Dublin Fusiliers were decimated.

The main problem affecting the British defence at this time was the chronic breakdown in communications between corps and division and the front-line brigades and battalions. Ordering and controlling attacks and counter-attacks was therefore very difficult, and on 24 May it was found necessary to withdraw the 4th Division on the left flank, after a French promise of support for a counter-attack was withdrawn – the *Official History* comments that the French now regarded the British passion for counter-attacks rather as their forefathers had viewed the Charge of the Light Brigade at Balaclava – magnificent, but not war.[6] This French view is at odds with their own doctrine that demanded unequivocally that any lost ground be re-taken immediately *whatever* the cost.

By 25 May, both sides were anxious to put an end to this second battle of Ypres, and for the same reasons; a shortage of artillery ammunition, great losses among the front-line divisions, and men weary beyond telling. On 27 May, French told the War Office that further offensive operations were impossible until his ammunition state improved and the Germans, with their reserves mainly committed to the Eastern Front, were equally anxious to close the battle down.

And so, almost by mutual agreement, the second battle of Ypres dragged itself to a close on 25 May. British losses here since the battle opened on 23 April came to 2,150 officers and 57,125 men, a total of 59,275, killed, wounded and missing – 10,519 officers and men had been killed. German losses were given as 860 officers and 34,073 men.

What had been gained from such losses? The short answer is very little. The Germans had taken much of the salient ridge but gained no strategic advantage, while the British, though retaining part of the salient, had done so only at great cost and would incur further losses while retaining what they held in the future. The basic rule of the Western Front, that he who attacks loses a quantity of men, was borne out again in this battle; the Germans lost men while attacking, the British while counter-attacking.

Many of the other problems were also made manifest here. Anglo-French cooperation varied from the slight to the non-existent. Communications were a nightmare and the BEF artillery had neither the guns nor the shells to provide the infantry with adequate support . . . and it has to be added that many of the infantry attacks would have been failures, even had such support been available.

The problem at Second Ypres was not the German use of gas – at least, not after the first few days. The main snag was that the Germans had the advantages of ground, machine guns and artillery – that dire Western Front combination – and the most crucial element here was the ground. It was necessary to retake the salient ridge and that task was beyond the power of the infantry units sent to take it.

The 'donkeys' allegation at Second Ypres rests largely on that point, and with some reason – without support, from artillery and the French, these attacks had little chance of success. The ridge had to be retaken, however, or the bulk of the salient was untenable; the French were unable or unwilling to undertake the task and so the BEF had no option but to take it on and attempt the impossible, with predictable results.

It is very easy to criticize the handling of many attacks at Second

Ypres, that of Hull's Brigade and that of the Lahore Division on 27 April in particular, but the need to mount counter-attacks and retake the ridge, or withdraw from the salient, is surely understandable. On balance, it is likely that Smith-Dorrien was right; neither Smith-Dorrien nor Plumer was a 'donkey' and the wisest and least costly course would have been to withdraw from the salient entirely. The snag is that this might have been a short-term solution with long-term consequences; what line in the north could the BEF have held once Ypres had been abandoned? Since Ypres was held, though at great cost, we shall never know.

7

The Battle of Aubers Ridge, 9 May 1915

> Breaking through the enemy's lines is largely a question of expenditure of high explosive ammunition. If sufficient ammunition is forthcoming, a way can be blasted through the line.
>
> Field Marshal Sir John French, January 1915

WHILE THE SECOND Army was fully engaged with the battle of Second Ypres, the First Army had not been idle farther south. The action at Aubers Ridge on 9 May was largely a continuation of the attempt to reach the ridge from Neuve Chapelle in March. Like that earlier attack, it was mounted to support a French attack on Vimy Ridge, which was in turn part of Joffre's now resumed Artois offensive.

Anglo-French discussions on how that offensive might be revived had begun just two weeks after the battle at Neuve Chapelle. The German offensive at Second Ypres had led to a delay in the implementation of the subsequent plan for Aubers, but in every other respect Second Ypres and Aubers Ridge were *discrete* battles.

These French attacks in Artois and Champagne had a dual purpose. First, they were part of the overriding French strategy for 1915, which had the aim of driving the enemy from the soil of France with the least possible delay; the elimination of the Noyon salient was a step to this end. Second, they were an attempt to take advantage of the German switch of forces to the Eastern Front and, by preventing the dispatch of more German units to the east, to help the Russians resist Austrian and German pressure along the Polish frontier. This last point was given increased importance from 1 May, when the German and

Austrian armies launched a major attack at Gorlice–Tarnów, an offensive that was to evict the Russians from Galicia and Poland.

This British attempt at Aubers Ridge took place over much the same ground as the Neuve Chapelle attack in March. The ground was drier now as spring advanced but was still as difficult in every other way and more closely watched by an enemy determined not to be caught by a surprise attack. In that watchfulness lay most of the problems that Haig's men would encounter in this new attack. The First Army commander had learned several lessons from the affair at Neuve Chapelle. So too, unfortunately, had the Germans.

Neuve Chapelle had displayed the new face of warfare to anyone alert enough to notice, and pointed up the difficulties any commander would face in attempting to force a way through defences composed of trenches, barbed wire, machine guns, artillery and resolute men. The general conclusion – or at any rate the current conclusion of the British generals – was that the secret of success lay in the use of a great quantity of high-explosive ammunition, to reduce the enemy defences and dismay or kill the defenders.

Up to a point, this view was correct; the First World War rapidly became an artillery war, where much depended on the guns, but a sufficiency of guns and shells was only part of the answer. As Field Marshal French averred at the start of the year, given sufficient guns and a vast quantity of shells it appeared possible to force a breach in the enemy line. What had still not been solved was the thorny question of what happened then. Unless exploited, a breach in the enemy line was useless.

The Germans had also absorbed this lesson, however, and were determined to create a defence line impervious to the heavy guns the British would surely employ in increasing quantity as the war progressed. Creating a strong defence line when the water table was only a metre or so below the surface was difficult, but the Germans were not short of ideas. At Aubers they had created a sandbagged defence line with machine-gun dugouts let into the lower part of the emplacements, virtually undetectable by air reconnaissance and impervious to shellfire. When the BEF infantry appeared to their front, these German machine guns and field guns would rake them with a terrible fire.

Another, apparently ignored, lesson of Neuve Chapelle came after the initial breach, when further advances had to be made and enemy strongpoints, swiftly manned by resolute defenders, began to strafe the advancing troops. To overcome this problem, the second lesson of Neuve Chapelle dictated that a successful breach required a rapid follow-up; delays after an initial success could clearly be fatal. As we saw in Chapter 4, the exploitation phase also required artillery support; the rear of the enemy's front-line positions required careful attention by the artillery if the infantry and cavalry were to have any success with their subsequent exploitation.

To give Haig his due, some of these problems had been addressed by the time the First Army made this new attempt at Aubers Ridge – though on this occasion the problems of exploitation never arose. As we shall see, in spite of the experience gained at Neuve Chapelle, the British attack on Aubers Ridge on 9 May was quickly halted in no man's land.

To fill in the background to the battle of Aubers Ridge it is necessary to go back to 24 March, when General Joffre wrote to Field Marshal French, proposing another joint attack towards the east, again with the aim of achieving a breakthrough on a wide front. The French attack was planned for some time at the end of April, when, said Joffre, 'The French Tenth Army, acting in conjunction with the British First Army, will undertake an important attack north of Arras with a view to piercing the enemy line. In order to carry out this attack the Tenth Army will be strongly reinforced – it will consist of fourteen infantry divisions and about 220 heavy guns and more than 720 field guns and howitzers.'

Joffre hoped that his allies would support this endeavour and again requested that the British take over more of the front line by relieving two French corps at Ypres for employment in the coming French offensive. Field Marshal French might have pointed out that he could not take over more of the French line *and* build up reserves for a major attack, but he agreed to an extension of the British line northwards into the salient, and directed First Army to build up supplies of men and munitions for a further attack.

On 6 April, Joffre sent the field marshal his plan for a joint Anglo-French offensive north of Arras. The French Tenth Army of General d'Urbal, which occupied a front of more than 30 kilometres from the La Bassée canal to Arras, would attack between Arras and Lens, the main effort being concentrated on 6 kilometres of front astride Vimy Ridge, heading for the eastern rim of Vimy Ridge and so downhill to the Douai plain. This central attack would be carried out by three corps, with another two and a half corps and II French Cavalry Corps being in reserve. The detailed planning for this attack was entrusted to General Foch, now commanding the French Army Group (GAN) in the north.

Joffre requested that to support this attack Haig's First Army of three corps – I, Indian and IV – advance on d'Urbal's left to Aubers Ridge, hopefully tying down German forces there and preventing any units being moved to the Lens–Arras front.

Foch proposed that the Tenth Army should attack first. This attack would be supported by three subsidiary attacks, one at the same time as the main offensive, one on the day before and one on the day after. The first attack would fall to the south of the main attack in order to widen the French advance. The second preliminary attack was to be directed at the German positions at the Notre Dame de Lorette spur, which overlooked the flank of the main French advance. The final subsidiary attack by IX Corps would go in on the right flank in order to help the main assault reach the Douai plain.

According to Foch, the British First Army should mount another supporting attack between Festubert and Neuve Chapelle, spear-headed by I Corps and the Indian Corps with IV Corps in support, all thrusting in the direction of Aubers Ridge. This attack, said Foch, should go in the day after the Tenth Army made its main bid for Vimy Ridge. Though Field Marshal French – urged on by Henry Wilson – was usually putty in the hands of General Foch, he insisted that the British attack should go in at the same time or at least on the same day as the main French assault.

Given the recent situation at Ypres, where Foch had consistently failed to deliver those frequently promised French counter-attacks to restore the original salient, Sir John French was in no mood to pander to French requests at this time, even had he agreed with the basic strategy.

The field marshal's reason for rejecting the French proposal was simple; if anything went wrong with the French attack, the full might of the aroused enemy would then be deployed against First Army – and it was anyway a far sounder practice to engage the enemy all along the front with all the available forces at once, rather than mounting an attack by instalments. That at least was the field marshal's view; Foch believed that an attack, once launched, had to be kept up, and the pressure on the enemy increased as the battle spread along the front.

French, however, demanded a precise date for the launching of the combined offensive, for which he was prepared to commit ten infantry divisions, supported by 600 guns – 100 of them heavy – and no fewer than five cavalry divisions – a great increase on the force committed at Neuve Chapelle.

On 2 May, Foch informed the field marshal that the French attack would go in on 7 May and again requested that the British attack be made on the following day. French weakened and duly complied, ordering the British attack for dawn on 8 May, though, in the event, the weather intervened. Two days of rain interrupted the prior bombardment of Vimy Ridge by the French artillery which Foch considered essential, and both armies attacked on 9 May, the Tenth Army's attack going in at 1000 hours, five hours *after* the British began their assault – and after four days of French artillery fire on the German positions at Vimy.

The artillery preparation, and the time taken for it, illustrates one crucial difference between the French and British approaches to the problems of breaching the Western Front defences at this time. The Tenth Army's offensive was preceded by a prolonged artillery bombardment, during which the French artillery fired no fewer than 1,813,490 shells from their field guns, largely concentrated on the German wire, and another 342,372 shells from heavy guns directed at German trenches, wire and dugouts. In both cases a considerable amount of damage was done and the German defences on the Tenth Army front were much reduced.

As a result, the Tenth Army's attack on 9 May breached the German lines on the anticipated 6-kilometre front and penetrated beyond that front for 5 kilometres – a startling advance in Great War terms. Within two hours some parties of French infantry had even reached the crest of Vimy Ridge and saw the flat expanse of the Douai plain stretched out below them.

Further exploitation seemed possible and a major breach within their grasp. Then, unfortunately, an old problem arose. The French reserves were not on hand nor ready for such a sudden and surprising success. Before they could be brought up to enlarge the breach and press on downhill to the Douai plain, the Germans had brought in their reinforcements and counter-attacked, using a multitude of heavy guns to seal off the French advance and block the advance of reserves from the rear.

The French were pressed back from the crest of Vimy Ridge, and bitter hand-to-hand fighting went on for the next five weeks without any chance of regaining the ground captured and lost on the first day. Tens of thousands of lives were lost in this Artois offensive, and the French cemetery at Neuville-la-Targette, west of Vimy Ridge, is one of the largest military cemeteries in France. In this tragedy we find a classic example of how the prime lessons of the Western Front had only been half learned by the Allied commanders, and in view of the pervasive 'donkeys' allegation this French failure to think the problem through deserves analysis.

Even in an 'artillery war', success did not entirely depend on artillery. The guns could beat a path through the defences, but any resulting benefit depended on rapid exploitation by the infantry, which, for the various reasons already explained, was rarely possible in 1915. The root cause of that failure was the communications problem, which was not the fault of the generals, and a chronic failure to cope with this problem by placing reserves well forward, for which the generals are more culpable. The British had made that mistake at Neuve Chapelle; the French were to repeat it on a much larger scale on Vimy Ridge; the end result was the same.

The British artillery preparation for Aubers Ridge could hardly have been more different from that of their allies; the Aubers attack relied on surprise and the artillery preparation was scheduled to last just forty minutes. For the assault on Aubers Ridge, Haig and his generals were proposing to follow the tactical plan employed at Neuve Chapelle, tweaking that plan slightly in an attempt to avoid or greatly reduce the problems encountered in that engagement. The *Official History* quotes the belief of some officers that 'This should be Neuve Chapelle all over again and much more successful because we have learnt the lessons and shall know what to avoid this time.'[1]

From this hopeful comment two interesting thoughts arise. First, the strange idea that Neuve Chapelle had been a success, albeit a limited one. Second, that the losses there – 4,855 officers and men in the 8th Division alone, about 50 per cent of its rifle strength – were somehow acceptable as the price of that 'success', even without much larger army losses.

Even so, if lessons had been learned those losses had not been entirely in vain, and it is therefore worth examining the plan to see what tactical changes were employed for this new battle. Haig was still placing a heavy reliance on surprise so a short bombardment of just forty minutes was allowed for before the infantry assault. For this bombardment Haig had 121 heavy guns and 516 field guns and howitzers.

On the matter of exploitation, no definite objectives had been set for the initial advance; this time the assault divisions were ordered to press forward as quickly as possible to the La Bassée–Lille road and then to the line of the Haute Deule canal, well beyond Aubers Ridge.

As for communications, that chronic nightmare, these were to be improved by an increased use of aircraft. Before the battle the 1st Wing, Royal Flying Corps, which was still attached to First Army, was directed to send up fighting patrols and prevent enemy aircraft spotting Haig's preparations. As at Neuve Chapelle, other machines, equipped with wireless sets, would spot for the artillery and during the attack three aircraft would spot the forward movement of the infantry, which – a new departure – would be marked out by white panels deployed on the ground by the battalions; this time at least, the divisional commanders might hope to know how the battle was progressing. During the battle, in an attempt to impede the flow of enemy reinforcements, the RFC were to bomb and strafe railway stations and lines in the rear of the Sixth Army positions, another new development, albeit one in its early stages.

If the enemy line could be breached by the artillery, as at Neuve Chapelle, then Field Marshal French had a large reserve, consisting of the Cavalry Corps, the Indian Cavalry Corps, the 1st Canadian Division, the 51st (Highland) Division and the 50th (Northumbrian) Division. On the other hand, all was not quite as well as it appeared; the Canadian Division and the 50th Division had already been heavily engaged at Second Ypres and both units were short of men and very tired. On 10 May all these divisions were at two hours' notice ready to move, so one lesson of Neuve Chapelle, the need for rapid support by the reserve formations, appears to have been learned by the BEF commanders.

Finally, Haig had laid plans to assist the forward movement of artillery during the exploitation phase when batteries of heavy mortars would be attached to the assault battalions for use against enemy strongpoints. These mortars and some light artillery were to be sent forward on lorries or armoured cars; wooden prefabricated bridges and supplies of duckboards had been gathered to make a path across the mud and ditches. Clearly, another lesson of Neuve Chapelle, the need for the rapid shift forward of artillery support, had been noted by General Haig, and he deserves full credit for absorbing these lessons and making these preparations.

Field Marshal French, General Haig and the First Army corps commanders therefore viewed the coming battle with considerable optimism. They believed that they now knew how to breach the enemy line and how to exploit that breach thereafter, and the orders they issued to the brigades and battalions reflected this view.

French's orders decreed that 'The First Army will . . . break through the enemy line . . . and gain the La Bassée–Lille road between La Bassée and Fournes.' Fournes is a village well east of Aubers, so the commanders' optimism is well in evidence even at this early stage. For First Army, French continued, 'its further advance will be directed on the line Bauvin–Don'.

This line was on the Haute Deule canal, some 10 kilometres southeast of Aubers, and that geographical fact inspires caution. This order called for an advance of some 9 kilometres across country where no British soldier had yet advanced more than 1,000 metres – optimism indeed.

To execute these intentions, Haig was planning a divergent attack. The First Army plan was to breach the enemy line at two points, one on either side of Aubers village and 5 kilometres apart. Having breached the enemy line at these widely dispersed points, I Corps and the Indian Corps would advance due east, south of Aubers, while IV Corps pushed south-east from the north, the two advances eventually trapping the German defenders between them and so forcing a withdrawal.

It was a good enough tactical plan but one that largely depended on the artillery, on the assaulting troops breaching the enemy line, and on the rapid movement of reserves to exploit forward thereafter – in short, on matters going a good deal better than they had at Neuve Chapelle two months before.

Haig explained this plan carefully to his corps and divisional commanders at two conferences on 27 April and 6 May; both meetings stressed the importance of rapid exploitation. Once through the German line, which had not budged since the end of Neuve Chapelle, these corps would converge for a solid advance on Aubers Ridge, 3 kilometres farther on, mopping up such strongpoints as they met on the way; the prime aim was to get on to the ridge before the Germans could establish a new defence line. Haig estimated that the number of German troops defending the line Neuve Chapelle–Aubers–Fromelles probably did not exceed six or seven battalions – say 7,000 men – supported by a few batteries of guns. With the ridge taken, the British would move on to their final objectives, crossing the La Bassée–Lille road to the Bauvin–Don position along the Haute Deule canal.

The attack would be supported by that short and violent artillery bombardment which, averaged across the front, amounted to three guns for every 100 metres of enemy trench, with the 18-pounders detailed for wire cutting. The *Official History* comments that in fact this was little more artillery support than that provided at Neuve Chapelle.

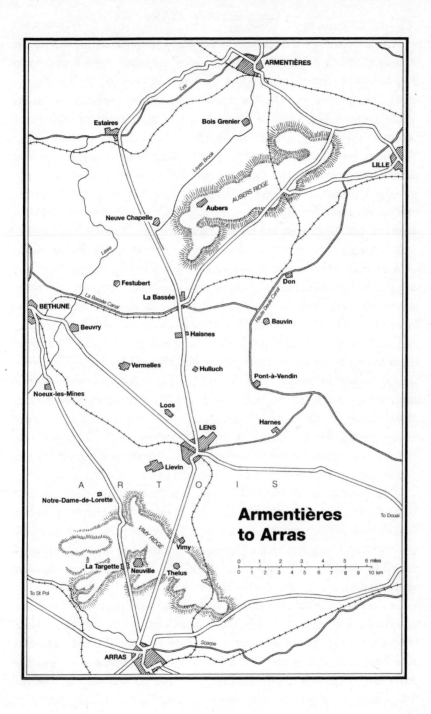

The prospect of success this time was somewhat improved by the fact that, although the Germans had good views over the British front line from the higher ground of Aubers Ridge, they apparently did not notice the preparations for the pending attack until the day before the battle began. The German defences, however, were already much stronger than they had been in March.

There were now three strong enemy divisions barring the First Army front between the La Bassée canal and Bois Grenier, the 14th, 13th and 6th Bavarian Reserve Divisions. Nor had these divisions been idle; every night for the last two months the German commanders had sent out parties to improve their defences in no man's land and build more strongpoints and machine-gun positions along the Aubers line.

The German trenches had been strengthened; parapets had been heightened and bunkers, equipped with pumps to keep the water down, had been dug into Aubers Ridge. Where dugouts were not possible sandbagged breastworks, too strong for the shells of field artillery to pierce, had been built and carefully camouflaged. The Bavarians had sited machine guns to enfilade the front and protected that front with dense thickets of barbed wire. To this can be added a quantity of artillery sighted to cover no man's land, the guns pre-registered so that defensive fire could be brought down even if the ground itself was obscured by fog. As ever, the Germans had made meticulous preparations to resist further attacks; as a result the battle of Aubers Ridge, if shorter, would prove to be as bloody as that of Neuve Chapelle.

The bombardment of the German line by 600 guns duly began at 0500 hours. At 0540 hours the guns lifted from the German front line and the infantry went over the top – and directly into a storm of rifle and machine-gun fire from German positions the advancing troops could not locate. Although every divisional assault met with disaster, an overall picture of the events at Aubers Ridge is better achieved by considering what happened on the various corps fronts.

On the I Corps front the assault was delivered by Major General Richard Haking's 1st Division, with Major General Henry Horne's 2nd Division in reserve, the latter a full 5 kilometres behind the front line. This attack was supported by ninety-six guns, 18-, 15- and 13-pounders, all tasked with wire cutting, and a further forty-six howitzers tasked with the destruction of the enemy trenches and strongpoints. These trenches were defended by fourteen companies of German infantry drawn from the 15th, 55th and 57th Regiments, with around twenty-two medium machine guns enfilading the front about to be attacked. Secure in their emplacements, the Germans were quite untroubled by the artillery fire.

Haking's leading battalions, drawn from the 2nd and 3rd Brigades, with the 1st (Guards) Brigade in reserve, had assembled overnight in the forward trenches and moved out into no man's land before zero hour; the width of no man's land here varying from 100 to 300 metres. When the barrage lifted from the enemy's front line the companies and platoons rose up to advance – and were immediately greeted with a curtain of fire from the unquelled defenders of the German line. When the British infantry attempted to get out of their front-line trench, 'Many fell dead on the ladders or parapet',[2] those falling back landing on the bayonets of the men waiting below.

Those already in the open rose and doubled forward, and a rough line was formed close to the German trenches, from which the enemy were now engaging them, many Germans standing on the parapet to fire their rifles at the men crouching in the open. When the barrage lifted and these men rose as one to rush the German line they were shot down at once or became entangled on the German wire. Within minutes the 1st Division's attack had stalled and losses were mounting rapidly.

The 1st Northamptonshire lost seventeen officers out of thirty-two and 543 men out of some 700 committed. The 2nd Sussex lost fourteen officers and 537 men, the 2nd King's Royal Rifle Corps (2/KRRC) eleven officers and 240 men and all the other battalions of the 1st Division committed to this attack suffered in proportion. In total, the six battalions of the two brigades that made the initial assault that morning lost 2,225 officers and men, some 60 per cent of their strength, without gaining a yard of ground. These losses will appear even more grievous when it is recalled that they fell almost exclusively among the rifle companies.

To the north of the 1st Division, the Indian Corps attack was led by the three brigades of the Meerut Division, the Dehra Dun, Garhwal and Bareilly Brigades, with the Lahore Division in reserve.

The prior bombardment was supported by the artillery of both divisions, with the 18-pounders devoted to wire cutting and seventy-two heavy howitzers tasked to demolish the 2,400 metres of German trench before the Indian Corps lines.

The first assault was made by the Dehra Dun Brigade with two battalions of the Garhwal Brigade in reserve and the Lahore Brigade on its left. The Dehra Dun Brigade assaulted on a front of 800 metres, doubling forward towards enemy trenches, but was stopped almost immediately by rifle and machine-gun fire. Losses in the Dehra Dun Brigade came to 893 men, all in a few minutes. The initial bombardment had completely failed to eliminate the enemy machine gunners or do much harm to the German defences, and with their own men milling about in no man's land even covering fire from their own trenches was denied the advancing troops.

Nor was this all. The enemy wire was found to be uncut and the artillery 'lifts' – that shifting forward of fire to the enemy's rear trenches – were found to be too quick, moving away from the enemy front line before the advancing Indian battalions could reach it. The enemy, which had been manning the front-line trenches even under the bombardment, was able to bring fire down on the attackers without any danger from shellfire.

Here was another problem. The way for troops to advance in the open is through a process called 'fire and movement'. One part of the advancing force fires on the defenders to keep their heads down while their comrades advance; then those in advance open fire while their comrades behind come forward; this 'leapfrogging' tactic, firing and moving, should bring the assault wave close to the enemy positions without undue loss. At Aubers Ridge, the task of delivering the 'fire' part of this process had been delegated to the guns and the assumption was that when the infantry went forward the enemy would be either dead, wounded or demoralized.

This did not happen. The guns had failed to reduce the enemy defences and the defenders were far from demoralized. They manned their positions and even stood up on the parapets to fire on their advancing foes, who had no time to regroup and employ fire-and-movement tactics before they were shot to pieces. As for the guns, their fire had moved on, away from the enemy front-line defences, and there was no means of rapidly calling the guns back. The telephone lines from the front line to the artillery battery positions had already been cut, and there is no evidence that the radios in the RFC spotting aircraft provided any alternative. Losses in the Meerut Division totalled 2,629 officers and men by the end of the day, most of these losses occurring in the first half-hour.

At 0605 hours the two divisional commanders decided to halt the attack, call down fresh artillery fire back on the front line and try again. Half an hour of shellfire duly fell on the enemy trenches but the gunners were unable to locate the German machine-gun positions and attempts to renew the infantry advance at 0700 hours led only to further losses.

News of this disaster was clearly reaching the divisional HQs. At 0720 hours General Haking reported the situation to corps HQ, asking for permission to commit the 1st (Guards) Brigade. He added that even if the entire 2nd Division came forward from reserve, it could not achieve much against uncut wire and undamaged defences. The survivors of the 1st Division were now pinned down in no man's land, unable to move forward, unable to fall back, sniped or machine-gunned whenever they attempted to move at all in either direction.

Yet another attack was mounted by the Meerut Division, however, commencing with a one-hour bombardment of the enemy line which started at 0745 hours. This provoked an immediate response from the German artillery, their fire descending on the battalions of the Bareilly Brigade, which was marching up to the front. This assault was cancelled after General Anderson, GOC of the Meerut Division, heard that the 1st Division would be unable to offer any support. The Meerut Division's troops therefore lay out in no man's land, under heavy fire, awaiting further orders.

By 0800 hours news of the check to the initial attack and the subsequent attempts to retrieve the position had got back to Haig's headquarters. Unfortunately, the full extent of this disaster and the reasons for it had not been realized, and Haig therefore decided to try again at noon, ordering I Corps and the Indian Corps to reorganize their units for another assault.

Haig then went to the headquarters of the Indian Corps at Lastrem and only then realized the seriousness of the position. He still decided to mount another attack, very much on the lines of the one that had just failed, ordering the artillery to repeat their original fire plan for the next attack and pound the German trench line thoroughly, switching the 18-pounders from wire-cutting shrapnel ammunition to high-explosive shells directed against the enemy trenches. Meanwhile the commanders of the 1st and Meerut Divisions were sending their reserves forward, in full daylight and observed by the enemy, who immediately engaged them with artillery fire, causing 'much confusion and many losses'.

At this point General Haig's actions must be queried. The success of his initial attack had been predicated on surprise; hence the short and – in the event – totally ineffective artillery bombardment. Yet now, with all surprise gone and his leading battalions decimated, he decided to repeat the attack on exactly the same lines; how he expected to avoid yet another, even more severe defeat is hard to understand. The Germans had not been damaged by these early assaults and their losses so far – some four hundred men – were being made good by reinforcements now arriving from the rear – a movement that had been spotted and reported to Haig's HQ by the RFC patrols.

Some changes to the attack plan were made. As the losses in the 1st Division were appreciated, Haig postponed the time of this second attack, first to 1440 hours and then to 1600 hours. During this time two battalions, the 1st Black Watch and the 1st Cameronians of the 1st (Guards) Brigade, came up to spearhead the new attack, and those units of the 1st and 2nd Brigades that had made the first attack and were able to withdraw came back from no man's land; many men were still pinned down in the open.

The British artillery had also been firing on the German support trenches all morning in an attempt to inhibit the movement of reserves. In this they were fairly successful, but the gunners did not have the weight of shot to dent the existing defences and their ability to continue firing was declining through a shortage of high-explosive ammunition.

When the infantry attack went in at 1600 hours, further losses followed. The Black Watch Battalion of the 1st (Guards) Brigade attacked when the barrage lifted but only fifty men reached the German parapet before they were driven back into no man's land, the Black Watch losing 475 officers and men in this futile attack. The Cameronians, coming up in support, lost nine officers and 240 men, most of them before the battalion got halfway across no man's land. At 1645 hours General Haking ordered a further assault, preceded by a ten-minute bombardment. This attack was duly put in, supported by the remnants of the companies pinned down in no man's land, but this simply led to more casualties.

The Meerut Division also suffered severely, for the German trenches on their front had not been seriously damaged and were strongly manned. The commander of the Bareilly Brigade, Brigadier General Southey, ordered his officers to press home their attack at all costs, and even after dark if need be; the attack was indeed pressed home with great resolution but with little success. Heavy fire fell upon the men as they left their trenches and very few got more than 20 metres forward before being hit. At 1640 hours, having lost over a thousand men in the last half-hour, Brigadier Southey called off the attack and reported to Division that it was impossible to commit the rest of his brigade in the face of such fire. By 1700 hours all movement on the 1st and Meerut Division fronts had halted.

General Haig now fully appreciated the situation and ordered that no more reserves were to be committed – but that the attack would be resumed at 2000 hours that evening. In the meantime, the ground taken – a few metres at most – was to be held and the 1st Division replaced by the 2nd Division. No attempt was made to switch the main assault to the IV Corps front, where the other events of the day should now be described.

The dawn attack by Rawlinson's IV Corps went in at Fromelles, to the north of Neuve Chapelle and some 6 kilometres to the left of the Indian Corps attack. This part of the German line was defended by four regiments of the 6th Bavarian Division, entrenched behind breastworks 6 metres wide and 2 metres high, well provided with machine guns. Even so, Rawlinson's assault got off to an encouraging start, partly because Rawlinson had dug mines under the German lines and the subsequent explosions reduced the number of strong-points on his front, and partly because General Davies, commanding the spearhead 8th Division, intended to use 7,000 men of the 24th and 25th Brigades for his first attack and so overwhelm the enemy by sheer weight of numbers.

The initial bombardment would be supported by seventy-two 18-pounders for wire cutting and thirty 6-inch and 4.5-inch howitzers for reducing the enemy trenches, while seven batteries of the Royal Horse Artillery would deploy their 13-pounders against the enemy communication trenches.

Once through the German front line, the plan was that the 8th Division should hold the breach while the 7th Division exploited forward towards Aubers Ridge. As elsewhere, the bombardment started at 0500 hours with some of the assault battalions moving out into no man's land to reduce the distance they would have to advance under fire. At 0540 hours the mines were detonated, the barrage lifted and the infantry advanced on the German defences at the double.

Even by this time, however, problems were starting to appear. The artillery fire appeared to be falling short, largely – it transpired – because the gun barrels were worn out and many shell fuses defective. One result of this was that the defenders were again completely unsub-dued and were openly waiting for the British attack, their bayonets flashing menacingly above their parapets.

The attack by the 24th Brigade was an immediate disaster, the assaulting troops being stopped within 50 metres of the British line, often by fire from German soldiers standing openly on their parapets. The battalions of the 23rd Brigade, coming up in close support, also suffered heavily, and by 0610 hours the advance of these two brigades had been stopped.

The assault by the 25th Brigade was initially very successful. Several platoons of the 1/13th London Regiment actually got into the German third-line trench, but this success was not duplicated elsewhere. The German line held and the attacking troops were soon pinned down in the open, taking heavy casualties. Forty minutes after the infantry had gone over the top, the 25th Brigade's commander,

Brigadier General Lowry Cole, arrived in the front-line trench to find it crammed with wounded men and the rest of his brigade scattered across no man's land, all forward movement having ceased.

Lowry Cole ordered more troops forward from the 2nd Lincolnshires, only to see the survivors from the leading waves running back in some confusion from the German trenches. While the brigadier was standing on the parapet, trying to halt this precipitate retreat, he was hit by machine-gun fire and mortally wounded. Brigadier General Pinney, commanding the 23rd Brigade, was ordered to take over the 25th Brigade as well, but there was now no possibility of renewing the attack. 'The British front and communications trenches were blocked with dead, wounded and leaderless men, the congestion being constantly increased by the endeavours of the rearmost waves to reach the front.'[3]

By 0830 hours the situation on the IV Corps front was grave. The infantry had managed to enter the German line at three points but could make no further progress. Nor could they be supported, reinforced or withdrawn, for German artillery and machine guns were raking the flat ground between the lines.

This dire situation was reported to General Haig but did not dent his desire to achieve some positive result at Aubers Ridge. This desire may have stemmed in part from reports reaching him from GHQ; the French were storming on to Vimy Ridge and needed strong support to keep their attack moving. Haig's ability to support this success with First Army was hampered by the defeats already inflicted on I Corps and the Indian Corps . . . and now on IV Corps. Here the 23rd Brigade was now being shelled in its forming-up position, the 2nd East Lancashires, to give just one example, losing 454 men before even leaving their trenches.

Haig still ordered General Rawlinson to press the IV Corps attack vigorously, but there was little the latter could do; the First Army's assault had foundered at the start and was now in total disarray. At 1800 hours Haig cancelled the order to attack at 2000 hours and summoned all three corps commanders to meet him at the Indian Corps HQ.

There they discussed the merits of a further attack in the dark, or a renewal of the offensive at dawn. The decision taken was to delay any further attack until daylight, but long before dawn the ammunition and casualty returns revealed how much the fight for Aubers Ridge had cost First Army.

In one brief day of battle, First Army had lost 458 officers and 11,161 men killed, wounded and missing, nearly as many as in the three-day battle of Neuve Chapelle – and not a metre of ground had been gained. The heaviest casualties – 192 officers and 4,490 men – had fallen on the 8th Division of IV Corps. The artillery, which had been firing all day and were still delivering harassing fire on the German trenches, reported that their stocks of ammunition were not adequate to sustain a further assault and that many of their guns were useless, their barrels and recoil mechanisms worn out by incessant firing.

It was now abundantly clear to all that the German defences could not be beaten down without artillery – and that artillery needed more heavy guns and larger supplies of high-explosive shell than any amounts currently available in the British line. It was also clear that the short bombardment and attacks relying on surprise were a thing of the past – battles would now need plenty of prior preparation by heavy guns and rely for their outcome on attrition.

These views, with a recommendation that the current attack on Aubers Ridge should be called off, were sent to Field Marshal French and any further attacks were cancelled, pending further orders, at 1320 hours on 10 May.

In the subsequent inquest, the blame for the failure at Aubers Ridge was placed entirely on a shortage of heavy guns and high-explosive shells and on the stark fact that the German defences were currently too strong for the methods available for reducing them. The generals appear to have escaped any condemnation, but the casualties caused in one fruitless day called for further explanation in which the blame was fixed on the government and the munitions industry.

This argument, over what came to be called the 'Shell Scandal', was fuelled by an article written on 14 May – just four days after the battle – by Colonel à Court Repington, the military correspondent of *The Times* and a crony of Field Marshal French, which stated that 'British soldiers died in vain on Aubers Ridge because more shells were needed.'

Further articles attacking the government duly followed in other papers and questions were asked in the House of Commons. It soon became clear that the figures relating to ammunition supply – though not necessarily the interpretation put on them by the press – were originating from somewhere close to Field Marshal French's HQ.

This disclosure proved a useful smokescreen for the other failures at Aubers Ridge, not least a failure to recognize that the enemy was intelligent and resourceful, equally capable of drawing lessons from previous battles and not least from the failures of his opponents. The Germans took steps to counter any moves the British might make for their next assault and created defences that proved more than adequate to halt the First Army advance in its tracks. That said, a shortage of heavy guns and enough high-explosive shell to pound those defences to pieces was a stark fact of life in 1915.

The 'Shell Scandal' rumbled on for months and occupies a great deal of space in many accounts – the biography of Sir John French devotes a twenty-two-page chapter to this one issue[4] – but the main outcome of the argument was the setting up of a Ministry of Munitions under David Lloyd George, who thereby took a long step towards Downing Street. Some of these allegations over the ammunition supply were true, but while they were being debated the BEF attacked again south of Ypres with an assault at Festubert. The war on the Western Front would continue.

8

Festubert, 15–27 May 1915

> Very considerable pressure was brought to bear on the British
> Commander-in-Chief both by General Joffre and General Foch,
> to induce him to continue offensive action.
>
> *British Official History, 1915*, Vol II, p. 45

ALTHOUGH THE BRITISH attack on Aubers Ridge had ended
abruptly after just one day, with very heavy losses incurred for
no visible advantage, matters appeared to be going somewhat better
with the French offensive in Artois. According to General Joffre, the
French were currently forging ahead along their front and, at last,
taking a quantity of ground at Vimy Ridge.

Joffre therefore insisted, frequently, loudly and at length, that Haig's
First Army must renew its attack on Aubers Ridge at once, if only
to prevent the Germans moving their forces south to counter this
advance at Vimy. For a number of reasons – the continuing action at
Ypres, the losses just incurred at Aubers Ridge and that chronic shortage of artillery ammunition – Field Marshal French was unable to
comply with these demands.

This being so, the days immediately after the end of the Aubers
Ridge encounter represented another low point in Anglo-French
relations on the Western Front – 'the most difficult in the relations
between the two Allied headquarters', to quote the Official History.[1]

For once, dissatisfaction between the Allied commanders was not
restricted entirely to the French. Field Marshal French was now
extremely peeved with his opposite number at GQG, and with General
Foch, and with good reason. Not only had the French 45th and 87th

Divisions given way before the gas at Ypres, thereby exposing the left of the British line to attack, but General Foch's repeated assurances that he would summon fresh forces and launch a massive counter-attack to restore this position at Ypres had come to nothing and still showed no sign of being implemented.

As for General Joffre, the *generalissimo*, his attitude towards the British was still based on ingrained beliefs, widely shared among the French generals. First, that the British were not pulling their weight in this struggle by taking over more of the line, supporting French efforts and putting in more attacks. Second, that the British generals should admit French superiority in all matters *militaire* and do as they were told without demur. If somewhat more tactfully expressed, the British view did not accord with these French sentiments, which were in any case based on a total and wilful misreading of the pre-war facts – and a somewhat exaggerated estimate of French generalship.

In order to understand the French point of view it is necessary to remind ourselves of the misconceptions that arose pre-1914 related in Chapter 1. From the moment the *Entente Cordiale* was signed, the French had spared no efforts to translate it into a full military alliance, in which aim they were aided by Brigadier Henry Wilson, Director of Military Operations at the War Office. Moreover, on several occasions during the years before the war the British government had pointed out to the French that any British participation in a Continental war would have to be decided on when that war arose and would be decided by 'the Government of the day' – not by some prior treaty or military alliance with the French.

All this seemed fair and logical to the British, but somehow, in the years from 1904, the French had convinced themselves – or allowed themselves to be convinced by Henry Wilson – that the British were equally anxious to confront the Hun and had thereby guaranteed to help France in the event of hostilities. This being so, any shortfall, actual or perceived, in the British commitment to French aims, post-August 1914, was seen as a failure, if not an actual betrayal by *l'Albion perfide*. To understand this deep divergence of views it is important to stress, yet again, that the British had never made any such commitment and had made that fact clear to the French government on several occasions, long before the outbreak of war.[2]

When the war began, this French delusion was helped and the British position obscured by the confusing orders given to the BEF commander by the British government. As related, these orders[3] directed Field Marshal French to comply with the demands of the French wherever possible but to remember that his was a separate command and he was not to place himself or his army under French command.

To his credit, Field Marshal French had tried to square these conflicting requirements to the best of his limited resources – and his equally limited abilities – but as the war escalated in 1915, his position became ever more precarious. With hindsight, it is possible to see that the British government should have taken a far tougher line with the French and not left the matter in the hands of the BEF commander; 'pussy-footing' around with Joffre and Foch did nothing for Anglo-French relations and simply fed the French sense of grievance.

In fairness, if all other factors were put aside, Joffre and Foch had a case at this time. In 1915 the French had the largest Allied army in the field and were holding by far the greater part of the line; it was clearly impossible for the British to go their own way in fighting this war and only sensible to fall in with French requirements and demands whenever possible, however unreasonable. It was also becoming clear, if not yet openly admitted, that some form of central control, or supreme command, was necessary to direct the diverse efforts of the *Entente* to some common strategic end. At the moment, the unco-ordinated efforts of the Allies were not sufficient to blunt the enemy's efforts anywhere; to win this war, the armies needed some form of strategic direction from the top.

That might be the case in the long term but the breaking point came when French demands ignored the realities of the BEF's current position – that it still lacked the men and the kit – the guns and shells – for major or extended operations. There was also the harsh fact that French strategy and French tactics and French doctrine – the '*offensive à outrance*', or all-out attack regardless of loss – had already cost the French armies a great number of lives for no apparent gain, and the British generals had no intention of going down that road. Firm

evidence supporting French claims to military infallibility was somewhat lacking in 1915; French courage cannot be faulted, but their
military competence can.

In any event, by May 1915 the French attack at Vimy was running
out of steam. Having penetrated the German line at Notre-Dame-
de-Lorette their advance had ground to a halt on the eastern slopes
of Vimy Ridge. This attack petered out for a reason that Haig would
have found familiar – a failure to hold the French reserves close
enough to the front for rapid intervention after the breakthrough.
Even so, the French attacks continued, gradually becoming yet
another costly battle of attrition. By the time this 'second battle of
Artois' ended on 18 June, the French Tenth Army had lost 2,260
officers and 100,273 men, and gained no useful territory whatsoever . . . a large casualty list is no indication of superior generalship.

Nevertheless, ever eager to help his ally and follow some part of his
confused instructions, Field Marshal French ordered Haig to resume
his attack as soon as possible. A fresh battle, another extension of the
Aubers Ridge–Neuve Chapelle engagement, the battle of Festubert,
duly began on 15 May.

The first move of this new encounter took place on 10 May, even
while the fighting at Aubers Ridge was subsiding, with the transfer of
the 7th Division from IV Corps to I Corps. The 7th Division went
into the line north of Festubert, a small village due west of Violaines
and some 5 kilometres south of Neuve Chapelle. On 13 May, the 1st
and 47th Divisions were formed into a unit known as Barter's Force,
commanded by Major General C. St L. Barter of the 47th Division.
With the Second Army fully engaged at Ypres, this new attack at
Festubert must again be mounted by Haig's long-suffering and very
tired First Army.

This move to Festubert indicated both a change of front and
a change of direction. The ground at Neuve Chapelle and Aubers
Ridge had proved too tough, secured by defences the First Army had
been unable to penetrate. This new attack from Festubert would thrust
east, north of the La Bassée canal, where Haig hope to find easier
ground and a less well-entrenched enemy; not all these hopes would
be fulfilled. Study of the map on page 150 will be helpful at this point.

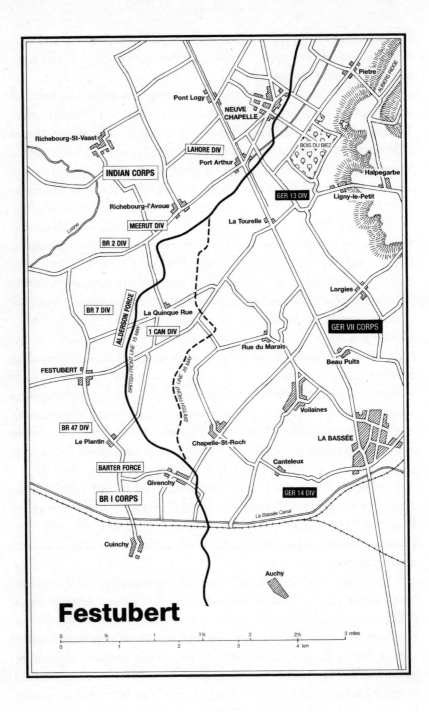

Pietre

Pont Logy

NEUVE
CHAPELLE

Richebourg-St-Vaast

BOIS DU BIEZ

LAHORE DIV

Port Arthur

Halpegarbe

INDIAN CORPS

GER 13 DIV

Ligny-le-Petit

Richebourg-l'Avoue

La Tourelle

MEERUT DIV

BR 2 DIV

L.Loisne

BR 7 DIV

La Quinque Rue

ALDERSON FORCE

Lorgies

GER VII CORPS

1 CAN DIV

BRITISH FRONT LINE 15 MAY

BRITISH FRONT LINE 25 MAY

Rue du Marais

Beau Puits

FESTUBERT

Voilaines

BR 47 DIV

LA BASSÉE

Le Plantin

Chapelle-St-Roch

BARTER FORCE

Canteleux

Givenchy

BR I CORPS

GER 14 DIV

La Bassée Canal

Cuinchy

Auchy

Festubert

| 0 | ½ | 1 | 1½ | 2 | 2½ | 3 miles |
| 0 | 1 | 2 | 3 | 4 km | | |

This part of the German line was held by VII Corps of the Sixth Army, which had all three of its regiments in the line, each occupying a front of 2 kilometres. Two battalions of each regiment held the front line with the third in billets, 3 to 5 kilometres to the rear. These units were well dug in, had a sufficiency of artillery and a limited number of reserves, all from VII Corps, consisting of a Jäger battalion and some cavalry. No further reserves could be expected from the Sixth Army as its two reserve formations, the 58th and 115th Divisions, had been moved to oppose the French Tenth Army at Vimy.

It appears therefore that the Germans opposing the British at Festubert were few in number, and this was indeed the case. As French pointed out to Haig, 'The strength of your Army is far superior to the hostile forces in front of you. The enemy has few or no reserves, other than local, which he can bring up.'

This assessment was accurate but misses the point; the enemy was well dug in and fighting on the defensive; numbers alone were not the issue. The British must assault the German defences, and weaken those defences before that assault with artillery fire – at Festubert, as at many of the battles before and afterwards, success largely depended on the guns and on a generous supply of artillery ammunition. This was likely to be a problem as ammunition was in short supply, not least because French had recently been obliged to send some of his slender reserve stocks to the Dardanelles.

Following the delays caused by the German defences at Aubers Ridge, Haig abandoned the elusive advantages of surprise for this new attack. This time, instead of the sudden, short bombardment of forty minutes or less, his guns would pound the enemy line for two full days and nights using heavy guns, 5-inch, 6-inch, 9.2-inch howitzers, to cut the wire and demolish the trenches. This steady shellfire would also, Haig hoped, demoralize the defenders and reduce their resistance to an infantry assault.

There was, inevitably, a snag. Joffre wanted the British to attack as soon as possible, claiming that the Germans had already moved their 58th and 115th Divisions to the Arras–Vimy sector. To move and register the guns and carry out this prior bombardment, however,

Haig had to put his attack back until 15 May; Field Marshal French approved of this delay while Joffre and Foch fumed.

Nor was this all; Field Marshal French also ordered some changes in the forces committed to this new attack, and by the time the preliminary bombardment began, the First Army position was as follows. I Corps had the 7th and 2nd Divisions deployed on a 5-kilometre front running from Festubert to Richebourg l'Avoue, a scattering of houses west of Port Arthur, and a scant 400 metres south of Neuve Chapelle. Both divisions were tasked for this attack, with the 1st Canadian Division, brought down from Ypres, in I Corps reserve. South of I Corps, Barter's Force – the 47th and 1st Divisions – held the ground as far as the Loos–Vermelles road while the Indian Corps occupied the front from Richebourg to the Bois Grenier.

Haig's plan followed the general lines of the one used at Aubers Ridge but on a less ambitious scale. The German line was to be breached in two places, by the 7th Division north of Festubert and by the 2nd Division 600 metres away to the south, not 6 kilometres away, as for the Aubers attack. Nor were the divisions asked to make a deep penetration. The depth of the initial attack was to be no more than 900 metres; when that much had been achieved the advance was to stop.

Given that a failure to exploit the initial success had been a prime cause of the problems met at Neuve Chapelle, this limitation might seem unusual or plain wrong, but Haig and French were not planing a major advance. The prime purpose of this Festubert attack was to help the French and stop the whinging from Joffre and Foch; any other successes or territorial gains would be a bonus. In military terms, Festubert was little more than a diversion.

Apart from the longer artillery bombardment there were a few new features, most notably the intention of Major General Henry Horne's 2nd Division to put in their initial attack by night and be established in the German first and second line by daylight. This attack, by two brigades of the 2nd Division, would be supported by a brigade of the Meerut Division and take place on a 2-kilometre front south of Richebourg l'Avoue.

If all went well, this first assault would be taken up at daylight by the 7th Division, attacking just to the south, their attack timed to coincide with a renewed advance by the 2nd Division's brigades. If all went according to plan – those fatal 'ifs' were already starting to accumulate – the inner flanks of the two divisions would meet on the line of the Festubert–La Tourelle road, a kilometre south of the 2nd Division start line. On this line the two divisions would halt and dig in. The flanking forces – Barter's Force and the Meerut Division – would also advance while the artillery battered the enemy positions farther south and prepared the ground for another advance. The *Official History* comments that the battle of Festubert was to initiate the policy known as attrition – 'the breaking down of a stubborn foe by the resolute use of superior numbers'.[4]

If this was indeed the new British policy it was one fraught with danger. Attrition is a dangerous game to play for, even if it works, the losses on both sides may be extreme. And it may not work; the enemy may refuse to engage in a battle based on manpower and may retire behind his defences, against which the attackers will waste their strength in vain. There is also the danger that in opting for attrition a general has abandoned all other possibilities and ceases to consider all his options – in effect, ceases to think entirely, abandoning every alternative in favour of a policy based on brute force and bloodshed.

The evidence so far indicates that General Haig was adapting his tactics as he gradually grasped the problems inherent in this Western Front situation and learned from the reverses that each battle delivered. He was also thinking broadly, notably in his use of the air arm for reconnaissance and communications – the RFC had not merited any consideration at all prior to August 1914 but now was proving of ever increasing use to the army staffs.

Any ignorance of air operations had been rapidly dispelled, especially since the formation of the trench system stopped the use of cavalry in the reconnaissance role. Aircraft were now used for this purpose, for artillery observation, to enhance communications, and for making attacks on enemy reconnaissance aircraft. During the Festubert engagement the RFC was also used in bombing operations behind the enemy front line, attacking German troop trains and military headquarters. An examination of Haig's planning and command during all three engagements at Neuve Chapelle, Aubers Ridge and Festubert gives evidence of a mind at work, evaluating each experience, adding to the existing range of command skills.

What is lacking is any evidence that Haig, or anyone else, was grasping the broad picture. Essentially, Haig was still trying to find a way of making the old methods work. Artillery still opened the attack, the infantry went forward to force a breach and the cavalry stood by to exploit success. This was the way it had always been; this was how battles were fought and won.

So far, admittedly, the battles had not been won, but there was always, apparently, a good reason for failure – a lack of artillery, poor communications, a delay in committing reserves . . . whatever. If these errors could be eliminated, perhaps the old ways would work, for surely the trick was to muster the traditional assets in some successful combination? What had not been appreciated was that in the current conditions governing warfare on the Western Front the old methods of offence would *never* work.

With the inestimable benefit of hindsight, much of that is obvious today, but it was not so obvious in 1915, and it would take another year before lessons learned in later battles such as the Somme in 1916 began to impinge on tactics. Until then it seemed to British generals, in company with their French and German counterparts, that the key to success was more and heavier artillery; and that failure was caused by the lack of it. As we have seen, sufficient artillery was not available to the British in 1915. Even if there had been enough artillery, it would not have guaranteed success, as the battles of 1916 and 1917 were to show. Ultimately, it was the *orchestration* of all arms, infantry, artillery, air and tanks in a co-ordinated deep battle that brought success, but that was a long way off in 1915, and ultimately it was only the British that achieved it – in 1918.

The artillery bombardment at Festubert began on a 5-kilometre frontage on 13 May and continued steadily, though not continuously, for two days, until the infantry assault went in on 15 May. Haig had mustered a greater number of guns than for either of the previous attacks and the majority had been properly registered. More than 100,000 shells, over one third of them heavy, fell on the enemy line;

the problem at Festubert was that a worrying number of these shells failed to explode, probably owing to the faulty manufacture of fuses in the British or US armaments factories.

Reports coming in to the divisional HQs indicated that the effects of this bombardment varied. The 2nd and 7th Divisions declared themselves satisfied but on 14 May, the day before the attack, Lieutenant General Anderson, GOC of the Meerut Division, stated that he did not consider 'that sufficient damage has been done to ensure the success of the assault . . . as regards wire cutting, we have not yet begun as the batteries detailed for it have had to shift their positions'.

Haig therefore postponed the attack for twenty-four hours, until the night of 15/16 May – a further irritant for General Joffre – and the infantry assault began at 2330 hours on 15 May when the 5th and 6th Infantry Brigades of the 2nd Division fixed their bayonets and advanced into no man's land. With them went the 4th Guards Brigade in support, and the Garhwal Brigade of the Meerut Division advanced 400 metres on their left flank; altogether these three assaulting brigades, two British and one Indian, mustered some ten thousand men.

This first attack was successful, at least in parts. The 6th Brigade got into the German front-line and support trench as the enemy fled to the rear up the communications trenches. The 6th Brigade then consolidated, having suffered very few casualties. The 5th Brigade and the Garhwal Brigade were not so lucky, as the enemy on their part of the front had been alerted by diversionary fire put down by the Lahore Division. The artillery barrage kept the enemy's heads down while the British and Indian troops got out of their trenches and formed up, but when the barrage lifted the advancing infantry ran into machine-gun and rifle fire, swiftly supported by artillery.

Nor was the cover of darkness much protection. The Germans had an adequate supply of excellent flares and rockets with which to illuminate no man's land, and were able to shoot the British and Indians down in quantity; only one battalion of the 5th Brigade, the 2nd Inniskilling Fusiliers, reached the German front line – and lost 649 men in the process, and in holding their position. Losses in the other 5th Brigade battalions were also severe; the 2nd Worcesters lost 395 men, the 2nd Oxfordshire 395, the 2nd Leicestershire 308; the 39th Garhwal Rifles lost 154.

After their previous experiences, the British commanders had been prepared for some reverses and a further artillery bombardment was put down, pending a renewal of the attack at 0315 hours on 16 May. Unfortunately, this three-hour delay in renewing the attack gave the Germans all the time they needed to bring up reinforcements; the position of the 6th Brigade was sealed off and when the new attack went in at dawn, it duly failed.

When Haig heard of this reverse, at 0540 hours, he ordered the Inniskillings of the 5th Brigade and the entire 6th Brigade to hold their positions while a fresh Indian formation, the Sirhind Brigade, moved up behind the 2nd Division; this was sound tactics, reinforcing success, however limited, while placing the rest of the force on the defensive and so limiting losses.

While the 2nd Division and the Meerut Division were thus engaged, the 7th Division went forward, spearheaded by the 22nd and 24th Infantry Brigades. Their attack went in north of Festubert at 0315 hours on 16 May and saw two sensible tactical innovations. Although the actual assault went in on a front of just 850 metres, the initial artillery bombardment fell on another 750 metres of German parapet, north and south of the intended breach, to prevent the infantry moving across no man's land on the breach being hit by enfilade fire.

In addition, this attack was closely supported by the fire of six field guns, 13- and 18-pounders, which had been trundled forward into the British front-line trenches. These fired high-explosive shells directly at the German trenches with some success, but the attack of the leading battalions in the grey light of dawn was still met with heavy machine-gun fire. The attacking troops then went to ground; the commanding officers of the 1st Royal Welch Fusiliers and the 2nd Queen's were killed; command of the Royal Welch Fusiliers was then taken over by a captain – and the assault was suspended for fifteen minutes until the enemy trenches could again be deluged with shellfire.

Fortunately, the battalions of the 20th Brigade were coming up on the left and by 0700 hours the 22nd Brigade had attained its objectives.

More it could not do; the Royal Welch Fusiliers had lost nineteen officers out of twenty-four and 559 men out of 806. The 2nd Queen's had lost twenty-one officers out of twenty-two and 433 men out of the 773 who advanced that morning.

The attack of the 20th Brigade, led by the 2nd Scots Guards and the 2nd Border Regiment, got off to a good start and then stalled as the Border battalion ran into the British bombardment and suffered heavily from their own gunfire. Even so, this advance reached and carried the German front-line trenches, but any further advance was inhibited by deep, flooded ditches and enfilade fire from German machine guns in the 'Quadrilateral', a position between the assault lines of the 2nd and 7th Divisions. One result of this fire was the death of the 2nd Border's commanding officer, Lieutenant Colonel Wood, and his second-in-command.

The fighting in and around the German front line then became hand to hand, British assaults being met by German counter-attacks; one of these counter-attacks completely wiped out an entire company of the Royal Welch Fusiliers, only one officer and three men surviving – as prisoners.

By 0900 hours on 16 May the situation was as follows. The 20th Brigade had advanced into the German trenches and was hanging on there. The 22nd Brigade had pushed forward for another 600 metres but was now under attack from artillery and machine guns. On the 2nd Division front the 6th Brigade and a battalion of the 5th Brigade were beyond the German front line but the rest of the 5th Brigade and all the Garhwal Brigade had failed to get forward. The gap between the 2nd and the 7th Division was still wide open and German artillery was now pounding the troops out in no man's land. Overall, the situation was not encouraging.

At 0900 hours, Lieutenant General Sir Charles Monro, GOC I Corps, visited the headquarters of the 2nd and 7th Divisions to assess the situation. The two divisions had not managed to link up their inner flanks and only one brigade of the 2nd Division had actually entered the German trenches. Electing to follow the First Army plan, General Monro therefore ordered the 2nd and 7th Divisions to press on and achieve a link-up. Their attempt began at 1000 hours, but the task proved extremely difficult across open ground pounded by artillery, machine-gun and aimed rifle fire. The attacks continued throughout the morning and were abandoned in mid-afternoon, with no success achieved.

During the afternoon General Haig came to visit the Indian Corps, I Corps and the 2nd and 7th Divisions. Having consulted the commanding generals and their staffs, he concluded that another attack to the east by the right wing – the 7th Division – offered the greatest chance of success, being less exposed to artillery fire. The units on the left flank, the Indian Corps and IV Corps – and Barter's Force to the south – were to remain on the defensive for the moment.

The objective of the battle now changed, from an operation designed to prevent any shift of forces to Vimy and perhaps seize part of the enemy front to one of stark attrition: 'the main object to aim at for the present is to continue to wear down the enemy by exhaustion and prevent him detaching troops to oppose the French'.[5]

The battle of Festubert was therefore renewed at dawn on 17 May. The prime objective now was the completion of the task attempted on the previous day, the link-up of the 2nd and the 7th Divisions. Unfortunately, the attacks for that day and 18 May were constantly hampered by communication difficulties. These increased with every day of battle, leading to a gradual breakdown in control, a situation aided, or even created, by the constant German artillery fire.

Nor was this all. Unknown to the British, on the night of 16/17 May the Germans had started preparing a second defence line, 1,000 metres behind their present front line, and were beginning to pull back towards it. This new line was observed and reported to First Army HQ by RFC patrols but its significance was not at first appreciated. The attack by the 7th Division duly began at 0245 hours on 17 May and by 0730 hours the German trenches, including many of their communication trenches, had been so damaged by shellfire that when the order to withdraw to the new line came the Germans were unable to pull back; around 450 men abandoned their shell-battered trenches and surrendered to the 1st/7th Battalion, The King's Liverpool Regiment.

The attack by the 2nd and 7th Divisions had meanwhile been postponed by General Monro, first to 0900 hours, then to 1030 hours, before being rescheduled to 0930 hours, after reports of German troops surrendering reached Monro's HQ.

This advance proved successful, though the troops ran into British as well as German artillery fire and another battalion commander, Lieutenant Colonel C. J. Stevenson of the 1st King's, was killed. The German line was taken on both divisional fronts and the advance continued to the new German defence line, where the attack was held. This success inevitably aroused General Haig's latent optimism, and at 1130 hours on 17 May he signalled to I Corps that 'There are signs of enemy resistance breaking down . . . Brigadiers on the spot will take the opportunity of pressing on; 7th Division against Chapelle la Roch–Canteleux–Givenchy, 2nd Division on Rue du Marais.'

Having stressed the importance of gaining this line, Haig added that Sir John French had now ordered that Aubers Ridge was no longer the First Army objective; the aim now was to take La Bassée and get access to the territory south of the La Bassée canal.

Anticipating further progress in this direction, Haig now put the 3rd Canadian Brigade at the disposal of I Corps. The attack was duly pressed but no further progress was made, and by mid-afternoon, four hours after that hopeful signal from General Haig, the advance of both the 7th and 2nd Divisions had stopped yet again. The advance was further checked when the infantry encountered wide dykes previously undetected and deep enough to drown those laden men who attempted to swim across. In the afternoon a further advance was stopped by enfilading machine-gun fire, which decimated the ranks of the 4th (Guards) Brigade of the 2nd Division, while an attempt by the Sirhind Brigade to support them also led to heavy losses. The Guards halted their advance and dug in, and all along the line other British units did the same. During this time yet another commanding officer was killed, Lieutenant Colonel A. Fraser of the 1st/4th Cameron Highlanders in the 21st Brigade; in the course of that day the Cameron Highlanders lost another twelve officers and 215 men.

The night of 17/18 May was wet and miserable and dawn was misty, hindering the artillery preparations for the next phase of the attack. These only began in the early afternoon with the infantry advance scheduled for 1630 hours, when the main thrust would be carried out by the 3rd Canadian Brigade, now attached to the 7th Division, and the 4th (Guards) Brigade, both advancing south-east across La Quinque Rue. The British commanders had not yet realized that the Germans had established a new defence line behind this position, which the preliminary bombardment had failed to touch.

The attack duly went in but was halted almost at once by enfilade machine-gun fire; the leading companies of the Guards Brigade lost so heavily in the first 100 metres that Brigadier Lord Cavan halted the attack, realizing that the planned advance of 550 metres was impossible. At 1930 hours the Guards attack was halted by orders from 2nd Division – losses in the 2nd Grenadiers and Irish Guards by then amounted to twenty officers and some five hundred men. The 3rd Canadian Brigade did not arrive in time to take part in this attack and then went to relieve the 21st Brigade on the right of the Guards.

Whatever happened to this attack by the 2nd and 7th Divisions, General Haig had decided that they had done enough and must be replaced in the line by the 1st Canadian Division and the 51st (Highland) Division. This change took place on 19 May; by the following day the Canadians and the Highlanders, now combined as 'Alderson's Force', named after the commander of the Canadian Division, Major General E. A. H. Alderson, occupied the front from north of Festubert to the junction with the Indian Corps. I Corps – 'Barter's Force' having been dissolved – now consisted of the 1st, 2nd, 7th and 47th Divisions.

The Germans had not been idle while these moves went on. During 19 May fresh reserves were brought up and their new defence line was strengthened. As a result, attacks on this line by the Canadians during 20–23 May met with little success; although the Canadians got into the German trench on 23 May they were quickly driven out again on 24 May by heavy machine-gun fire from both flanks.

Haig was still determined to press on and renewed the attack the next day with the 47th Division, after a full-day bombardment of the German line. The 47th Division, led by the 142nd Brigade, attacked at 1830 hours, just north of the Givenchy–La Chapelle road, and two battalions of the London Regiment captured the original German front and support trenches on a 1,000-metre front, after an advance of 400 metres – a highly commendable effort.

Unfortunately, this was as much as they could do. The leading battalions were immediately brought under machine-gun fire and were then struck by artillery concentrations – and blocked by German infantry occupying the newly discovered trench behind the original front line. Nothing further could be achieved; artillery ammunition was running out, casualties had been severe and the Germans stronger than before. Although local attacks continued until 27 May, the battle of Festubert was broken off on 25 May, after ten days of heavy fighting.

What had been achieved? Very little, at least in terms of ground gained; that desirable ground beyond Aubers Ridge was as unattainable as ever. The attack had managed to push back the German line for about a kilometre; the new British line now ran from just south of Port Arthur to just west of Givenchy, 4 kilometres to the south. As for the main objective, to assist the French with their battle in Artois, the French did not take Vimy Ridge and their attacks, which continued for another month, until 18 June, also proved very costly.

So too did the battle of Festubert, in which First Army lost 16,648 men killed, wounded and missing, again a heavy price to pay for so little gain. Nor did this attack do much to damage the Germans, who lost about five thousand men during the Festubert engagement.

These three attacks mounted by the First Army between Ypres and Vimy from March into May, all with the object of taking Aubers Ridge and convincing the French of British resolve, should now be analysed. What had they achieved and what lessons had been learned – if any? Three battles in three months with British casualties now exceeding 40,000 men; Aubers Ridge was still in German hands and Field Marshal French and the BEF had nothing to show for this effort and sacrifice but 4 kilometres of shell-torn, blood-stained ground, 1 kilometre wide at its widest section and plentifully littered with corpses.

Considering all this, is it possible to find some reason or merit in the strategy of Field Marshal French and the tactics of General Haig? The answer to the first question has already been put forward and remains starkly obvious; the Western Front could not be broken by the means currently available and some fresh methods must be found. As for why these attacks continued in such circumstances, it is apparent that the real reasons lie in that deep-seated desire to placate the French.

Field Marshal French was actually in an impossible position – 'between a rock and a hard place', as the Americans say, obliged to support the French in their offensives but without the men, kit or munitions to do so. The *Official History* concedes this point: 'The BEF was not in 1915 in a condition to make the effort our French Allies expected of the British Empire in a life and death struggle.'[6]

Until a fresh strategy was found, the war on the Western Front would continue to produce heavy casualties and be fought with traditional tactics. From the results we have so far, at Second Ypres, Neuve Chapelle, Aubers Ridge and now Festubert, can we judge whether the generals, and most notably General Sir Douglas Haig, were showing any sign that they were beginning to grasp the true nature of this new kind of war?

For the last ninety years, many Great War critics and historians have employed the benefits of hindsight to castigate the generals for their incompetence and callousness. Much of this criticism is uninformed or unfair, for after the battle is over we can all 'play general'.

History, however, albeit viewed backwards, is lived forwards. To evaluate the actions of the Great War generals we must start at the beginning, before the battles began, and evaluate what they knew then, not evaluate them with what we know now. We can now see that the defensive combination of barbed wire, heavy artillery and machine guns could not be overcome by any force or method presently available to the Anglo-French armies. True as this is, that fact was not so obvious in 1915.

Besides, to concentrate on the Western Front, important as it was, is taking the narrow view. Looking back, it is easy to see that Germany had already lost this war. The Schlieffen Plan had failed in 1914 and Germany was now fighting a war on two fronts, a war the German Imperial Staff previously stated could not be won and which the Schlieffen Plan had been devised to avoid.

In 1915 the Russians were still in the field and fighting hard; the British were growing stronger by the day. Even while the battle at

Festubert was in progress Italy joined the war on the side of the *Entente* powers, by declaring war on Austria-Hungary – if not yet on Germany. In recent weeks a German U-boat had sunk the liner *Lusitania* off the coast of Ireland with the loss of 1,198 lives, 128 of them American; if this sort of thing continued the United States might well enter the war. Everywhere Germany's list of enemies was growing, and in this there was hope of eventual victory for the *Entente* powers.

Apparently, therefore, the best course of action, for the moment at least, was to hang on in the west and keep fighting – but what was the best way to do this in the present situation? The Western Front and the German armies manning it were both intact. Any initial defeats on the Eastern Front had been quickly contained, Austria-Hungary could hold her own against the Italians, if not against the Russians, and Turkey was in the process of inflicting a further defeat on the Allies at Gallipoli, where Allied troops had gone ashore on 25 April. Overall, both sides had reasons for anticipating eventual victory and the war would therefore continue until one side or the other was totally defeated.

This returns the question of the Western Front battles to the generals currently fighting them. Were they making a useful contribution to the outcome of this war? Did their current tactics and command skills offer any hope of victory in the field? The evidence for this is scanty. Sir Douglas Haig had both planned and commanded in the last three battles but had achieved very little. He had failed to achieve a breakthrough or gain his prime objective of Aubers Ridge – and had lost a large number of good men in his attempts to do so.

On the other hand, can it be fairly alleged that he had mishandled his army, or acted like a donkey? Surely not, when all the circumstances and difficulties of the time are taken into account. A fair if critical view of the evidence suggests that Haig was using his brains in fighting this new kind of war, and that the BEF did not yet have the resources, in guns and shells and manpower, to fight it properly. For that lack of resources the blame must rest squarely with the pre-war British government, which would not then – and will not now – pay for a large, well-equipped army in times of peace.

Certainly, Douglas Haig had not so far shown much in the way of original thinking or strategic innovation. Like French and Joffre and all the other commanders, he was sticking to the old ways and trying to make them work – but with variations and improvements. The well-worn allegation that Haig always attacked in the same way is not borne out by an examination of these recent three engagements. He had a limited number of cards but he appeared to be playing them well.

When something went wrong in one battle – a breakdown in communications, a failure to hold the reserves at readiness – Haig took steps to remedy that error for the next engagement, at least as far as the situation permitted. His attempts to improve matters did not always succeed, and there was always the small matter of the enemy, who was never less than resourceful. The Germans too were constantly deepening their positions and improving their defensive tactics, but Haig was certainly trying to make some sense of this war, and he deserves full credit for making those efforts, whatever the outcome, rather than decades of constant denigration.

To balance this praise, it also has to be admitted that these heavy First Army losses in three hard-fought battles had not been rewarded with any success – quite the contrary. The net result was little short of zero, and in such circumstances it is hard to defend Douglas Haig against the 'donkeys' allegation, until the overall situation is taken into account and one attempts to put forward some element that would have made a difference.

The main allegation, that since these attacks were getting nowhere and only driving up the casualty figures they should be stopped until some means of breaking the enemy line was discovered, is sensible but not acceptable. The French, for one, would not accept it.

They wanted the enemy expelled from France in short order and were not going to wait for years for that happy outcome – even if it cost them, and their British allies, a great number of men. This being so, the only option now was to bind up the wounds, bury the dead, train more soldiers, find more guns and ammunition and, as soon as possible, do it all again.

After Festubert, the war on the Western Front subsided for a while,

while the heavy losses of the spring were absorbed and plans were laid for a new offensive in the autumn. This pause gives us time to consider events elsewhere, in Russia and at Gallipoli, in order to place the Western Front campaign in context, before we return there for the early stages of what became the battle of Loos.

9

Operations Elsewhere, 1915

The German lines in France may be looked upon as a fortress that cannot be carried by assault . . . with the result that these lines may be held by an investing force while operations proceed elsewhere.

Lord Kitchener, letter to Field Marshal French, 2 January 1915

THESE BATTLES ON the Western Front in 1915, at Ypres, Vimy, Champagne, Aubers and Festubert, were not discrete events. They were part of that constantly growing, worldwide struggle that became the Great War, and they have to be put in that context, especially when parts of that worldwide struggle had a direct bearing on the military situation in France. It is therefore wrong to believe either that the war was currently concentrated exclusively on the Western Front, or that the events and problems of 1915 were typical of other years in that war, or arose from the immediate situation. The events of that year on the Western Front have to be seen in the context of the war as a whole.

When Lord Kitchener wrote his perceptive letter, quoted above, to the BEF commander in January 1915 he was referring indirectly to a proposed operation in the eastern Mediterranean, one that had recently been discussed in cabinet and eventually became the Dardanelles landing and the subsequent Gallipoli campaign. At this time the notion that 'operations elsewhere' were even being contemplated would have been unwelcome news to Field Marshal French. He fully agreed with General Joffre that France was the only theatre where decisive results could be achieved, and that all available divisions, guns and shells should be sent there and nowhere else.

This belief, while understandable, is highly contentious. At this point in the story of 1915 it would be as well to leave the Western Front for a while and consider those actions, or 'operations', that were taking place 'elsewhere'. Apart from widening the argument, a consideration of these 'operations elsewhere' will also help to dispel any notion that the national governments or the various commanders-in-chief were adopting a totally blinkered approach to the war or hoping to end it by simply repeating, on an ever increasing scale, those frontal attacks on the Western Front which had so far proved both futile and extremely costly.

Frontal attack would indeed continue on the Western Front, but it forms only part of the picture. In 1915, while the Allied generals were striving to find a way to break the enemy line with the old methods, the various problems brought about by the creation of the Western Front were receiving active and thoughtful consideration by the powers that be at the War Office and in Whitehall. The 'donkeys' accusation assumes that the *Entente* generals and the politicians thought that the only way to break through on the Western Front was to beat their heads against it, but this is not the case; many other avenues were being explored, and some of these should now be considered.

To begin with, there was always a possibility, albeit a remote one, that the embattled nations, faced with lengthening casualty lists, would finally come to their senses and talk peace. Curiously enough, the growing number of casualties had the opposite effect. On both sides of the line the rising death toll only stiffened national resolve to continue the war. After losing so many men it seemed impossible, if not plain wrong, to stop the fighting now and reach some compromise with the foe, thereby tacitly admitting that the hundreds of thousands of men who had died in this war so far had died for nothing.

One wonders whether, had it been possible to consult those men, that expanding army of the Great War dead, they would have been so obdurate. Perhaps they would have seen one stark fact; that if this war continued more millions would join them in the graveyard. Seen in that context, peace, if hard to achieve, was a necessary and desirable option.

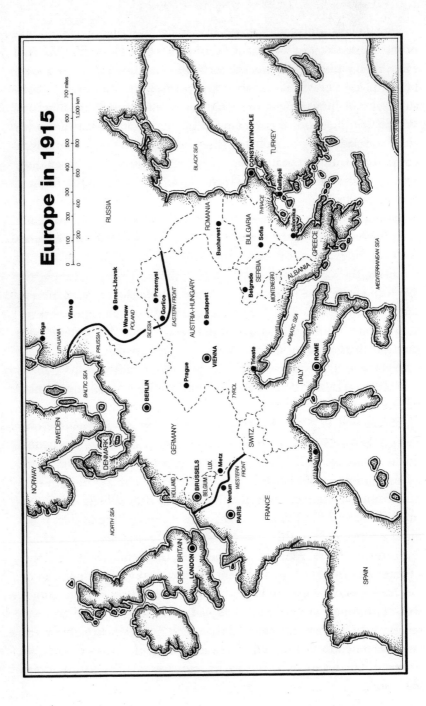

Europe in 1915

Such an option had been urged upon the nations by the president of the United States, Woodrow Wilson, in 1914, before the war had even begun. In May 1914, Wilson had sent his emissary, Colonel Edward M. House, a Texan millionaire, on a peace mission to Britain and Germany. Colonel House – the rank was honorary – had helped Wilson win the presidential election in 1912, and the two men were close colleagues. Wilson charged House with approaching Sir Edward Grey, the British foreign secretary, and the Kaiser, and exploring avenues for a peaceful settlement of the naval arms race. Sir Edward and the Kaiser both expressed interest in the idea of an Anglo-German conference, and one had been tentatively arranged in Kiel during July 1914 before hostilities intervened.

President Wilson had not ceased his efforts as the war gained momentum. Some of his concern was undoubtedly based on a fear that if the war continued the USA would inevitably be sucked into it, a fear intensified by the Germans' use of the submarine weapon against neutral shipping, and in particular by the sinking of the liner *Lusitania* by the submarine *U-20* off the coast of Ireland in May 1915, with the loss of 1,198 lives, including 128 Americans.

This event, terrible as it was, was only the latest in a long series of tragedies since August 1914, ranging from the sack of the Belgian university town of Louvain to the recent execution of the British nurse Edith Cavell, which ensured that if the USA ever entered this war it would do so on the side of the *Entente*. Against this has to be set the fact that there were some 15 million Americans of Irish descent who were totally opposed to helping the British at all and another 11 million German-Americans largely devoted to supporting the Kaiser.

To this can be added the fact that the US Army was very small, a force mustering just 80,000 men, most of it currently deployed on the Mexican frontier, fending off the revolutionary bandit Pancho Villa. For the moment at least Wilson's peace policy was widely supported by the American public and US industry profited greatly by supplying arms and munitions to the combatant powers. Even so, a fear of 'escalation', that the USA would gradually be sucked into this conflict, remained a major political issue.

This fear of escalation was only part of it; Woodrow Wilson genuinely hated war, and in late January 1915 Colonel House was again dispatched to Europe, tasked to discover whether the bloodshed in this war so far had produced any active desire for peace among the warring nations. His conclusion was that neither side was now serious about wanting peace. For the moment they appeared content to await the outcome of the coming year's offensives and were simply playing for time.

There were, however, some national differences. The British were not opposed to a negotiated peace, provided the Germans asked for it. 'When Germany really wishes peace she should approach all the Allies or President Wilson, who could then communicate with all the Allies fairly and straightforwardly,' declared Sir Edward Grey. The Germans and the French were less willing to compromise, the French because the Germans were on their soil, the Germans because they had taken a great deal of territory and wanted some compensation and reward in return for giving it up.

Colonel House duly toured Europe throughout the spring of 1915, and began by asking the nations to declare both their 'war aims' and the terms they would expect in return for peace. Britain and France declared that their terms would include the German evacuation of Belgium, the unequivocal return of Alsace and Lorraine to France and full compensation for the losses and damage caused by the German Army. In the circumstances these aims did not seem unreasonable to Colonel House, but Germany did not hesitate before rejecting them.

In spite of this rebuff, Colonel House then asked the German Chancellor, Herr T. von Bethmann-Hollweg, to state Germany's war aims – and must have been staggered by the reply. To begin with, for any return to peace Germany required the guaranteed retention of Alsace and Lorraine, taken from France in 1871 and a major cause of the current war. She also wished to retain the Belgian city of Liège and to the Lorraine and Alsace industrial centres to add the French industrial basin of Longwy-Briey. Bethmann-Hollweg added that the *Entente* powers, not Germany and her Austrian and Turkish allies, must also pay the full cost of the war.

With her industrial base secured, Germany also wanted to ensure commercial survival and a market for her industrial products. A further demand was for the post-war creation of a new commercial Europe – *Mitteleurope* – a massive extension of the nineteenth century German *Zollverein* or Customs Union, a commercial pact among the North German states dominated by Prussia and created in the 1840s. The creation of the *Zollverein* had marked the start of Germany's rise to economic and military power and, with the assistance of three wars against Denmark, Austria and France, had led to the creation of the German Reich in 1871.

The Kaiser, his minions and the German industrialists of the Pan-German League now wished to expand their commercial power base to most of the Continent, and the *Mitteleurope* notion was a massive project, not unlike the post-Second World War European Common Market and Union. Apart from Longwy-Briey, Germany would annex Belgium and the French Channel coast as far south as the Somme estuary. German troops would occupy France on a line drawn east from the Somme to Verdun; the French population in these areas would be encouraged to leave. The French naval base at Toulon was to be handed over to Germany, the French population again evacuated and replaced by Germans. The list of demands goes on for pages, but the clear aim was to create a German-dominated state or empire in the heart of Europe. Once completed, the plan called for *Mitteleurope* to embrace Austria, Bulgaria, Denmark, Finland, Holland, Romania and Sweden.

Nor was this all; the Russians would have to retreat to the east of the Nieman river, the Russian western frontier of Napoleonic times, giving up most of Poland and the Baltic provinces, while ceding Lithuania and land on the eastern frontier of Germany as '*Lebensraum*' – 'living space' for Germany's expanding population. The list of German demands included Africa where, to secure their long-sought 'place in the sun', the German people would take over the Belgian Congo and certain French territories and create a new block, *Mittelafrika*.

These demands were so arrogant and so extensive that one can only wonder whether the German government was serious. There was no real possibility that the *Entente* powers would agree to any of this, and if any one nation felt inclined to weaken their allies would surely have stopped them. The British, for example, would never agree to France ceding Germany territory on the Channel coast, should such a concession even be contemplated. Colonel House returned to the USA in June 1915 and reported to the President that 'he saw no hope for a negotiated peace' and 'confessed that he could see no alternative to America being drawn into the war'.[1]

In fairness to Germany, it has to be admitted that the *Entente* powers, whatever lofty motives for fighting they declared openly, also intended to profit from their victory in this war. Russia declared that one of her war aims was control of the Dardanelles and the Bosporus seaway, most of the western side of the Sea of Marmara and the Turkish province of Thrace.

The Turkish empire, already failing, seemed ripe for dismemberment, and all the other *Entente* powers, most notably Italy, were equally interested in a share of the eastern spoils. Italy, which had only joined the *Entente* on 25 May 1915 – and then only against Austria – expected to be rewarded in the post-war share-out with the Austrian Tyrol, the Dolomites and the port of Trieste. France declared that she must have control of Syria and Britain promptly put in a bid for Palestine and Sinai to gain control of both sides of the Suez Canal. Further British expansion, into Arabia and Mesopotamia – later Iraq – was also being considered. This war, which had ostensibly started to help 'poor little Belgium', was becoming a war of conquest and territorial expansion.

The net result of Colonel House's missions in 1914 and 1915 was precisely zero. The war would therefore continue until further shedding of blood inspired the Americans to try again. This being so, we can switch our attention back to the Western Front, and consider what ways were being put in train by Britain and France in their attempts to achieve a breakthrough in 1915.

There were only two ways to solve the costly dilemma created by the Western Front defences; one could break through them, or go round them. Getting round the Western Front would be difficult, for one flank rested on the North Sea and the other on the frontier of neutral Switzerland. Therefore any attempt to outflank the Western Front must be made a long way from western Europe.

That fact had been appreciated long before the BEF made its first attempt at a breakthrough at Neuve Chapelle in March 1915. Even by January 1915, just five months into the war, the difficulties had been appreciated, and both ways – breakthrough or outflanking – had their devotees – with the First Lord of the Admiralty, Winston Churchill, a devotee of both. The first led to the birth of the tank, to which Churchill served as midwife. The second led to the Gallipoli campaign, for which Churchill would be roundly condemned.

It had already become clear that to exercise the first option, to break *through* the defences of the Western Front, some new piece of kit was needed. The infantry could not do it on their own; once they left their trenches they were fully exposed to fire and, all too frequently, were held up by the enemy wire. Artillery could help them, up to a point, but what they really needed was some device that could wade through mud, flatten barbed wire, roll over trenches and defy machine-gun bullets and shell splinters. This list of requirements, this specification, called for what later became known as an Armoured Fighting Vehicle or AFV, the machine better known to the general public as the 'tank'. This name came into being when questions were asked as to what lay under the large canvas covers that draped the first machines. The most acceptable answer was 'a water tank' . . . and so the name 'tank' was born.

Steps to develop a viable AFV were proceeding throughout 1915, but had begun as early as Christmas 1914, following an idea put to the Secretary of the cabinet, Colonel Maurice Hankey, by a Royal Engineer officer, Lieutenant Colonel Ernest Swinton. Colonel Swinton had been visiting the Western Front as an official war correspondent, an unusual role for an army officer, and during his visit had been struck by that dire combination of factors – mud, wire, machine guns – that had so far impeded any advance across no man's land. He had also been appalled by the casualty figures.

Putting these harsh facts together and considering a solution, Swinton came up with the idea of a tracked armoured vehicle to overcome this combination, a vehicle based on an agricultural machine, the Holt Caterpillar Tractor that was then coming into use on British farms. Armoured plate was not a problem, the Royal Navy had plenty of that; indeed, in 1914 the Royal Naval Air Service had used Rolls-Royce cars, draped with armoured plate, to rescue RFC and RNAS pilots shot down by enemy fire. Swinton wrote down his ideas, roughed out a few sketches of what this new machine might look like, and passed them to his chief, Colonel Maurice Hankey.

At Christmas 1914, Hankey wrote a memorandum to the War Cabinet supporting this idea, and this memorandum came to the attention of the First Lord of the Admiralty, Winston Churchill, a man who was always interested in new ideas. The war secretary, Lord Kitchener, was much less interested in new-fangled notions, so the early development of what became the tank began as a naval project; to keep the army quiet, the machine was at first known as a 'landship'.

By January 1915, Churchill had drawn up an outline specification for the prototype landship. This called for a tracked vehicle, 40 feet long and 13 feet wide, carrying a quarter-inch of armoured plate on the roof, with slightly thicker armour on the front and sides. This first vehicle, which never got into production, was seen as a troop carrier, a kind of Trojan horse, designed to carry fifty men armed with the portable Lewis machine gun, which was being introduced to the army at this time. Carried in safety to the enemy line, these men would sally forth from the landship and spread alarm and despondency up and down the enemy trenches, hosing the defenders with automatic fire.

This idea was barely out of the planning stages when the disasters at Gallipoli forced Churchill from the Admiralty and the War Cabinet Committee, but later in 1915 the idea was revived and re-examined by the new minister of munitions, David Lloyd George. This later machine was based on further proposals from Ernest Swinton, embodied in a document, *The Necessity of Machine-gun Destroyers*, which he sent to the cabinet in June. Swinton had been doing some serious thinking, and his new idea was a considerable advance on the troop carrier concept of January.

This new vehicle would be armoured, have a projected speed of 4 miles per hour – about the pace of a fit infantryman – and be able to cross a trench a metre wide. It would also be armed, either with machine guns (the 'female' version) or 2-pounder guns (the 'male' version), though in the end the tank – now a proper fighting vehicle or AFV – would be armed with both machine guns and a brace of 2-pounder or 6-pounder guns.

This outline was sent to the War Office – the Admiralty bowing out at this time – and a full specification was prepared for the first prototype of the tank, code-named Little Willie. This first tank was assembled rather than invented, for the four main elements – armour, tracks, guns and the internal combustion engine – already existed. Construction of the prototype began in August 1915, the machine changing constantly as the work continued. Development progressed rapidly, with the first tank lumbering out of the workshops on 8 September 1915. This vehicle was larger than the proposed prototype and therefore christened Big Willie.

Work continued, and by the time a production model was produced in January 1916 Willie was 31 feet (10 metres) long, 8 feet (2.5 metres) high and 14 feet (4.5 metres) wide, and weighed 28 tons. Big Willie carried a crew of eight and was armed with machine guns and a 6-pounder gun, the latter carried in a projecting sponson mounted on the side armour. Field trials then commenced in Britain and in considerable secrecy, before small invited audiences. The powers that be were generally impressed with this machine, but Lord Kitchener, the man who had to decide on their employment in the field, remained non-committal. He rejected suggestions that a thousand of these AFVs should be ordered at once, opting instead for just forty, though this initial order was later increased to one hundred.

The manufacture of these machines during 1916, the raising of dedicated tank units – the Tank Corps – and their eventual employment at the battle of Flers-Courcelette in September 1916 are events that fall outside the context of this book, but the point is surely made. From the early months of the war, certain active minds were at work, brooding over the problems of the Western Front and attempting to find solutions; it is hardly likely that a diehard, hidebound 'donkey' of the old cavalry school would ever have contemplated a radical creation like the tank, yet Haig, the vector of all the 'donkey' allegations, was a stout supporter of the tank from the first time he saw one.

There were, however, two problems that were never solved during the Great War. The first was a firm decision on what sort of weapon the tank actually was. Was it an 'infantry support' weapon, in effect a mobile fort that could accompany the infantry as they advanced and provide local fire support, with a top speed of 4 miles per hour, which appeared the most likely role? On the other hand, given the basic problem of the breakthrough, the need for speed in the exploitation phase, should these tanks have been designed and built as armoured cavalry, fast, heavily gunned, armoured machines, capable of moving at speed over the battlefield as horses had done in days gone by?

This problem was not settled until the Second World War when the British – wrongly – opted for the infantry support tank, such as the Matilda, heavily armoured, slow moving and with a 2-pounder gun, and the Germans opted for the armoured cavalry approach – the Panzer III, IV, V and Mk VI Tiger – with the tank becoming the land element in their blitzkrieg (lightning war) offensives of 1940/41.

Getting *round* the Western Front defences was a more complex problem, one that required strategic thinking rather than some tactical innovation. Some form of amphibious operation, a landing north of the Belgian border or on the Baltic coast of Germany, had been contemplated, but the difficulties of mounting such an operation were considerable. Holland was neutral, the kit and competence for a major amphibious assault did not exist, the army and the Royal Navy could not agree on the basic concept – and the German Army would certainly be able to bring up men and supplies to contest the landing faster than the Royal Navy could land more troops and *matériel* to expand the bridgehead.

These facts were not fully appreciated in 1915 when the cabinet and the War Office began to study the strategic possibilities of an attack in the eastern Mediterranean, specifically an attempt to force the narrow passage of the Dardanelles and so drive Turkey out of the war. The reasons for this interest were strategic; beyond the Dardanelles lay Constantinople, then the capital of Turkey, a member of the Central Powers. Beyond Constantinople lay the Bosporus, the sea road to the

Black Sea . . . and Russia, that beleaguered member of the *Entente*, in urgent need of help.

If the *Entente* powers could force the Dardanelles, the strategic possibilities were certainly considerable. Turkey – long known as the 'Sick Man of Europe' – could be driven out of the war. That would remove a threat to the Suez Canal and the Persian Gulf oilfields, so vital to the British fleet. Free access to the Black Sea would enable the western *Entente* powers to supply arms and equipment to Russia, making the German task of defeating that country immeasurably more difficult. The collapse of Turkey would also strengthen the influence of the *Entente* powers in the Balkans – though that aim might also be achieved by an attack on the Balkans via the Greek port of Salonika.

Above all, though, opening a new front in the eastern Mediterranean would divert German strength from the west and – perhaps – offer some relief to the French and British generals in their only alternative strategy, that of making further costly offensives against unreduced German defences. This strategic thinking, which began in early 1915, marked the start of a long argument between the 'Easterners' and the 'Westerners' over where the Great War should be fought and won. The 'Westeners' believed that victory could be obtained only on the Western Front while the 'Easterners' held that victory could be obtained only somewhere else.

This thinking, which led to the Gallipoli expedition, came to a head in January 1915. Although the Dardanelles are a long way from the Western Front, this operation had a profound effect on Western Front activities and should therefore be examined – if only to point up the fact that errors of judgement were by no means confined to the fields of France and Belgium.

The Anglo-French fleet had been chipping away at the Dardanelles from the time Turkey joined the Central Powers in October 1914. In November 1914 the Allied fleet carried out a short bombardment of the outer forts, and a British submarine entered the Sea of Marmara and sank a Turkish ship.[2] These pinprick operations achieved very little, other than to alert the Turks and their German advisers to the dilapidated state of their defences in the Dardanelles.

The first move towards any decisive attack came in that Christmas memorandum from Colonel Hankey to the War Cabinet referred to above. While urging the development of the tank, Hankey also suggested that the way to attack Germany was via her allies, and he proposed that a force of six divisions should be deployed for an attack on Turkey, supported by troops from Greece and Bulgaria. This proposal met with stout opposition from Sir John French, who wanted every available division sent to France. This rejection coincided with an appeal by the Russian commander, the Grand Duke Nicholas, for some British effort in support of his forces under attack in the Caucasus.

This last appeal seems to have tilted the balance in the War Cabinet, and the idea of an attack in the Dardanelles was supported by both Kitchener and the First Sea Lord, Admiral Sir John Fisher, though the strength of their commitment varied. Kitchener was proposing only a 'demonstration', some action to suggest that Constantinople was threatened, while Fisher wanted an all-out amphibious assault, for which he was prepared to offer the assistance of some elderly battleships to force the Dardanelles, the sea route 13 kilometres long and 2 kilometres wide that led up to the Sea of Marmara and Constantinople.

Fisher's political master, the First Lord of the Admiralty, Winston Churchill, realized that Kitchener was not seriously interested in this venture, and on 3 January 1915 he cabled Admiral Carden, the commander of the British fleet in the eastern Mediterranean, asking whether the navy alone could force the Dardanelles. Carden replied that it might be done but it would not be easy – it would take a considerable amount of time and would require a considerable number of ships. He did not, however, reject the idea entirely, and from that moment the Gallipoli operation began to develop – and unravel. Also unravelling was Churchill's relationship with Admiral Fisher, who stated bluntly, and correctly, that 'the Dardanelles operation was futile without soldiers'.

The study of any military operation should begin with a close look at the ground, and a survey of the Dardanelles straits should have revealed the fundamental problem confronting any attacking force; the straits are very narrow and the Turkish Army held both sides.

Granted, the various forts along the shore were not in good condition, and a post-war report from the Turkish government frankly admits that 'until the end of February 1915, a landing in the Dardanelles would probably have been successful and the capture of the straits by troops comparatively easy'.[3] But no landing was contemplated in January or February 1915; the task of forcing the Dardanelles was entrusted to the navies of Britain and France and a small number of obsolete battleships and cruisers.

The story of the Gallipoli operation falls outside the scope of this present work but should be briefly covered, if only to illustrate the existence of some basic errors. The first error was the belief that warships alone could force the Dardanelles straits. Their attempt to do so began on 18 February with a bombardment of those outer forts that had been shelled the previous November. This second bombardment lasted a day, but was then called off owing to bad weather and was not resumed until 25 February. After that the naval bombardment went on sporadically for some weeks. This naval gunfire obliged the Turks to abandon the outer forts, and landing parties from the Royal Marines went ashore and blew up parts of the defences on 26 February, but the main effect of this action was to refocus Turkish attention on the state of their defences in the Dardanelles.

The Turks reacted by sending in troops and guns to repair and man the coastal defences and by sowing a quantity of mines in the narrow waters of the straits. Admiral Carden was soon aware of this large Turkish minefield astride the Dardanelles but was unable to clear it before a cable arrived on 11 March, urging him to press on at once with the attack. Carden had not done so by 18 March when he fell ill and was replaced by Admiral de Robeck, his second-in-command. Meanwhile, matters were stirring in Britain; the 29th Division, the last Regular Army division, was tasked for the Middle East, where an expeditionary force of some seventy thousand men, British, Indian, Gurkha and ANZAC (Australia and New Zealand), was assembling under General Sir Ian Hamilton.

The next naval attack duly went in on 18 March and quickly ran into another new and unsuspected Turkish minefield. Heavy naval gunfire was silencing the forts when the French battleship *Bouvet* struck a mine and sank inside two minutes with great loss of life. The attack continued until 1600 hours, when two more battleships, HMS *Inflexible* and HMS *Irresistible*, struck mines and developed heavy lists. Admiral de Robeck ordered a retirement, but even while this was in progress another British ship, HMS *Ocean*, sent to assist *Irresistible*, struck a mine and both vessels sank. The result of this attempt to force the Dardanelles by sea power alone was the loss of three ships sunk and three more badly damaged. De Robeck's conclusion, that the straits could be forced only after the shores had been secured, was therefore totally correct . . . and came just a little late.

Nor was that the only problem. An attack requires surprise, but this blundering about by the navies had thrown away that possibility; the Turks were now well aware of Allied intentions and responded by bringing up troops and guns – before the Allies tried again, the Dardanelles had become a fortress. Nor was this all, for this venture led to another tragedy; the Turks, alarmed at this intervention, turned on their Armenian population and massacred all they could find – some 750,000 Armenians perished in the subsequent bloodbath. While this slaughter was going on the Turkish Army was expanding rapidly; six new divisions marched to the Dardanelles, commanded by a very competent German officer, General Liman von Sanders, and under his direction the hills around the straits were turned into a series of fortresses.

Kitchener had now become closely involved, declaring in early March that 'having entered into the project to force the straits there can be no idea of abandoning this scheme', and he ordered the 29th Division to join Hamilton's force in the eastern Mediterranean. The French also raised a division, and this force was then augmented from Egypt by the two-division strong Australian & New Zealand Army Corps (ANZAC), which made its debut at Gallipoli on 25 April 1915.

By the time the Anglo-French forces went ashore at 0500 hours on 25 April the Turks were well prepared and waiting to receive them. The troops, British, French, Indian and ANZAC, were held on the beaches or just inland, and everywhere the landing forces, as on the Western Front, failed to exploit the initial successes. Nor was this initial success universal; while the troops landed unopposed on several beaches, the landing on 'W' Beach was a costly shambles and the

Dublin and Munster Fusiliers were cut to pieces when they came ashore from the SS *River Clyde* on 'V' beach. As on the Western Front the troops were rapidly reduced to digging in and holding on.

Matters deteriorated over the summer with rapidly rising casualties – 38,000 by the end of May, 60,000 men lost on either side by the end of August. On 6 August another landing was attempted at Suvla Bay, with the same result; the invaders achieved surprise but failed to exploit it. The Turks held their ground and casualties rose towards the 100,000 mark.

This fresh failure at Gallipoli had repercussions at home. Asquith was forced to restructure his Liberal government as a coalition, Admiral Fisher resigned and Churchill was forced from office. In October General Hamilton was replaced by General Monro, who, having visited the battlefield, decided that evacuation was the only option. This evacuation took some time to arrange and finally took place in December 1915 and January 1916, when 180,000 troops were evacuated from the beaches without loss – the only successful part of the entire Gallipoli campaign.

Gallipoli is a prime example of how not to conduct an amphibious operation. The big mistake came at the start with the notion that the Allied navies could force the straits on their own. Their attempt to do so simply led to a steady increase in the Turkish commitment. But the Dardanelles operation was more than a waste of men and resources. The strategic concept was excellent but the execution did nothing to reduce the German strength on either the Eastern or Western Fronts and diverted scarce munitions and troops from the BEF. The failure at Gallipoli stemmed from a total lack of experience of the planning and conduct of an amphibious operation, another facet of total war that was then outside the experience of the military commanders.

There remains the matter of Russia, where the military situation was causing great anxiety. After their defeat at Tannenberg in 1914 the Russian plan for 1915 was to secure their western frontier against further German attacks before thrusting into Silesia. This attempt went on throughout the winter, with battles along the Polish frontier and in the Carpathian mountains. In these battles it became apparent that while the Russians could cope with the Austrians they were no match for the Germans, and the battles here were hard fought and costly. In March, however, the fortress of Przemysl at last fell into Russian hands, a victory countered by German successes in forestalling the Russian advance on East Prussia, an action that led to more Russian losses in fighting around the Masurian lakes.

Von Falkenhayn's strategic plan for the campaigning season of 1915 was to reduce the pressure on the Austrians and inflict large casualties on the Russians. To this end he proposed a major offensive between the towns of Gorlice and Tarnów, a push forward through the Russian centre between the Carpathians and the Vistula.

This Gorlice–Tarnów attack was entrusted to General von Mackensen, who had under his command the German Eleventh Army of eight divisions newly arrived from the west and the Austrian Fourth Army of six divisions. This force, supported by over a thousand guns, was opposed by just six poorly equipped Russian divisions, and their attack went in on a 30-kilometre front on 2 May, after a four-hour artillery bombardment that flattened the Russian defences.

Reviewing the plans for this attack, it is interesting to note that Mackensen's chief of staff, General von Seeckt, had analysed the problems inherent in the Western Front attacks and ordered that his troops must 'strive to keep the advance continually moving', and that reserves must be close to the front in a position to follow up any penetration.

As on the Western Front, at Neuve Chapelle and elsewhere, the initial attack on 2 May achieved complete surprise. The difference here was that the exploitation phase was equally successful. Not only was the entire Russian front rolled up between Gorlice and Tarnów, the advance continued for another twelve days until the German and Austrian armies had reached the River San, more than 120 kilometres from their start line. There the advance slowed for a few days, the Austrians disturbed by the entry of Italy into the war. Then more troops arrived from France and the advance continued. The fortress of Przemysl was recaptured in early June when the Russian front was cut in two.

Unfortunately for von Falkenhayn, the armies, German and Austrian, were not used to such rapid and extensive advances and had now outrun their supply lines. Nor had the Russians been subdued; their armies had absorbed and replaced their losses so far – totalling some 400,000 men – and were willing to fight it out all summer.

So the eastern battles continued into August, by which time the Germans had racked up some formidable successes; Poland was now entirely in their hands, as were over 700,000 Russian prisoners, and with this much accomplished von Falkenhayn elected to break off the eastern offensive, turn the eastern armies for an attack on Serbia and send a number of divisions back to France in anticipation of an autumn offensive by the Franco-British forces. The continuation of the war on the Eastern Front was entrusted to Field Marshal Paul von Beneckendorff und von Hindenburg, the Commander-in-Chief of the Eastern Front, who attacked again on 9 September, sending two armies against the Russians manning the front around Vilna, and to the Austrian commander, Conrad, who attacked the Russians south of the Pripet marshes.

Both these attacks met with only limited success. The Russians, fighting on the defensive around Vilna, were able to bring the Hindenburg offensive to a halt before the Austrians opened their attack on 26 September. The Russians again stood their ground and had halted Conrad's force by mid-October and inflicted no fewer than 230,000 casualties on the Austrians in the process. These attacks in the summer and autumn of 1915 were the last major offensive the Russians mounted in the Great War, but they were still able to contain the German Army, and so keep many German divisions employed in the east until the revolution of 1917 took Russia out of the war.

These various alternative possibilities in 1915 – attacking at Gallipoli, inventing the tank, supporting Russia, and the dim prospect of a negotiated peace – were not the only thoughts on ways to bring this war to a successful conclusion; it was also thought possible to attack the Germans at home. Kitchener had described the German position in 1915 as resembling a fortress, and the traditional way to capture a fortress was by starvation. From this it followed that another way to bring Germany to its knees was by a close naval blockade, cutting off Germany's supply of food and strategic materials.

There was nothing original in this proposal, though the outcome would take time to achieve. Nor was this attempt one sided; Germany was currently attempting to starve Britain out of the war by a submarine offensive in the Atlantic and the Western Approaches. Their offensive was hindered by the need to avoid sinking neutral shipping, especially ships from the USA. On the other hand, the German submarine offensive was aided by the British Admiralty's stubborn refusal to introduce the convoy system. This permitted merchant ships to sail independently – and be sunk in quantity.

It will be seen, therefore, that the options for 1915 stretched far beyond the narrow confines of the Western Front. There were, in effect, five cards on the table, all bidding for the defeat of Germany: the advent of the tank, an outflanking attack in the eastern Mediterranean, a successful continuation of the war on the Eastern Front, a negotiated peace settlement, probably involving the good offices of the United States, and a naval blockade of Germany, leading eventually to civilian starvation.

This last option proved at least partially successful and certainly contributed to Germany's eventual defeat in 1918. Around half a million German civilians died of starvation during the First World War and many more died during the influenza epidemic that came after it, their bodies debilitated by years of malnutrition. The problem of feeding the civilian population had, however, already become apparent by 1915.

Germany had a population of some 66 million, and with so many men called from the land to the colours in 1914 the harvest that year was disappointing – by the winter of 1914/15 German households were already starting to feel the pinch. Fats and sugar were almost unobtainable and meat and butter were soon available only on the rapidly expanding black market.

In an attempt to stop the black economy in Vienna, Austria introduced a form of food rationing in April 1915. After food riots in Berlin in October, Germany followed suit in November 1915, imposing three meatless days per week, a measure shortly followed by the rationing of bread. By the spring of 1916 most German foodstuffs were on ration and civilians were reduced to a weekly diet of black bread, sausages, a kilo and a half of potatoes, one egg, and a few kilos of turnips. The effects of this on civilian morale should not be under-estimated, now the effects of the war were hitting home.

The troops at the front did rather better, but at a considerable cost; in one week the German Army consumed 10 million kilos of meat, mostly horsemeat, 35 million kilos of bread and 100 million kilos of potatoes – every week a single army corps could devour 1,300 cows, 1,100 hogs and 4,100 sheep – and men serving at the front were not available to till the land or tend the livestock; by the end of 1915 the German Army too was on short rations.

Three facts emerge from this sad litany of 'operations elsewhere'. First, that the Allies were not devoting their attention exclusively to outdated methods of war and attempts to penetrate the Western Front. Second, that these efforts to end the war, or at least expand it into more profitable areas, were either under active consideration or actually being applied. Third, that technical innovations were also being considered, most notably the tank. Mistakes were made in 1915 and mistakes would continue to be made throughout this war, and in all other wars. The evidence presented above should, how-ever, disprove any notion that the commanders of the BEF in 1915 were either uniquely devoid of imagination or unwilling to con-template whatever device or course of action was available to help end this war.

The Road to Loos, July–September 1915

In so far as France is concerned, the only thing that can be
counted on is that the French will never be friends of anything
other than their own interests.

Manuel de Godoy, 1801

ROM THE MOMENT the BEF landed in France in August 1914,
Anglo-French relations and the actions of the BEF were largely
dictated by the wishes of the French, most notably those of the French
generalissimo, General Joffre. As has been related in previous chapters,
to a certain extent this French dominance in 1915 was inevitable;
the Western Front war was being fought on French territory, France
supplied the logistical assets in the shape of ports, roads and railways,
and the French currently had more forces in the field. Military
demographics alone gave the French the larger say in Anglo-French
military affairs.

To this must be added that self-inflicted wound, the orders issued
by the War Office to the commander-in-chief of the BEF in 1914.
These conflicting requirements – see the Appendix – would have
taxed the patience and negotiating skills of someone far more talented
and subtle than Field Marshal Sir John French. To his credit, the field
marshal tried to obey these orders, but in doing so he frequently
impaled his command on the sharp thorns of unworkable requirements. At no time was this more true than during the preliminary
moves before the battle of Loos.

Given the precious gift of hindsight, it is easy to see that there was
merit in the French desire for an overall commander, certainly on the

Western Front, if not for the conduct of the war as a whole. To have a situation where the coordination of the Allied struggle largely depended on goodwill was clearly unsound, and some form of supreme command was desirable.

Indeed, as long ago as 1906, in their post-*Entente Cordiale* discussions with the British government on aspects of command in the event of hostilities, the French had proposed that they should have the overall command on land and the British should have overall command at sea. No decision was taken on this point for, at that time, the British had no intention of committing themselves to any formal military or naval alliance with the French whatsoever, declaring that any such decision must be left to 'the government of the day', when and if hostilities with any other power – but in reality with imperial Germany – should ever come about.

When that eventuality arose in 1914, the instructions on command issued to Field Marshal French were about as far as the British government was ready to go, but these instructions were clearly ambivalent and created a situation the French were usually able to exploit.

Joffre could not issue direct orders to the BEF but, via Henry Wilson, he made it very clear that he expected the British commander to comply with his wishes whenever possible. This also left the French – military, government and people – free to complain, if the British did not support French plans in every respect, that they were not pulling their weight in the common struggle against the Hun.

This matter of cooperation, on how it should be defined and how far it should go, gradually became a struggle of wills, between French and Haig on the one hand and Joffre and Foch on the other. The struggle was to dominate Anglo-French relations in the weeks before the battle of Loos and committed the BEF to a battle the former pair were most anxious to avoid.

It is fair to say that by the middle of 1915 the British commanders were becoming somewhat disenchanted with their French allies. Time and again since August 1914 the BEF had been committed to battle, often in unfavourable circumstances and usually with the promise of French support, which, in the event, had frequently failed to materialize either in adequate amounts or on time. This failure occurred even when the British effort had been made to support the French.

This had been the case at Second Ypres and at Neuve Chapelle, during Aubers Ridge, and most recently at Festubert. These battles had been launched either to support French efforts or to demonstrate British determination in the common cause. It cannot be said that the French efforts in this period, though certainly on a larger scale than those of the BEF, were rewarded with better results. French losses in the first six months of 1915 were appalling, and evidence of military genius among the French commanders was extremely hard to come by.

The engagement at Festubert petered out on 27 May. By that time Joffre's attack in Artois – the second battle of Artois – had already proved another disastrous failure, though Joffre did not actually call this battle off until 18 June. Undaunted by this reverse, Joffre intended to renew his attack on the Noyon salient as soon as possible – and again required full and close support from his British allies.

Joffre can at least be credited with the virtues of consistency. In 1915, while the BEF had been busy in those fruitless attempts to carry the Aubers Ridge position, Joffre had concentrated his efforts on eliminating the Noyon salient, that great German dent in the French line, which had its apex at Noyon, 90 kilometres north-east of Paris. All attempts to cut the salient had so far failed, and Joffre attributed this failure in no small measure to a lack of support by the BEF, either in declining to take over more of the French line, so freeing French divisions for the Noyon battles, or by a failure to press on with supporting attacks, regardless of loss.

Joffre's next attempt to eliminate the Noyon salient was ambitious and would require the bulk of the French Army and half the BEF. The basic idea was for two attacks on the salient, one east from Artois and one north from Champagne, two linked, coordinated offensives which would meet up and isolate the three German armies – the First, Second and Seventh, totalling 300,000 men – now occupying the salient and force their withdrawal, not least by cutting the railway lines from the east which supplied them across the Ardennes and the Douai plain. These two attacks, if successful, would be followed up by a general advance by all the Allied armies on the Western Front and, said Joffre, 'compel the Germans to retreat beyond the Meuse and probably end the war'.

This had been the *generalissimo*'s strategic plan for 1915 and Joffre, who was nothing if not stubborn, had not given up on this intention even after the disappointments and losses of the spring. By the early summer, though, he had realized that his previous attacks, made only from Artois against the western face of the Noyon salient, had been blunted by the strong German defences and by the German ability to concentrate their troops on that part of the line, while maintaining a strong front in Champagne.

For his next attack, Joffre would tackle both these problems. This attack would be both stronger in terms of men and guns and would come from Champagne, as well as from Artois, so as to diffuse the German opposition. Against the three German armies in the salient Joffre would hurl four French armies, the Fifth, Fourth, Second and Third, north from Champagne, while the French Tenth and the British First Army drove east from Artois. All these armies aimed to converge in the Ardennes, trapping the German armies behind their advancing lines.

There were a number of snags with this master plan, especially in Artois. First, in spite of several gallant and costly attempts, the French had not taken Vimy Ridge, that bastion in the German line which overlooked the Douai plain from the west. Second – and inevitably – the French needed to shorten their line in order to build up strong reserves for these forthcoming offensives. This requirement meant that the BEF must take on more of the front, a constant demand of General Joffre, and – equally inevitably – this was an action that Field Marshal French was currently unwilling to take. He was aware that the French held a disproportionately large share of the front but he had his own problems and for once these took priority.

Like Joffre, French had to build up his reserves if the BEF were to play any significant part in the forthcoming offensives. He could not do this and also take over more of the French line. Granted, more British divisions were coming out to France, but the British professional army of pre-war days was gone and the troops coming out now were either territorial formations or the first of the New Army divisions. Six territorial divisions – the 46th (North Midland), 47th (1st/2nd London), 48th (South Midland), 49th (West Riding), 50th (Northumbrian) and 51st (Highland) – had all arrived by April 1915, and the first of Kitchener's New Army divisions – the 9th (Scottish), 12th (Eastern) and 14th (Light) – were in France by the end of May.

In spite of the growing requirements of Gallipoli, other divisions, New Army or territorial, were also on the way, but these units needed more training, more equipment, especially artillery, more ammunition for that artillery, and some experience of Western Front conditions. Committing untried divisions to the full rigours of the Western Front without some prior time in the line with more experienced formations was not regarded as a viable option.

Nor was the British sector of the line quiet in the weeks after Festubert. Even in 'normal' times, BEF casualties were running at around three hundred a day – nine to ten thousand men a month, roughly the rifle strength of an entire division – and this when no major battle was in progress. Even after closing down the Festubert attack the BEF fought further small-scale battles in the Ypres salient, at Givenchy, Bellewaarde and Hooge, local actions that gained no ground but pushed up the casualty figures . . . and there was, as always, the chronic problem of finding sufficient high-explosive artillery ammunition and heavy guns.

General Joffre knew all this but he was not to be denied. On 4 June he sent Field Marshal French a draft of his plan for his new offensive with the express wish that the BEF should be ready to attack by early July. Their support should consist initially of taking over another 35 kilometres of French front south of Arras, and then, most significantly, by aiding the attack of General d'Urbal's Tenth Army in Artois with a major attack on the German line south of the La Bassée canal and north of Lens. Field Marshal French concurred with this plan, at least in principle, and on 19 June he told Foch, now commanding the French Armies in the North (or GAN), that he would be able to put in this attack on or about 10 July. This attack would be made by Haig's First Army on a 10-kilometre front running from Grenay, 6 kilometres north of Lens, north to the La Bassée canal. To this end Haig's First

Army would now be reinforced by two more infantry formations, the 15th (Scottish) Division and the 47th (London) Division.

Having agreed this much with Foch, on 21 June French asked Haig to inspect the Lens–La Bassée front and prepare detailed plans for the attack. The field marshal was extremely disconcerted when, three days later, Haig, having visited the sector, declared that in his opinion the ground was quite unsuitable for an attack and any assault there would be a disaster.

General Haig's assessment was quite right, and the prime reason for this opinion was the ground. The ground between the La Bassée canal and Vimy Ridge, the setting for the battle of Loos, has not changed much since 1915. The countryside hereabouts is arguably one of the most depressing parts of France, largely flat and feature-less, briefly redeemed by the looming bulk of Vimy Ridge to the south. This is mining country, grimly described in Zola's *Germinal*, a land dotted with grimy villages and the great black humps of slag heaps – *crassiers* – and dominated by the winding gear of the pits. Both of these features, the *crassiers* and the pit-head towers, provided the Germans with perfect observation points, while the open nature of the ground denied any advancing infantry cover from the sweep of enfilade machine-gun fire.

The fields around the villages are small and soggy, those inhabitants not engaged in mining devoting their time to market gardening and small-scale arable farming. There are numerous isolated farm build-ings and a number of small woods and copses, while the open land is criss-crossed by ditches, hedges and fences. Apart from Vimy Ridge, the only rising ground lies to the east, beyond the large village of Loos, where a low ridge offered perfect observation points and a useful, second-line defensive position to the Germans. In sum, from the La Bassée canal to Lens the countryside is flat and open, virtually devoid of cover, a paradise for machine gunners, a perfect 'killing ground' for any infantry attempting to cross it.

German guns covered every metre of ground in front of the British line, and their defences – machine-gun posts, deep trenches and thick-ets of barbed wire – were growing stronger every night, with French civilians and prisoners of war pressed into service, creating two thick defence lines north of Lens, well wired and covered by machine guns and field artillery. To this can be added the fact there was another defensive advantage south of La Bassée, for here the low water table of the Ypres salient gives way to chalk, and the Germans were able to excavate deep dugouts in this shell-absorbing, easily worked material.

With the possible exception of the Somme, it would have been hard to find anywhere in France less suitable for an infantry assault, and Haig said so, in detail and at length, in his subsequent memorandum to the BEF commander. Field Marshal French therefore went to see the ground for himself, and came back in full agreement with the First Army commander. An attack on the French left at Loos was simply a recipe for further disaster – and the BEF had seen enough of those in recent months.

This being so, Haig proposed that if an attack on the left flank of the French Tenth Army was deemed so essential, subsidiary attacks could be made south of the La Bassée canal while his army launched yet another major assault on Aubers Ridge, that costly but still desirable objective. Haig also pointed out that, given the BEF's current shortage of artillery ammunition and heavy guns, a major offensive of any kind was inadvisable and would probably remain so until 1916. In this too General Haig was quite correct. French duly endorsed the first part of this proposal – an attack on Aubers – and passed Haig's views on to General Joffre, where they met with a frigid reception.

Joffre's reaction is understandable for, in his view, doing nothing for another year was not an option. With that point accepted, it could then be argued that unless the French and British armies were prepared to do nothing for another year until all the British manpower and logistical problems had been solved there was little else the Allies could do other than follow the strategic plan he had put on the table . . . and that, said Joffre, meant an attack at Loos.

As it was, with French and Haig firmly against an attack over the flat land north of Loos, any notion of a combined attack in early July had to be abandoned while other issues intervened. During the rest of June a series of meetings was held between the French and British munitions ministers – M. Thomas and David Lloyd George – at

Boulogne, to thrash out the chronic question of artillery support and ammunition supply.

In this the German armies had a clear advantage, possessing some 10,500 artillery pieces of which 3,350 were of 5.9-inch calibre or above, an average of one heavy gun for every three field guns. The BEF, on the other hand, had only seventy-one heavy guns in France, compared with 1,406 field guns, a ratio of 1:20 – and, it should be noted, far fewer guns of any kind. To remedy this shortage would take until at least the spring of 1916. The French had plenty of the fast-firing 75-mm but were also very short of heavy artillery and were currently stripping heavy guns from their forts on the eastern frontier, an action that was to have dire effects during the Verdun fighting of 1916.

The ammunition situation was even more worrying. According to current estimates, the Germans and Austrians could produce 250,000 rounds of artillery ammunition per day, of all calibres, the French about 100,000 . . . and the British just 22,000. The supply of shells to the BEF was totally inadequate and likely to remain so until the British munitions industry expanded or the large number of shells already on order arrived from the USA. It was also necessary to find a wire-cutting shell, one equipped with a fuse of sufficient sensitivity to detonate it on contact with wire. This device – the Direct-Acting Fuse No. 106, a 'graze fuse' – was only just at the testing stage. The war had come suddenly upon the British and time – more of that precious time – would be needed to solve the problems that had not been tackled in the pre-war years. In the matter of shell supply, again no real improvement was anticipated before 1916.[1]

This, however, was only one aspect of the problem. That year's offensives so far had shown that the secret of success depended on plenty of heavy artillery, an attack on a wide front – and rapid exploitation. The latter factor was currently unobtainable since the armies lacked mobility, but the first two were closely linked. If the attack front were expanded to avoid the creation of a narrow salient, this would inevitably increase the task of the guns while thinning out the number of guns available to cover the front – at least until that time in the dim and distant future when the Anglo-French armies had artillery to spare.

The artillery commanders of the BEF brooded over this problem for some time and eventually came to the conclusion that the
ideal attack would be delivered on a front of at least 40 kilometres,
would be delivered by no fewer than thirty-six divisions and would
be supported by the fire of 1,150 heavy guns and howitzers and
perhaps twice that number of field guns. This number of guns would
not be available until 1916 – if then. When asked at Boulogne to give
a date for the provision of this firepower, the French and British munitions ministers – like General Haig – suggested the spring of 1916.
Needless to say, this endorsement of the British view by M. Thomas,
the French munitions minister, carried no weight whatsoever with
General Joffre.

This analysis of the artillery problem during the Boulogne conference caused a general decline in enthusiasm for the Noyon offensive,
but on 11 July General Joffre called another conference at French's
HQ at St-Omer to thrash out the problem yet again and bend the
British to his will. During this conference Joffre told the British commanders that he totally disagreed with any notion of postponing
offensive operations until 1916 – and also with Haig's proposals for an
attack north of the La Bassée canal. He followed this with a letter to
French on the following day in which he urged the BEF to mount a
powerful offensive to the north of the French Tenth Army, and stated
that if the British looked carefully, 'and avoided the built-up area of
Lens and Liévin, your attack will find particularly favourable ground
between Loos and La Bassée'.

General Joffre did not explain why he thought this ground so favourable and he failed, in this instance at least, to change the field
marshal's mind. French continued to recommend that the First Army
attack should go in north of the canal and some 16 kilometres from
the left flank of the Tenth Army. Typically, however, the field marshal
then wavered. When Joffre disapproved of this proposal, French
promptly compromised and agreed to put in the main attack alongside the French north of Vimy, provided the French advance south of
Lens was sufficient to neutralize the German artillery. Various other
arrangements were agreed and the joint attack was postponed until the
end of August while these were put in place.

Neither at the time nor later did General Joffre offer any evidence to support his contention that the flat, open ground north of Vimy Ridge was suitable for an attack, and there followed a considerable amount of debate on this point between the two Allied headquarters. On this point at least the French were clear; they wanted an all-out infantry attack between Loos and the La Bassée canal, and they kept up a relentless pressure on their ally until they got it. This pressure slowly wore the British field marshal down.

Field Marshal French's resistance was also eroding over other issues. He offered to help by relieving two French divisions north of Ypres, but that still did not satisfy General Joffre, who always wanted to keep the BEF divisions at some distance from the Channel ports, possibly fearing that the BEF might attempt to use them for an evacuation. French then agreed to position his newest army, Lieutenant General Sir Charles Monro's Third Army, astride the River Somme, between the French Tenth and Sixth Armies, so taking over a wide section of the French line. Field Marshal French did not like this move, for it placed a French army between the British First and Third Armies, but he never resisted Joffre's demands for long. This relief could not take place before 8 August, which put back Joffre's Artois–Champagne offensive until the end of that month at the earliest, even if the ongoing argument over the site for the Artois attack could be settled.

General Haig was still pressing for an attack north of the La Bassée canal. On 22 July, he reiterated his objections to the attack at Loos and again the field marshal changed his mind and fell in with Haig's views . . . at least for a while. There was then another meeting with Foch, held at Frévent on 27 July.

At this meeting Field Marshal French, while stressing his eagerness to aid the Tenth Army attack, pleaded that he could do this equally well and far more usefully – and at a much lower cost in lives – by sending in his men against the Messines–Wytschaete position on the southern edge of the Ypres salient – or against Aubers Ridge. The BEF had fought for Aubers Ridge time and again in recent months; why not repeat these attacks with more men and artillery, and a greater chance of success, and so lift the BEF out of the damp and dismal Lys valley before another winter arrived?

Foch would not hear of it. He admitted that an attack against the Lens–Liévin position would probably be a disaster, 'with no chance whatever of success',[2] but maintained that if the First Army attacked north of this position and the Tenth Army attacked south of it – and this time took Vimy Ridge – eventual success was guaranteed, in spite of heavy losses. The two armies could then advance across the Douai plain, driving the enemy back to the Meuse and beyond, with victory now in sight. Foch did not believe that an attack anywhere north of the La Bassée canal would have the useful effect of keeping German reserves away from the French attack at Vimy.

For once, after this meeting French returned to his headquarters totally unconvinced, not only about the prospects for a successful British attack at Loos, but about the whole Artois offensive by the Franco-British forces. He did not think the French could break the German line with the resources currently at their disposal and believed that, at best, this attack would only create another salient in the German line. Therefore, on 29 July, he wrote again to Joffre summarizing the discussions at Frévent, expressing his doubts about the plan and offering, yet again, to attack at Aubers Ridge. Unfortunately, he concluded this letter by assuring Joffre that 'the British Army would assist in the general operations in whatever manner and direction the French High Command thought best'[3] – a statement that completely undermined the position French had just described.

Joffre therefore saw no reason to modify his views and, having discussed this letter with General Foch, wrote back on 5 August saying that he still insisted on an attack around Loos. 'It seems to me', he wrote, 'that no more favourable ground than that which extends from the north of Angres – west of Liévin – to the La Bassée canal can be found on which to carry out the general offensive of the British Army.'

This statement was completely untrue. The ground over which Joffre and Foch wanted the BEF to attack was almost devoid of cover for the advancing troops; any competent general would have seen this at a glance, so either Joffre and Foch had not seen the ground – which is most unlikely – or they were completely determined to have their way in this matter, whatever losses that insistence imposed on their ally. This last seems the most obvious reason, for Joffre continues: 'I agree entirely with General Foch, and I cannot suggest a better direction of attack than the line Loos–Hulluch and the ground extending to the La Bassée Canal, with the final objective Hill 70 and the Pont à Vendin.'

The obvious disadvantage of the ground refuted this argument completely, and on 10 August Field Marshal French sent Joffre another proposal, stating first that the *generalissimo*'s letter had not caused him to revise his previous opinion, that the First Army could deliver more effective and less costly help by attacking north of the La Bassée canal. But again, French went on to say that since the French were set on a British attack at Loos, he 'would direct the movements of the British Army in accordance with the wishes which you as *generalissimo* expressed'.

This statement may have pleased Joffre but any satisfaction was immediately contradicted by the next paragraph, which stated that the British attack would take the form of 'neutralizing the enemy's artillery and by holding the infantry on its front'. In other words, there would be no frontal assault north of Lens by the British infantry; the First Army would cooperate with the Tenth Army using artillery fire alone. Instructions to this end had been sent to Haig three days previously, on 7 August, confirming this decision: 'The attack of the First Army is to be made chiefly with artillery, and a large force of infantry is not to be launched to the attack of objectives which are so strongly held as to be liable to result in the sacrifice of many lives.'

On receiving French's letter on 11 August General Joffre became extremely perturbed. In his reply on 12 August he pointed out that an artillery bombardment was not what he wanted and not what he had been promised; an artillery attack would not do at all. According to Joffre, the plan required an all-out infantry assault and he would settle for nothing less. French could be equally stubborn and, backed by Haig, he declined to amend his latest offer. The Allied plan for the forthcoming offensive was deadlocked.

Unknown to Field Marshal French, however, Joffre had already taken steps to get round the constant obstructions put up by the BEF commanders. If the British would not support his schemes willingly, perhaps they could be coerced into compliance by pressure from above? On 30 July, while this argument over Loos was in train, Joffre had made a proposal to M. Millerand, the French minister for war, suggesting a new formula for the conduct of the Franco-British High Command, one that Millerand should put to the British government:

> During the period in which the operations of the British Army take place on French territory and contribute to the liberation of this territory . . . the initiative in combined action of the French and British Armies devolves on the French Commander-in-Chief notably as concerning the effectives to be engaged, the objectives to be attained and the dates fixed for the commencement of each operation.

This proposal – or formula – graciously concludes: 'The Commander-in-Chief of the British Forces will, of course, fully retain the choice of means of execution.' In short, if this formula were accepted the French would decide whom the British would attack, where they would attack, when they would attack and for how long they would continue to attack. The British commanders would have to do as they were told – and any failures in the execution could still be laid at their door.

To press this proposal forward, General Joffre then invited Lord Kitchener to visit the French Army. After a lavish three-day tour of the French front between 16 and 19 August, M. Millerand presented this formula to Lord Kitchener, and after a prolonged discussion Kitchener apparently agreed to it – but for the forthcoming Loos operation only. Kitchener then had to announce this decision to Field Marshal French and General Haig, and the latter recounts how it was broken to him.

'Lord K came to my writing room,' writes Haig in his diary for 19 August,

> saying he was anxious to have a few minutes talk with me. The Russians had been severely handled and it was doubtful how much longer they could withstand the German blows. Up to the present he had favoured a defensive policy in France until all our forces were ready to strike but . . . he now felt that the situation had arisen in Russia in which the Allies must act vigorously to take some of the pressure off Russia if possible.

When with the French he had heard that Field Marshal French did not mean to cooperate to the utmost of his power when the French attacked in September and were anxiously watching the British on their left . . . and *he had decided that we must act with all our energies and do our utmost to help the French even though by so doing, we suffered very heavy losses indeed* [Haig's italics].[4]

Haig replied that his army was ready to attack and wanted only ammunition – he made no mention of the ground nor raised any of his previous objections. Kitchener promised to provide all the artillery ammunition he had and thanked Haig 'profusely' for his help. This collapse of Haig's resistance was swiftly followed by a similar reaction from Field Marshal French.

The *Official History* is in no doubt that this sudden compliance with French demands was a serious mistake.

Under pressure from Lord Kitchener at home, due to the general pos-ition of the Allies, and from Generals Joffre and Foch in France, due to the local situation in France, the British Commander-in-Chief was therefore compelled to undertake operations before he was ready, over ground that was most unfavourable, against the better judgement of himself and General Haig, and with no more than a quarter of the troops, 9 divisions instead of 36, that he considered necessary for a suc-cessful attack.[5]

Even if the reasons for Kitchener's decision were valid, he had therefore totally undermined the position of the BEF commanders and committed the First Army to a doomed attack. The Russians had been driven out of Warsaw on 5 August and lost a great many men in the 1915 campaign, but how was a fruitless – even disastrous – British attack in Artois supposed to remedy that far-off situation?

We do not know whether Kitchener visited the ground north of Vimy and reached his own conclusion on that point, but he certainly did not consult French, the BEF commander, before arriving at this decision. Here lies another failure in command; the British Secretary of State for War – and a British field marshal – was ordering his sub-ordinate generals to launch an attack that they had already decided – correctly, and for very good reasons – would be a disaster. It was highly probable that this attack would cost thousands of British lives for no tactical gain whatsoever. The French had rejected every alternative, and it is hard to avoid the conclusion that Kitchener went along with Joffre and Millerand's plans simply to please the French and so put an end to this constant bickering.

It appears that Kitchener knew that the French were being intransigent, and realized that the attack would be costly – indeed, he admitted as much to Haig – but he still wanted Haig to attack. Perhaps Kitchener believed the Russian situation to be really serious, or perhaps he felt that Joffre must be supported and his wishes met in the interests of Allied unity. He may even have believed that the attack would succeed.

If so, he was the only one to do so. The French had already been offered full British support anywhere else but at Loos, and everything at Loos short of a full infantry attack, but they had refused to accept anything other than total compliance with their demands . . . and Kitchener now ordered Haig and French to meet these demands, in full and without further argument.

To make an attack in the full knowledge, belief or conviction that it will fail is little short of murder, an action that falls within the limits set by Liddell Hart's dictum that 'to throw away men's lives where there is no reasonable chance of advantage is criminal'. This, however, is the course that the BEF was now set upon, and there was no way out of this dilemma. French and Haig could have resigned rather than accept this order, but their soldiers could not resign, and what generals knew the situation on the Loos front better than these two? They had to stay in post and do their best to limit the disaster they believed was pending.

These meetings, conferences and exchanges of letters, proposals and counter-proposals in July and August 1915 reveal the deep divisions that existed in the Anglo-French command. The French commanders saw the BEF as an ancillary unit of the French Army, most useful for holding part of the French line and pinning down German reserves during French attacks but of no particular account in a major battle like the one pending at Vimy–Loos.

Therefore, if the British attack did not succeed and resulted in heavy losses among their infantry divisions, that did not matter.

Provided Haig's army occupied the attention of the German commanders and held German units and reserves between Lens and La Bassée while the French broke through elsewhere, the French did not care whether the First Army attack succeeded or not. Their only concern was that the First Army should mount a major attack, one on a sufficient scale to occupy and engage large elements of the German Army opposing the French at Vimy.

From the French point of view this attitude, if harsh, was reasonable. There was a war on, the two nations were allied, French losses had far exceeded British losses, and sacrifices should be shared. Field Marshal French and General Haig did not – could not – agree with this blunt formula. They were willing to commit their forces, but only on the understanding that the attack should stand some chance of success.

It should be added at this point that the French were not nearly so inflexible when it came to the question of the ground affecting the actions of their own forces. On 31 August, having won the argument, Joffre informed Field Marshal French that their joint offensive could not begin before 15 September. A few days later the attack was put back yet again, to 25 September. It then transpired that Joffre had now taken a look at the ground in front of his Tenth Army – that ground just south of Haig's army – and decided that it would need a good deal more softening up by artillery before the French infantry went in.

Nor was this the only change to the French offensive. Joffre also decided to shift the attack in Champagne to another, more open, habitation-free area of the front; the ground originally chosen was now considered unsuitable for an attack, since it contained too many villages and farmhouses offering strong defensive positions to the Germans. The existence of villages, farmhouses, miners' cottages and German strongpoints barring the First Army front at Loos had not struck Joffre as a reason why the *British* attack should be moved to more suitable ground.

This overview of the discussions between the French and British commanders in July and August 1915 points up another harsh fact; in the end, whatever the tactical situation, the British felt that the Franco–British alliance must be maintained, whatever the cost to the front-line soldiers. It is arguable that the most sensible answer would have been for Kitchener, French and Haig to present a united front to Joffre and Foch and to flatly refuse to launch an attack at Loos.

They could then have gone ahead with an attack at Messines and Aubers Ridge and, having failed to convince the Secretary of State for War that their demands were reasonable, the probability is that the French would have accepted this offer. For the reasons already explained, however, this did not happen, and Haig was now committed to an attack that he knew would cost his army dear. From the moment Kitchener agreed with Joffre and Millerand that the BEF must accept the French proposals, the fate of the First Army at Loos was sealed. Kitchener did, however, offer one asset that may have helped Haig swallow this hard decision – poison gas.

The centre of Ypres in 1915

Having taken the German front-line trench at Bellewaerde, Liverpool Scottish hold up a flag to signal success and indicate that the advance is continuing. The officer with a cap is an artillery forward observation officer. The soldiers are taking cover under the parapet of the trench, on the British side

Germans experimenting with gas before it was used for the first time in the First World War at Ypres on 23 April

Allied soldiers had no protection against gas in April 1915. The first gas masks were goggles and pads of cotton waste. Highlanders hold bottles, possibly of soda water to moisten the pads; if soda water was not available, urine was used instead

Right: Men of the 1st Cameronians (Scottish Rifles) in the Bois Grenier section using a Vermorel sprayer which contained a solution of thio to absorb and neutralize the chlorine in the gas

Below: The 2nd Lancashires in a mine crater blown before the battle for Aubers Ridge

Smith-Dorrien photographed as a major general in 1901, and signed by him. He was sacked as Commander, British Second Army, in May 1915

A photograph taken in 1918 with (*left to right*) General Sir Herbert Plumer (GOC Second Army), Lieutenant General Sir Herbert Lawrence (Haig's Chief of Staff from February 1918) and Field Marshal Sir Douglas Haig (C-in-C BEF)

Above: Captured German trenches, Festubert, 1915. The man in the foreground is probably a telephone operator with an artillery forward observation party. He unreels the wire connecting him with the guns behind him as he advances. The wire, seen on the ground beyond his right boot, has not been buried and is very easily cut by shellfire

Right: An officer looking through a periscope from a trench at Bois Grenier. The sergeant is warming his hands on a brazier made from a biscuit tin. The man smoking is in his dugout, the entrance facing away from the enemy

Left: A Vickers machine gun being fired at a German working party east of Hebuterne, July 1915. The gunner has trained the gun on to the target, clamped it down, and slid back under cover before opening fire. He is slightly less vulnerable to return fire by small arms and enemy machine guns, but not to artillery

Below: A section of the Loos battlefield. This is part of a panorama possibly taken early in 1916

The opening day of the Battle of Loos, 25 September 1915: troops advancing to attack through gas. A private photograph taken by a member of the London Rifle Brigade

Pipes and tubes for releasing the gas or 'accessory', similar to that used at Loos. Later in the war both sides used gas shells which were much more reliable and could deliver the gas more accurately, reducing the risk of gassing their own side. Photograph taken in 1916, after steel helmets had been issued.

The Loos road, a mass of shell holes and wrecked transport

Walking wounded in Vermelles, returning from the attack on the Hohenzollern Redoubt, 13 October 1915

11

Planning Loos, 19 August–25 September 1915

> The Commander in Chief wishes you to support the French
> attack to the full extent of your available resources and not to limit
> your action in the manner indicated in his letter of August 7.
>   Orders from Field Marshal French to
>   General Sir Douglas Haig, 23 August 1915

WHEN THE GERMANS introduced poisonous chlorine gas on the opening day of the battle of Second Ypres in April, the British did not hesitate to condemn this action as further evidence of German barbarism. In doing so they quoted extensively from the Hague Declaration of 1899, the one that condemned the use of 'asphyxiating gas', and also from Article 23(A) of the 1907 Hague Convention on the Laws and Customs of War, which specifically forbade the use of 'poison' or 'poison weapons'.

This outburst of righteous indignation in April 1915 did not prevent the British from rapidly developing their own chemical weapons. They had begun to do so by 3 May, a mere two weeks after the German gas attack at Ypres, and the first British gas tests took place at Porton Down on 13 May. Since scientific development usually takes somewhat longer than three weeks, it is apparent that the British had plans afoot for the employment of poison gas long before the Germans struck first at Second Ypres. Indeed, by the end of the war the British had launched more gas attacks than any other combatant, but the first British employment of the gas weapon in action was at the battle of Loos in the autumn of 1915.

Haig's rapid, indeed eager, acceptance of Kitchener's order to support the French at all costs raises a further question. For some months Douglas Haig had been supporting Field Marshal French in the latter's efforts to resist French pressure for an infantry attack at Loos; there is no indication in his diary that Haig urged similar caution on Lord Kitchener or that he took the secretary of state to the ground north of Vimy and allowed him to see the situation for himself. One might wonder why not, for if Haig's previous objections had any validity, the results of this attack would be the same, with or without Kitchener's endorsement. The British infantry would go over the top and be slaughtered in great numbers.

Exactly why Haig and French's resistance to an attack at Loos suddenly collapsed at this point is not clear. Perhaps they were convinced by Kitchener's arguments that the Russians must be helped and the French supported. Perhaps they were simply worn out by this constant bickering and found Kitchener's support for Joffre the last straw. Another possibility is that French and Haig fell for the dire notion that they owed their ultimate loyalty to their political master, Lord Kitchener, the Secretary of State for War, and must carry out his wishes, whatever the cost.

This notion is dire because none of these officers would pay that cost; the men they commanded would pay it with death and wounds on the battlefield. The prevailing belief seemed to be that loyalty went in only one direction – upwards, to the senior officer – while loyalty to the men under command came a poor second. This flies in the face of the basic rule for any officer of any rank, that his prime duty is the welfare of his men. Granted, in war a commander has a higher duty; he has to obey orders and, above all, he has to win. If the lives of his men were truly paramount he could never order attacks at all, for even successful attacks cost lives.

It is possible to argue this from several angles, but the prime point about the battle of Loos and the reason for raising this issue now is this: three senior British commanders, Kitchener, French and Haig, knew all along that an infantry attack at Loos would be a disaster, would cost a number of British lives and would achieve very little – yet they went along with the French anyway, comforted by the thought, perhaps even the belief, that the use of poison gas might make a difference.

Haig certainly gave the use of gas as a reason for changing his mind when he spoke to his corps commanders at Hinges on 6 September. Previously, he told them, he had doubted the chances of success for any attack south of La Bassée because of a lack of heavy artillery. But now, owing to the possibilities arising from the use of gas on a large scale, he had altered his views. The use of gas compensated for the lack of guns and would allow him to attack on a wider front than his guns alone warranted. There was a prospect that the German defences might be completely overrun and that the first tactical successes might be turned into a strategic victory.

The opportunity to assist the infantry assault at Loos by using gas certainly eased Haig's mind. Writing to Sir William Robertson on 16 September, he declared that 'with gas decisive results were to be expected – on the other hand without gas, the fronts of attack must be restricted with the result of concentrated hostile fire on the attacking troops, considerable loss and small progress. In my opinion the attack ought not to be launched except with the aid of gas.'

Convinced that this was so, Haig's diary entries over the few days after his meeting with Kitchener show that he was pushing ahead rapidly with plans for a gas-supported attack.[1] On Saturday, 21 August, three days after the meeting, Haig was in close consultation with Lieutenant Colonel Foulkes, RE, a 'gas expert' sent out from the UK. On the following day Foulkes laid on a gas demonstration for the IV Corps commander and his staff as well as for some of the First Army's divisional commanders. These meetings continued as the plan for the Loos attack developed, and eventually some 5,500 gas cylinders were distributed among the front-line units, ready for discharge before the assault.

The main problem confronting Haig at Loos – as well as a host of subsidiary ones – was over the matter of ground. As related, this was generally unfavourable for any kind of infantry advance – the *Official History* states that 'a more unpromising scene for an great offensive can hardly be imagined'[2] – but since the attack must now proceed, Haig could only take all the various problems of the ground into account and make the best possible arrangements to overcome them. Any study of the battle must therefore begin with a study of the ground

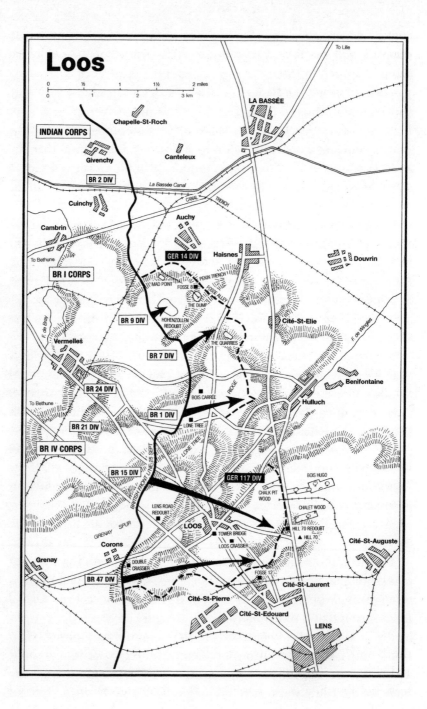

Loos

0   ½   1   1½   2 miles
0   1   2   3 km

To Lille

INDIAN CORPS

Chapelle-St-Roch

LA BASSÉE

Givenchy

Canteleux

BR 2 DIV

La Bassée Canal

Cuinchy

CANAL   TRENCH

Auchy

Cambrin

GER 14 DIV   Haisnes

Douvrin

To Bethune

BR I CORPS

PEKIN TRENCH

MAD POINT   FOSSE 8

FOSSE ALLEY

THE DUMP

BR 9 DIV

HOHENZOLLEN
REDOUBT

Cité-St-Elie

F. du Biez

THE QUARRIES

Vermelles

BR 7 DIV

RIDGE

Benifontaine

BR 24 DIV

BOIS CARRÉE

Hulluch

To Bethune

BR 1 DIV

BR 21 DIV

LONE TREE

BR IV CORPS

LONE TREE

BOIS HUGO

BR 15 DIV

GER 117 DIV

CHALK PIT
WOOD

CHALET WOOD

LENS ROAD
REDOUBT

GRENAY   SPUR

LOOS

HILL 70 REDOUBT

▲ HILL 70

Cité-St-Auguste

Corons

TOWER BRIDGE

LOOS CRASSIER

Grenay

DOUBLE
CRASSIER

FOSSE 12

Cité-St-Laurent

BR 47 DIV

Cité-St-Pierre

Cité-St-Edouard

LENS

and the enemy positions established on it. As ever, study of the map opposite will be helpful, and the various points on the battlefield should be carefully noted.

The opposing front lines ran north from Lens to La Bassée, roughly parallel to the main road running behind the German line north from Lens to La Bassée. This road passes though a 60-metre-high feature, Hill 70, and past the villages of Hulluch, Cité-St-Elie and Haisnes and a low ridge east of the road which offered the German defenders good observation over the entire attack front. Particular obstacles to any advance along this front were, starting from the south, the great bulk of the Double Crassier, a vast slag heap that offered the enemy both shelter and observation. Just south of the Double Crassier lay the village of Cité-St-Pierre, while to the north-east lay the village of Loos itself. Loos was overlooked in the centre by the great, pylon-like structure known to the British as 'Tower Bridge'.

The opposing lines, which varied in distance from 200 to 400 metres apart, lay on either side of a long, low spur, known as the Grenay spur, which meant that the front-line trenches were concealed from each other, at least in the southern sector, as far as the Vermelles–Hulluch road, which ran west to east across both front lines and, on the BEF side of the line, marked the boundary between IV and I Corps. Between the lines, just south of the Vermelles–Hulluch road, was a position marked by the remains of a cherry tree and therefore known as 'Lone Tree', while about 800 metres north of this road was a major German defence work known as the Hohenzollern Redoubt. North of the redoubt lay the village of Auchy-la-Bassée.

Two points of particular note are Hill 70 in the south, close to Loos, which would be attacked by the 15th (Scottish) Division, and Fosse (Pit Head) 8 in the north, which would be the prime objective for the 9th (Scottish) Division. All these places were to feature in the forthcoming engagement and should be noted now.

The attack front, which lay between the village of Grenay, on the British side of the line, and the La Bassée canal, ran for some 10 kilometres across open country tangled with pits, small villages and scattered farmhouses. It was immediately obvious to Haig that the strongest part of the German defences lay around the Hohenzollern Redoubt and Auchy in the north and in the complex of *crassiers* and villages – Loos, Lens, Cité-St-Pierre, Cité-St-Auguste – in the south. He therefore elected to make his main thrust in the centre, between these strongpoints, on a front of 6 kilometres, between Grenay and the La Bassée canal, aiming to push across the open ground towards Hulluch, make a breakthrough there and press on to the Haute Deule canal, which lay a further 10 kilometres to the east.

To widen the breakthrough, on breaching the enemy line two divisions, the 2nd Division in the north and 47th Division in the south, were directed to pivot outwards and make a front guarding the flanks of the attack. This 'blossoming out' action would also protect the field artillery, which would be hurried forward in support of the continuing advance towards the east.

For his initial attack Haig intended to employ six divisions of two corps, Sir Henry Rawlinson's IV Corps in the south and Lieutenant General Sir H. Gough's I Corps in the north, with three divisions of Haking's new XI Corps in reserve. IV Corps consisted, from the south, of the 47th Division, positioned alongside the left flank of the French Tenth Army, the 15th (Scottish) Division in the centre and the veteran 1st Division with its right flank resting on the corps boundary, the Vermelles–Hulluch road. North of the road I Corps had the 7th Division, the newly arrived 9th (Scottish) Division and finally the 2nd Division. Four of these divisions would push east while two would form a front on either flank, facing north and south. Taken together, the Tenth Army and the First Army's combined attack front stretched to 32 kilometres.

The six divisions of First Army could muster a total of 75,000 men, and they were supported by four times the number of field guns and howitzers available to the enemy, who was holding this 10-kilometre front with just four rifle regiments and a Jäger battalion of the 117th and 14th Divisions, a total of thirteen battalions or some 11,000 men.

At this time, the seven German armies covering the Western Front from Verdun to the sea could muster a total of seventy-two divisions, roughly a division every 6 kilometres, though the front from Arras to the sea, held by the Sixth and Fourth Armies, was held by thirty divisions, one every 5 kilometres. The Sixth Army would oppose the British and French attack in Artois, for most of the German armies were now in the east, campaigning against Russia. The Allied strength in the west at this time consisted of six Belgian divisions, ninety-eight French divisions and twenty-nine British divisions, only eleven of them Regular, giving the British a total of some 916,000 men in France. For the moment, and on the Arras to La Bassée front, the Allies had the advantage of numbers.

This discrepancy in numbers alone would appear to endow Haig with a significant advantage. The usual, accepted attacker-to-defender ratio is 3:1; while this is only a working figure and subject to considerable qualification and amendment, with an attacker-to-defender ratio of 7:1, as here, the basic advantage of numbers clearly seemed to rest with General Haig. The fact that this superiority in numbers proved of little help at Loos is eloquent testimony to the power of the defence during these Great War battles.

These German regiments usually kept one battalion in the line, one in the support trench anything up to 1,000 metres behind the front line, and the third in billets far to the rear; a battalion currently consisted of between 700 and 800 men. The available reserve was the 2nd Guards Reserve Division, stationed on the Douai plain, 11 kilometres behind the front, and the 8th Division, which was at Douai, 20 kilometres farther back.

The Sixth Army's general reserve, consisting of three Landwehr divisions, was kept in Lille and Valenciennes and was not expected to reach the battle area until twelve hours after the attack began. Therefore, to repel the initial attack, the Germans had far fewer men and far fewer guns, but they were in well-wired defensive positions with established strongpoints in the cellars of the farms and villages, and possessed excellent observation – and plenty of machine guns for sweeping the attack front with enfilade fire.

As for the French Tenth Army on the right flank of the British First Army, they would attack on a 20-kilometre front to the south of First Army, and employ no fewer than seventeen infantry divisions, 420 heavy guns and 670 field guns, mostly 75-mms. For exploitation, this force also had two cavalry divisions in reserve. The First Army was not so well endowed, with nine divisions, including reserves, supported by 114 heavy guns and 841 guns of smaller calibre. The ammunition supply was still inadequate, though better than before – on 25 September the batteries had half a million rounds of field ammunition and 35,000 rounds of heavy artillery ammunition. Much of the latter would be expended in the days before the assault in a bid to cut the German wire.

This wire was to constitute the major hazard to the advancing infantry. The enemy had built a thick wire fence right down their front, 7 metres wide and 3 metres high. This wire lay some 20 metres before their front-line trenches and was backed by another wire fence between their front and support lines. These trench lines also contained deep dugouts, which provided shelter even from direct hits, and four days of prior bombardment did little damage to either the wire or the men sheltering in the dugouts.

The objectives and achievements of the various British divisions employed at Loos will be given when their experiences come to be described, but the overall plan is worth considering. From the time Haig and Field Marshal French were coerced into taking a full part in this French attack, they had a month to evaluate the enemy strength and defences, work out a viable plan and incorporate the use of gas into the various divisional advances.

The essentials of this plan were simple; after a prior drenching with gas and after several days of shellfire, the enemy lines would be assaulted on a 10-kilometre front by six divisions of infantry. When these divisions had breached the enemy line, a further three divisions from XI Corps would pass through the breach and exploit towards the Haute Deule canal. It should be noted that XI Corps had been formed only on 30 August – a scant three weeks before the battle of Loos began. This plan should also be compared to the recent, previously calculated requirement for a successful breakthough – an attack by more than thirty divisions on a very wide front. Granted, the First Army attack would be in conjunction with that of the Tenth Army, but the latter would attack five hours after the First Army went forward and much could go wrong in that time. The compensation for all this was poison gas.

Gas warfare was still in its infancy and the gas here – referred to only as 'the accessory' as a security measure – would be discharged from cylinders positioned in the British front-line trenches. In the days before the battle, scores of gas containers were moved into the British trenches. Haig intended to start his attack with a forty-minute discharge of gas, pushed across into the enemy trenches by the prevailing west-erly wind and on into the enemy's artillery positions. German gas masks were known to be effective for only half an hour, and it was hoped that this discharge would last long enough to overwhelm the gun crews.

It was also hoped that the chlorine gas, being heavier than air, would seep down into the deep German front-line bunkers and into the cellars of the farmhouses. The belief was that gas would asphyxiate the machine gunners positioned on the flanks of the attack from where, unless quelled by gas and accurate shelling, they could pour enfilade fire on the British infantry crossing the open ground. It will be seen from all this that hope, rather than certainty, governed the plans for the attack.

The surprise element employed at Neuve Chapelle and Aubers Ridge was now regarded as less important than the cutting of the thick German wire, and that could be done only by a prolonged prior bom-bardment lasting here for four days. The artillery commanders calcu-lated that they had enough shells for this and for up to six days of subsequent fighting. To ensure artillery support after the anticipated breakthrough, some guns would be shifted forward as soon as pos-sible after the initial assault, their movement protected by the fanning out of the two flanking divisions.

Steps were also in hand to improve observation by RFC observers, whose aircraft were now equipped with wireless sets in direct contact with the gun batteries. Only after the shelling and the gas had done their work would the assault infantry go forward, and only after the breach had been secured would the reserve divisions be committed. Apart from the basic fact that the ground was totally unsuitable and the presence of the reserves uncertain, there is very little wrong with this plan – provided it worked.

Haig explained this plan to his corps and divisional commanders at a conference held at Hinges on 6 September, a few days after the opening date for the battle had been moved back to 25 September. At this conference, as related, Haig presented an optimistic scenario for the coming engagement, largely because of the gas.

Gas, he averred, would more than compensate for a shortage of heavy guns and 'provided we and the French take reasonable precautions as to secrecy and advance with the necessary vigour and strength on the general line Douai–Valenciennes, decisive results are likely to be obtained'.[3] From this it appears that success or failure at Loos depended largely on what happened in the first few hours; that was certainly Haig's opinion and the crux of his plan.

The first task was to break though the German first and second lines on a 6-kilometre front between Loos and Haisnes – the open space between the two mining zones – and then push on eastwards in the direction of Pont-à-Vendin and the Haute Deule canal. The divisions were to do this, said Haig, 'to the extreme limit of their power, adequate reserves are behind us and all attacks will be pressed forward with energy until the enemy's resistance is crushed'. There were to be no pauses – the attack was to be pressed home and kept moving.

At this point it would be as well to introduce and examine the matter of reserves, as this became a cause of much contention later. As the previous battles in 1915 had most painfully revealed, initial success, even where it was obtained, was quite useless unless it could be exploited. Exploitation meant the rapid introduction of follow-up forces from the reserve formations, for the units involved in the first attack would be at best disordered, if not much reduced, during the fighting that would surely mark the opening hours of battle.

But, as we have seen, the prompt introduction of reserves to maintain the struggle and exploit the breach was always fraught with difficulty. This was largely due to two chronic First World War conditions over which the generals had no effective control – communication difficulties and the problem of moving infantry and horse units forward quickly, on narrow and congested roads. If the attack at Loos was to avoid these difficulties, great attention must be paid to the question of reserves.

The matter of deploying reserves close to the action, so that they could rapidly follow up and exploit any success, was a matter

French and Haig had carefully considered while planning this attack. Whether they had reached an agreement on this is quite another matter, but the need was clear. Since every man in I and IV Corps would be needed for the initial assault, even corps reserves had been committed to the first attack, so leaving the First Army without any reserves of its own.

This left available only the GHQ Reserve, a force under the direct control of Field Marshal French, for the exploitation phase, and this force was duly committed to the Loos attack – or so it seemed. The current GHQ Reserve formation was XI Corps referred to above, a force consisting of two New Army divisions, the 21st and 24th, plus the newly formed Guards Division, all under Lieutenant General R. C. B. Haking. Haig naturally wanted this corps under his direct command before the battle started.

Field Marshal French disagreed. He intended to retain control of these divisions as long as possible, only releasing them to Haig at the appropriate time, after the initial breakthrough had been achieved. Therefore, together with the Cavalry Corps, which was also tasked to exploit any breakthrough, XI Corps was dispatched to an assembly area around Lillers, 26 kilometres behind the BEF front line before Loos. Twenty-six kilometres was a good day's march for an infantry division, so these reserves were not in any practical sense under Haig's control.

In his post-action dispatch, French claimed that 'in view of the great length of the line along which the British troops were operating, it was necessary for me to keep a strong reserve under my own hand. The XI Corps were detailed for this purpose.'

This comment seems to suggest that XI Corps was kept in BEF reserve, for deployment anywhere along the BEF front, and not fully committed to First Army for the Loos battle. General Haig, on the other hand, believed that this corps was promised to his army and would be under his control, his operational orders for Loos stating plainly that 'the XI Corps are in Army reserve'.

On 19 September, Haig sent a formal request to French, asking that XI Corps should be in the line Noeux-les-Mines–Beuvry, some 5 kilometres behind the current front line, by dawn on 25 September.

French agreed to this, and Haig therefore thought his views regarding the commitment of XI Corps to First Army had prevailed.

This, in fact, was not entirely the case. Although XI Corps was positioned where Haig wanted it, Field Marshal French still retained operational control. Haig could not use these divisions until French released them to First Army.

The divisions marched up to the Noeux–Beuvry line from their bases around St-Omer, a distance of some 60 kilometres, taking two nights for the journey. The two New Army divisions had only just arrived in France and were totally inexperienced in battle. They had not been in the line, had inexperienced staffs and, thanks to these long night marches in pouring rain, were very tired even before the battle began. General Haking, the XI Corps commander, had been assured that his men would be committed only after the breakthrough, and used to pursue a beaten and retreating enemy. As we shall see, it was not to work out like that.

There was one interesting exchange during this period, on 12 September, when General Foch paid a visit to Haig's headquarters. Various matters were discussed but, said Haig, 'I gathered that the real object of his visit was to find out whether we British really meant to fight or not. I reassured him on that point and told him that Joffre's orders were the same to me as those of Marshal French. I told him the men were never in better heart and longing to have a fight.'[4]

Whether 'the men' were that keen on fighting is debatable, but those in the front-line divisions were certainly well trained. In the weeks before the battle Haig took each brigade out of the line in turn and had the officers and men go over a rehearsal area where the ground and the obstacles they would face had been marked out with tape. He had also decided to mix smoke shells in with the gas, in an attempt to screen the advancing troops from direct, aimed fire. New weapons, such as the Stokes 3-inch mortar and the portable, if heavy, Lewis light machine gun, were incorporated into the battle tactics.

It is therefore fair to say that Haig did everything he could do to produce a workable plan and give all the assistance in his power to the men making the attack – there is little evidence to support the 'donkey' allegation – but some of the old problems remained. First of all the attack was on too narrow a front and lacked sufficient artillery; second, the French assault would go in five hours after that of First Army – and some matters were anyway beyond Haig's control.

For example, it was clear to Haig that the success of the Loos assault depended almost entirely on gas – but the deployment of gas depended largely on the strength and direction of the wind at the time of the attack. To get the gas cloud flowing over the German trenches depended on a good, steady, westerly wind, but winds are notoriously fickle. There was always a risk that the gas would either hang about in no man's land and so impede the attack, or drift back into the British trenches.

Haig had been fretting over the wind for days and pestering Ernest Gold, a weather expert from Cambridge University, on the prospects for 25 September. Gold's forecasts were not encouraging on the evening of 24 September, but Haig ordered the assault troops into the front-line trenches, ready for whatever the dawn might bring.

At 0500 hours on Saturday, 25 September 1915, General Haig was waiting anxiously on the wind in the garden of his advance headquarters. When dawn broke the air was still, the wind rising briefly for a few minutes, only to fall away again. After a while, Haig asked one of his staff officers, Alan Fletcher, to light a cigarette . . . the smoke drifted away towards the east and the enemy trenches, borne on a slight but definite south-westerly breeze. Haig therefore ordered the release of the gas at 0550 hours, and forty minutes later, at 0630 hours, the infantry went over the top to begin the battle of Loos.

12

The First Day at Loos, 25 September 1915

Manning the front trench, the Germans opened a heavy fire on the mass of the 2nd Brigade held up by the wire in front of them.

British Official History, 1915, Vol. II, p. 211

WHAT HAPPENED DURING the battle of Loos was determined long before the infantry left their trenches, and it is not the author's intention to describe here the events beyond that point in any great detail. Nor is it necessary to do so; a broad outline of the actions of the various divisions provides a vivid picture of what happened on each section of the front, and each account reveals the growing catastrophe that became the battle of Loos.

Loos is the archetype of every Western Front battle. Every image that has come down the decades from the Great War was a stark reality here: choking gas and plunging shellfire, chaos and confusion, men trapped and slaughtered in the open, held up before great thickets of barbed wire and flayed by machine guns; infantry charging forward over shell-torn ground kicking footballs to the sound of bagpipes. Every Great War nightmare was a living reality at Loos, where any idea that modern war was glorious finally died.

In the south, on the right flank of General Sir Henry Rawlinson's IV Corps, the 47th Division had the difficult task of attacking with one flank in the air, since the French Tenth Army on their right were not planning to attack for another five hours. The neighbouring French division, the 81st, was holding its ground, but the artillery of the French XXI Corps was helpfully engaged in pounding the

German line on the British front from soon after dawn, and continued to do so until the British infantry went forward.

The 47th (London) Division, a Territorial Force (TF) formation commanded by Major General C. St L. Barter and currently holding 2.5 kilometres of front astride Grenay, was to advance through the Loos defence line just south of the village and then on to the Lens–La Bassée road. Their attack faced two significant obstacles; the first was a high slag heap on their right flank called the Double Crassier, about 1,000 metres in length and 35 metres high, at the southern end of the Grenay spur.

Another slag heap, called the Loos Crassier, 800 metres long and 50 metres high, ran south of Loos to Fosse 12, the pit that had produced the spoil that formed the Loos Crassier. At the north end of the Loos Crassier stood a pair of linked pit-wheel houses known to the British troops as 'Tower Bridge'. As related in the previous chapter, the 47th Division had to form a flank at the southern edge of the attack front to screen the general advance. Two infantry brigades, the 140th and 141st, would therefore take up position between the two *crassiers* where, since their advance would be overlooked by the German second-line position on the Cité spur and prevent them digging in, they would occupy some German trenches.

The 47th Division attack must therefore be made through a confined area of slag heaps, mine workings, hamlets and cottages, leading to the narrow gap between Loos and the villages of Cité-St-Pierre and Cité-St-Edouard. All the advantages of ground rested with the enemy, drawn here from the 22nd Reserve Regiment of the 117th Division, well dug in with plenty of dugouts and several machine guns offering enfilade fire across the divisional front.

The 47th Division got off to a good start, leaving their trenches at 0630 hours, forty minutes after the release of gas. The gas had already flowed down the slope of the Loos valley and seems to have been of some assistance during the advance. The infantry found that the gas had reached the German trenches and the smokescreen laid by the Stokes mortars concealed their advance, though it caused a certain amount of confusion and led to some troops going off line.

The initial advance was contested by unaimed fire into no man's land, but most of the defenders fled as the Londoners, bayonets fixed, came charging out of the gloom, the men of the 1st/18th London Regiment kicking a football before them. Enfilade fire from the flanking machine guns in Cité-St-Pierre caused considerable loss in the attacking battalions, but by 0730 hours the Londoners had got into the German support line between the Double Crassier and the Béthune–Lens road and were preparing to hold it against an antici-pated counter-attack.

This success had a price. The 47th Division lost sixty officers and 1,352 men killed, wounded and missing in the first few hours of the battle, including the commanding officer, second-in-command and adjutant of the 1st/19th London Regiment, but by 1000 hours the division had taken most of its objectives and held the right flank firmly. Field artillery was now being manhandled forward in support, so in this sector at least the assault appeared to be going well.

The same cannot be said of the attack put in on their left by the 15th (Scottish) Division, commanded by Major-General F. W. N. McCracken. This division had to assault on a 1.5-kilometre front between the Béthune–Lens and Vermelles–Loos roads, but the main divisional objective was the village of Loos itself. After that had been taken the division was to press on to the ridge crossed by the Lens–La Bassée road and take Hill 70, which overlooked the attack front. The main obstacles here were various strongpoints, particularly the Lens Road redoubt and the Loos Road redoubt, as well as Loos itself, Hill 70 and the Hill 70 redoubt.

Once captured, Hill 70, the Scots' second objective, was to be pre-pared as a defensive position against any counter-attack, and a full bat-talion had been detailed for this single task. Behind these front-line defences lay the German second line, which was another divisional objective, and the hope was that the enemy, bustled out of his front line, would not be able to occupy this position before the Scots were upon him. The *Official History* comments that 'no provision had been made to tackle the defences in the suburbs of Lens; it was hoped that the Germans would be kept on the run and not hold their second pos-ition in any strength'.

It was rather late in the war for this kind of thinking; all previous evidence and the harsh experience of the current year should have shown that the Germans, however few in numbers, would make a fight of it. As we shall see, the crux of the battle on this part of the front was Hill 70.

The sum total of all this is that the new, unblooded 15th Division had to tackle one of the strongest defensive systems on the entire First Army front. There was a strong possibility that its advance beyond Loos would be quickly enfiladed by machine guns from either flank, from German positions in the Bois Hugo and Chalet Wood, north of their front line, and from the suburbs of Lens to the south. The Scots, like the 47th Division, hoped that the Germans could be pushed quickly out of their front-line trenches and be unable to hold their second line in any strength – neither hope would be fulfilled.

The attack began at 0630 hours, the Scots advancing in extended line formation, with fifty paces between each line. They ran at once into machine-gun fire, which cut down a number of men before they could close with the enemy and silence the machine guns with grenades. The gas had not flowed well forward here; pockets of it hung about in no man's land, choking the Scots as they ran forward, suffocating the wounded who took shelter in the shell holes. The British gas masks were not only gas-proof; they were also air-proof, and had to be lifted or removed from time to time so that the wearer could breathe.

Apart from the limited effect of the gas, the smokescreen was too thin and the German machine guns inflicted considerable damage among the advancing troops, while snipers in the enemy front line took a particularly heavy toll of officers. The 9th Black Watch lost 158 men crossing no man's land and the 8th Seaforth lost a similar number, including the commanding officer and the second-in-command; here, as in other Great War battles, the battalion commanders and their staff, moving with the rifle companies, suffered heavy losses. This in turn led to a gradual loss of command and control as the day wore on.

Nevertheless, on the Scottish battalions went, bagpipes skirling to urge the men on, over the German front line and into Loos, bombing their way across the trenches and supports of the Loos defence line, which they found unoccupied, and pressing on towards Hill 70. At their back Piper Laidlaw of the 7th King's Own Scottish Borderers (7/KOSB) marched up and down the British parapet, playing his pipes under fire until he was shot down and wounded, an action that earned him the Victoria Cross.

After ninety minutes – at 0800 hours – Loos was in their hands, and by 0915 hours the leading companies of the assault battalions had reached the Lens–La Bassée road. Poor visibility due to smoke and pockets of gas, however, plus the constant raking by machine-gun fire and heavy losses among the company officers, was already leading to confusion.

The platoons and companies of the 44th and 46th Infantry Brigades, tasked to capture the Lens Road and Loos Road redoubts, had now collapsed into one jumbled knot of men, perhaps 1,500 in all, massed in a narrow front some 600 metres wide at the eastern side of Loos village. In this jumbled formation, totally out of order, the Scots went surging out of Loos to attack Hill 70, 500 metres to the east, appearing, to one observer, like 'a Bank Holiday crowd'.

By this time, around 0930 hours, the smoke and gas had largely cleared. The slope of Hill 70 was in plain view ahead, and no orders were needed to direct these troops on to their next objective; crammed together, walking or trotting, the Scots moved towards the hill. This was all to the good but a bigger problem was looming; the 15th Division was getting out of position. Hill 70 lay south-east of Loos and the division had been ordered to advance due east, across the flank of Hill 70 rather than over the crest. The advancing troops were now swinging out of line and gradually veering to the south.

This swing to the south was mainly due to poor visibility, again caused by smoke and gas, compounded by the fact that a great many officers, especially company and platoon commanders, had been lost in the first hours of fighting. The troops were increasingly leaderless and therefore advanced to attack whatever obstacles stood directly in their path or appeared most obvious, their original orders being either unknown to the junior officers and senior NCOs struggling to take charge or ignored in the general excitement as the Scots chased the Germans fleeing towards Hill 70.

To give just one example, the 44th Brigade, which should have moved with its *right* wing aligned on Hill 70, had its *left* wing fixed on that position. This shift pushed the 46th Brigade to its right well over to the south, where the battalions promptly came under heavy fire from German positions in the Cité-St-Auguste. The junior officers and men of the 15th (Scottish) believed in any case that they should maintain contact with the 47th Division on their right flank, and tended to drift south in order to keep that contact, instead of pressing east.

In the face of increasing enemy opposition the advance continued. As the Scots crossed Hill 70, driving the enemy before them, their leading platoons were heading almost due south, towards the Cité-St-Laurent, a northern suburb of Lens, an area their commanders had been most anxious to avoid. The Germans concealed there met the Scots with a hail of fire, bringing their advance to a halt only 70 metres from the St-Laurent line, and by 1130 hours the 15th Division attack had been stopped. The Germans were now pounding and raking the survivors with fire while preparing a counter-attack. At Hill 70, around nine hundred Scots from various units had crossed the crest and were descending the far slope, when they were brought under fire from the German second-line position straight ahead and enfilade machine-gun fire from the flank.

This fire gradually brought their advance to a halt but, after lying down in the open for a while, the survivors rose and attempted to storm across the German wire. The wire here was 10 metres wide, chest high and partly concealed in long grass. Unable to go forward or retreat back up the open slope, the Scots then attempted to dig in on the chalky ground before this barrier, losing men to snipers until all were either killed or had surrendered. By 1100 hours the division attack here had also been halted.

Fortunately, at noon the French attack began south of Lens, their infantry going forward at 1245 hours, some six hours after the British advance. As a result no German troops could be spared to assault the Scots hanging on grimly north and east of Lens, and they were able to consolidate their position, though the Germans retook the Hill 70 redoubt and the hill crest. The division spent the rest of the day consolidating the ground already held and attempting to evacuate the wounded from no man's land – a task not completed for another full day.

The 15th (Scottish) Division had taken Loos village and gained positions between the German first and second lines on a front between the Double Crassier and Chalk Pit Wood beyond the Bois Hugo, but the cost had been very high; 124 officers and 4,151 men were lost from the 44th and 46th Brigades alone. The 44th Brigade was said to be 'in fragments' and some of the battalions had been virtually annihilated. The 8th Seaforths had lost nineteen officers and 700 men, the 9th Black Watch twenty officers and 672 men. At dusk, the 47th and 15th Divisions held a position somewhere between the German first and second lines – the question now was whether these positions, gained at such cost, could be held when the enemy returned.

Nor was any help available; a reserve formation, the 62nd Brigade from the 21st Division of XI Corps, should have been on hand by 1000 hours but had not arrived. Their leading files did not arrive in the old British front line trench until 1930 hours, and on arrival were, in the words of General McCracken, 'not in a condition fit to enter such a fight'. This was bad, but worse was to follow.

To the north of the 15th (Scottish) Division was the veteran 1st Division, commanded by Major General A. E. A. Holland. This was a Regular Army, 'Old Contemptible' formation, a mix of 1st and 2nd Battalions from a dozen famous regiments, plus two battalions of the Territorial Force, the 1st/14th London Scottish and the 1st/9th King's. The 1st Division was one of the original BEF units, though very few veterans of Mons and Le Cateau remained in its ranks after a year in the field. The 1st Division had been the IV Corps reserve but was now committed to the initial assault, attacking on a line between the Vermelles–Hulluch road and a point just north of the Vermelles–Loos road. In the centre of their front, well out in no man's land, stood the scarred trunk and leafless branches of 'Lone Tree'.

The German trenches here were only some 275 metres from the shallow 'jumping-off' trenches called 'Russian saps' which had been dug in no man's land before the attack. These trenches had been sited on the reverse slope of the Grenay spur, which meant that troops moving east to attack the German line would be immediate and obvious targets on coming over the crest. The 1st Division objectives were the Lens–La Bassée road, which lay just to the rear of the German line, and beyond that the German second-line position south of the village of Hulluch. After that, all being well, the division would press on for another 10 kilometres to the Haute Deule canal. Taking the initial objectives alone would involve an advance of some 2,500 metres, through two defence lines and past various strongpoints, a highly ambitious aim.

The divisional plan allowed for two brigades, the 1st and 2nd for the initial attack, with the 3rd Brigade in reserve. The 1st Brigade was to assault on the front between the Vermelles–Hulluch road and Lone Tree. The 2nd Brigade was to assault from south of Lone Tree, as far as a German trench line known as the Northern Sap. Having crossed the German front and support lines, the 1st Brigade would advance due east, but the 2nd Brigade would edge south-east from there to get in touch with the left of the 15th (Scottish) Division on the Loos–Hulluch road.

A feature of this attack was the gap of some 550 metres between the right flank of the 1st Division and the left of the 15th (Scottish). In addition, since the two brigades would diverge as they advanced, a two-battalion formation known as 'Green's Force', consisting of one battalion from each brigade, was formed under the command of Lieutenant Colonel E. W. Green of the 2nd Royal Sussex. Green's Force consisted of the 1st/9th King's (Liverpool Regiment) and the 1st/14th London Regiment (London Scottish). Green's Force would fill in the gap in the centre, between the two assault brigades.

The gas was duly discharged and rolled across no man's land, and at 0630 hours the 1st Division's assault began. Then the wind suddenly veered and drove the gas back into the British trenches, forcing men to leap out and take cover from enemy fire behind the parados, the rear of the front-line trench. Many men were already feeling the effects of the gas as they advanced into no man's land, where, apparently untroubled by the gas, the Germans at once opened fire on them with machine guns and trench mortars. Then the 2nd Brigade discovered, on crossing the crest of the ridge, that the wire on its front, south of Lone Tree, set like a hedge on the reverse slope, was 10 metres thick . . . and quite undamaged.

Wire alone was no particular obstacle, and some of the men had wire clippers. The problem was that this wire hedge was covered by machine-gun fire, and as the men from the 2nd KRRC and the 1st Royal North Lancashire Regiment tried to cut a path through they were ruthlessly cut down by machine-gun fire and snipers. Their advance was rapidly brought to a standstill and they fell back, with many of the dead and wounded left hanging on the wire. This repulse of the 2nd Brigade gave the Germans here time to man their trenches in strength, while the British supports soon fell back, leaving the first wave of attackers completely isolated. The attack by 2nd Brigade had stalled within an hour of starting and losses were already mounting rapidly. By mid-afternoon, in spite of all their efforts, the 2nd Brigade had not penetrated the enemy line at any point.

North of Lone Tree, the 1st Brigade was rather more fortunate. Though the gas attack here had failed to quell the defenders, the assault wave advanced in three extended lines, and in spite of intense machine-gun and rifle fire pressed home its attacks and took the Bois Carré, 500 metres north of Lone Tree, the Germans abandoning their front-line positions and fleeing back towards Hulluch.

This success was not achieved without heavy losses. The *Official History* records that 'The 10/Gloucestershire had been destroyed as a battalion and only sixty survivors continued the advance.' The rest of the brigade, the 8th Royal Berkshire and the 1st Cameron Highlanders, pressed on east, towards the outskirts of Hulluch, and dug in there to await the arrival of Green's Force. The much-depleted battalions of the 1st Brigade now had to hang on east of the German front line until Green's Force and the 2nd Brigade came into line on their right.

News of this expensive success encouraged the 2nd Brigade, still hung up before the wire or pinned down in no man's land, to try again. The 2nd Royal Sussex, with two companies of the 1st Northamptons attached, was ordered to push ahead, picking up the remnants of the assault battalions as they advanced. At 0805 hours this attack was reported as successful, but at 0901 hours another report came back to divisional headquarters, saying that the Royal Sussex and the Northamptons were held up by uncut wire south of Lone Tree and were being cut to pieces by machine-gun fire and shelling.

The fate of the 2nd Infantry Brigade at Loos is the stuff of nightmares. The brigade had now put in two attacks, each one ending with the advancing soldiers impaled on the enemy wire. The soldiers had been choked by their own gas, lacked any cover from smoke and had taken casualties from flanking machine guns untouched either by bombardment or the gas. Now they were pinned down before the wire and enemy artillery and machine guns were raking no man's land to their rear, so denying them either retreat or support. The Germans were now working their way along their trench system to outflank the brigade, and although this advance was being contested by elements of the 1st Brigade, the 2nd Brigade was in serious trouble and in need of prompt relief.

The divisional commander, Major General Holland, was now confronted with the need for a difficult decision. He knew that the 2nd Brigade attack was stuck in front of the German wire but that the 1st Brigade had managed a limited breakthrough and were behind the German line. He also knew that the divisions to his south, the 15th (Scottish) and 47th (London), had broken through and taken Loos. His problem lay in the centre, with the failure of the 2nd Brigade to maintain its advance, a failure that put the entire divisional position in jeopardy.

Two courses of action were open to General Holland. He could either send his reserve formation, the 3rd Brigade, in behind the 1st Brigade, ordering it to work south and prise the enemy off the 2nd Brigade, or send it into the gap between his division and the 15th Scottish and order it to advance north and clear the enemy trenches. A decision had to be reached quickly, amid the noise and chaos of battle, but either decision stood a fair chance of easing the problem confronting the 2nd Brigade – provided it came off.

For some reason, however, General Holland opted for a third solution. He believed that there was only one weak German battalion on the 2nd Brigade front. He also believed that the enemy must soon surrender as they were outflanked on either side and about to be overwhelmed, either by his own 1st Brigade or by the Scots of the 15th Division, now bombing their way north along the German trenches.

He therefore decided to abandon any idea of a flanking attack and to reinforce the 2nd Brigade for another frontal attack. He elected to do this by putting Green's Force in on the left of the 2nd Brigade while the 3rd Brigade went up on the right of the 1st Brigade. He then ordered Green's Force to make yet another assault on the uncut German wire.

Orders for this attack went out at 0910 hours, but three runners were killed trying to get them forward to the battalions and the order did not reach Lieutenant Colonel Green until 1055 hours. It was therefore after midday before this attack went in, with one battalion deployed on either side of Lone Tree.

The result was an extension of the existing catastrophe. The men of Green's Force were shot down as they rose from cover and ran forward to join the survivors of 2nd Brigade, who were still pinned down before the German wire. In half an hour the 1st/14th London Scottish lost 260 men and the 1st/9th King's 235; all this in addition to the 1,728 men killed, wounded and missing already lost by the 2nd Brigade that morning – a total of 2,223 men killed or wounded, without the brigade penetrating by as much as a metre through the German wire.

General Holland had committed a basic military mistake; he had reinforced failure. By reinforcing failure, sending in more troops at a point where the attack had already failed, Holland simply added to the casualties and achieved nothing. This indeed was 'donkey' behaviour and quite inexcusable; Holland knew what was going on on his front and flanks and how and why his attack had stalled.

Yet he made a decision based either on excessive optimism or a complete misjudgement of his enemy – which is a second elementary military mistake. To assume that these German soldiers, who were currently shooting his attack to pieces and were securely encased in bunkers and trenches behind a hedge of barbed wire, would elect to surrender before their position became untenable was simply cretinous.

To mount another assault was now extremely difficult. The wire across the divisional front was now under enfilade machine-gun fire and largely uncut. Machine guns were not usually employed spraying bullets to their front, in the manner so often depicted in the cinema; to obtain the best results, machine guns were fired *across* the front and to the flanks – this made best use of the banana-shaped 'beaten zone' produced by the fire, and carpeted the ground with bullets for hundreds of metres. If, as here, several machine guns were laying enfilade fire across the front and the wire, their 'beaten zone' would be impassable and the area thus covered a perfect 'killing ground'.

At 1315 hours General Holland abandoned frontal attacks and sent what was left of his infantry round to the south, ordering the 2nd Brigade and Green's Force, which were still out in no man's land, to leave some men to hold the line while the survivors came back and went south, crossing the German line through the gap created by the 15th Division and wheeling north to get behind the Germans. This much more sensible move succeeded; the Germans who had savaged the 2nd Brigade, 400 men of the 157th Infantry Regiment, now commanded by a captain, were taken in the rear and surrendered two hours later. They had held up the British advance here for nine full hours, causing terrible losses; their own casualties had been negligible.

As these men surrendered, a strong German counter-attack towards Lone Tree came in from Hulluch but was repulsed by fire from the 1st Brigade. With the enemy removed from their front the survivors of 2nd Brigade and Green's Force then moved up to the Lens–La Bassée road, which they reached at 1720 hours. There they dug in, exhausted.

It had been a hard day for the 1st Division. About half the men in the rifle companies had gone. Of the 6,000 men in the two brigades who had attacked that morning only 1,500 were still fit to fight at dusk. Moreover, the 600-metre gap, which Green's Force had been created to fill, was not closed during the day. Nor was it closed overnight, and this failure was to cause further losses and fresh disasters when the battle was renewed the next day.

On the left of the 1st Division, north of the Vermelles–Hulluch road, I Corps, commanded by Lieutenant General Hubert Gough, took over the attack from IV Corps. Gough's corps contained three divisions, the 2nd, 7th and 9th (Scottish), and these divisions were responsible for breaking through the German line on a 3-kilometre front up to the La Bassée canal and then pressing east through the German second line to the Haute Deule canal.

Hubert Gough was the right man for this task. General Gough was, in cavalry terms, a 'thruster', a general officer noted for his ability to push men forward, if for little else. Thrusting would be important, for this advance of some 10 kilometres was to be achieved without any pause that might give the Germans time to gather and commit their reserves. Gough's corps had no reserves; the hope was that they would be supplied by the 21st and 24th Divisions of Haking's XI Corps, which were supposed to be on hand early on the first day . . . but had yet to appear.

This advance on the Haute Deule canal sounded a formidable task, as indeed it was. The BEF had not advanced 10 kilometres – or anything like 10 kilometres – through the enemy lines since they had landed in France the previous year. On this occasion just three German regiments opposed General Gough's divisions, and he there- fore felt confident of success. In fact, General Gough was *always* con- fident of success, a characteristic that endeared him to that quiet optimist, General Sir Douglas Haig.

The ground over which I Corps was to advance sloped away north of the Vermelles–Hulluch road. The terrain was open but well sup- plied with slag heaps, quarries and groups of miners' cottages typical of the region. Most of these features, especially the cottages, had been turned into mortar- and machine-gun-equipped bastions, surrounded by thick belts of wire. Particular obstacles overlooking the I Corps front included the Quarries, a chalk excavation, 100 metres long and 7 metres wide, straddling the crest of the Grenay spur, which curved back behind the German line north of the Vermelles–Hulluch road. Then there was Fosse 8, another coal mine, surrounded by cottages and workings, with its own slag heap known as 'The Dump'. Closer to the canal was the large village of Auchy, while behind the German second line lay the large villages of Hulluch, Cité-St-Elie and Haisnes, as well as the town of La Bassée. Study of the map on page 206 will be helpful.

Five lines of trenches, each 100 metres apart, barred the British front, and the entire I Corps advance would be overlooked by the looming Hohenzollern Redoubt, that German strongpoint which lay just inside the 9th (Scottish) Division area. These defences were virtually untouched by four days of artillery bombardment and were manned and ready for action when the British assault went in.

Major General Sir T. Capper's 7th Division attacked on a 1,500-metre front between the Vermelles–Hulluch road and the southern edge of the Hohenzollern Redoubt, and was tasked in particular with taking Hulluch and the Quarries position. Gas release was inhibited by the fact that the south-westerly wind would tend to blow it over the British front hereabouts, so not all the cylinders were turned on, though where gas and smoke were employed they worked fairly well.

The real problem here was the depth and strength of the defences. These consisted of the usual trenches and dugouts, plus several strongpoints, of which one, the Pope's Nose redoubt, formed a small salient in advance of the German line from which any infantry advancing into no man's land could be raked with enfilade fire. There was also an intermediate line, some 600 metres behind the front line, straddling the crest of the Grenay spur. Very few of these defensive positions had been damaged by the artillery bombardment. The only consolation was that this position was weakly held by just two companies, perhaps 300 men, of the 11th Reserve Regiment, with another two companies in support. One of these companies occupied the Quarries position.

The leading battalions of the 7th Division, from the 20th and 22nd Brigades, managed to enter the German front line in less than fifteen minutes. They suffered heavy losses, for the wire had not been well cut and their advance was contested by machine-gun fire from the Pope's Nose redoubt, while the 20th Brigade battalions ran into their own gas cloud. Casualties were especially high among the battalion officers; in the 8th Devonshire Regiment only three officers out of the nineteen who went over the top made it to the German line. By the end of the day this battalion had lost all its officers and 600 men out of the 750 who had gone into the assault that morning. Other battalions were also decimated. All the officers of the 2nd Royal Warwickshire were killed or wounded, and only 140 of the battalion's NCOs and other ranks were unwounded at the end of the day.

The 7th Division advance was therefore made at great cost. Even so, the division crashed through the enemy defences and took its first objective on the Vermelles–Hulluch road. Though originally detailed to press on to the German second line and the Haute Deule canal, by evening the division had already lost around five thousand men and had only a tenuous grasp on the Quarries and the German second line. At 1930 hours Gough ordered the division to consolidate and hold the ground gained north-west of Hulluch, roughly between the German first and second lines. The survivors started to dig in, the guns came forward, sappers came up to improve defences and lay telephone wires, and by dusk three brigades of field artillery and some howitzers supported this new front line.

This sounds promising, but a closer reading of the evidence suggests that the 7th Division had been badly damaged. The 20th Brigade suffered heavy losses, especially to the 2nd Gordons and the 8th Devons. The Gordons hacked their way through uncut wire to the German parapet, losing many men, including their commanding officer, in no man's land. Equally severe losses fell on the 8th Devons, which lost the CO, second-in-command and the adjutant and all but 100 of their casualties in the first hour of the attack. The 22nd Brigade, which had also run into uncut wire, had been swept by enfilade machine-gun fire and cut to pieces and was described as 'a skeleton of its former self' by that evening. The other battalions were in no better state; no man's land before the German line was now littered with the bodies of dead and wounded men.

The 9th (Scottish) Division, commanded by Major General G. H. Thesiger and going in on the left of the 7th Division, had a very difficult task – and had never been in action before. The two assault brigades, the 26th and 28th, had to take some notably strong frontline positions, including the Dump, Fosse 8 and the Hohenzollern Redoubt – and the latter position jutted forward close to the 9th Division's front line, so enfilading the attack front. The assault brigades were also tasked with taking 1,500 metres of the enemy's front-line and the communication and support trenches in the rear. When that much had been achieved, the division had to press on to the Lens–La Bassée road, moving on from there to reach the Haute Deule canal.

Reading this list of tasks suggests that the 9th Scottish Division was given too much to do – and so it proved.

The initial phase of their attack went well; the gas did useful work and the artillery fire damaged the German wire. The assaulting troops of the 26th Brigade, led by the 7th Seaforth Highlanders, bombed and bayoneted their way into the Hohenzollern Redoubt within the hour and were soon in the German front-line trenches. The 26th Brigade should then have continued towards the village of Haisnes, but their advance was hampered by a lack of success on their left flank, where the 28th Brigade had been held up before a group of cottages and trenches called the 'Madagascar' position, partly because the gas had failed to take effect, and partly because the wire here had not been adequately cut.

The infantry therefore suffered severely; one battalion, the 6th KOSB, was reduced from 750 to just fifty men in half an hour, and now the whole 9th Division front was being raked by machine-gun fire, which 'practically annihilated' the 10th Highland Light Infantry. Casualties in this battalion, fifteen officers and 631 men, represented 85 per cent of the officers and 70 per cent of the men; most of these casualties were caused in the first few minutes of the attack.

At 1115 hours, General Gough ordered a renewed attack by the 28th Brigade, assisted by the artillery of the 9th and 2nd Divisions. The losses of the first attack had not been reported and Corps HQ did not know that three German strongpoints on the 28th Brigade front – 'Strongpoint', 'Mad Point' and 'Railway Redoubt' – were still in action. This second attack also failed with great loss, and at 1330 hours the 28th Brigade commander reported that his force was 'unequal to further offensive action'[1] and it was ordered on to the defensive.

This reverse at Madagascar Trench affected the entire 9th Division. The Scots now had to devote their strength to defending their north-eastern flank in front of Fosse 8, for the attack of the 2nd Division to their left had also failed. There was still the 9th Division reserve, the 27th Brigade, which came up to support the 26th Brigade, but there was then a breakdown in communications between the 27th Brigade commander, Brigadier General Bruce, and Divisional HQ, a signals lapse that led to another disaster.

General Bruce had been given two conflicting sets of orders. If the attack of half the 26th Brigade on Fosse 8 failed, he was to reinforce them. On the other hand, if this attack went well, Bruce was to support the other half of the 26th Brigade in its advance towards Haisnes. In the event the attack went well. Fosse 8 fell at 0800 hours and so Bruce was cleared to move on Haisnes . . . but the timing for this move was unclear.

The divisional commander, Major General G. H. Thesiger, wanted Bruce to wait for an order to proceed, whereas the latter understood that he should move his men as previously ordered, as soon as he had definite news that Fosse 8 had fallen. Soon after 0800 hours word was received that Fosse 8 had fallen and Bruce therefore ordered his three leading battalions to advance on Haisnes.

The 9th Division commander, unaware that Bruce had already acted, now sent an order that only two of 27th Brigade's four battalions should assist the attack on Haisnes. Ten minutes later, Gough, who seems to have taken a close interest in the brigades of the 9th Division, told Thesiger that the 7th Division had taken Hulluch and he was to send the whole of his reserve – Bruce's 27th Brigade – to take Haisnes. There were clearly too many people giving orders for the 27th Brigade, but Bruce and three of his battalions were now en route for Haisnes, so Gough's intervention should not have been a problem.

Then it transpired that a gap had opened up between the positions of the 26th Brigade and the much-battered 28th Brigade. Bruce therefore received *yet another order*, to send only three battalions against Haisnes – which he was already doing – and send the fourth to plug the gap between these brigades. Order and counter-order usually add up to disorder, and so it proved here.

In view of all these conflicting orders, Bruce elected to proceed with his current plan, supporting the 8th Gordon Highlanders in their move on Haisnes, which had been held up by German resistance at Pekin Trench. There the assault battalions were caught up in a maze of trenches, German artillery began to range on the advancing troops, and the balance of the 9th Division battle, which had so far been in the British favour, started to slip. General Bruce was unable either to restore the position or to advance, and by nightfall his brigade had been stopped.

Dusk found the 9th Division embedded in the enemy line at several places, although the 28th Brigade was back in its original trenches and the artillery, which had come forward in support during the afternoon, had been forced to withdraw again. Apart from a certain amount of meddling by Gough, the 9th Division had been well handled, but the results were meagre and had cost over five thousand men killed, wounded or missing. Among those who died that day was the divisional commander, Major General Thesiger, killed by shellfire near the Hohenzollern Redoubt, one of several general officers to be killed in this battle. General Gough was of the opinion that more could have been done that day if a greater degree of support had been available and the reserves had come up from XI Corps, and the latter part of this opinion was spreading among the commanders of the assaulting corps as night fell on the first day of the battle of Loos.

The 2nd Division of I Corps was commanded by an artillery officer, Major General H. S. Horne, and their fate that day was an unhappy one. The *Official History* sums this up exactly: 'The 2nd Division awoke to a day of tragedy, unmitigated by any gleam of success.' This was all too true, and as an extension of what was happening at other points along the front the fate of the 2nd Division should be briefly recorded.

The prime task of the 2nd Division was to form a defensive flank in the north-east to protect the four assault divisions in the open centre of the battlefield and provide cover for the forward movement of the guns. To do this, the three brigades of the 2nd Division were drawn up astride the La Bassée canal and given specific tasks: on the north bank the 5th Brigade was to advance east through Canteleux and Chapelle-St-Roch. On the south bank the 6th and 19th Brigades were to attack towards the big village of Auchy and occupy a German communication trench, Canal Trench, which ran parallel with the canal. Once Canal Trench had been captured these brigades were to turn it into a defensive flank.

As well as gas and artillery fire, this attack was to be assisted by the explosion of three mines under the German front-line trench, which was just 90 metres from the British line. This plan was thwarted by the fact that the Germans had recently evacuated their front line here and moved to the support position a short distance to the rear . . . and this new position was held by six battalions. The German support line was now a proper front-line fire trench, equipped with a fire step and a loopholed parapet, all creating a strong defensive position covered by enfilade machine-gun fire from the brickworks in La Bassée.

When matters go wrong in war they often go wrong at the start, and so it was here. The gas and smoke were duly launched at 0550 hours but the gas promptly came drifting back into the British trenches. Two of the mines went off at 0620 hours and the attack went in at 0630 hours, but by now many of the men had either been gassed or were wearing fogged-up gas masks. There was no smoke to conceal their advance, and the Germans were fully on the alert.

The result was inevitable – a slaughter. The19th Brigade advanced at first in extended line but was forced to bunch at the mine craters and to pass through gaps in the British wire, so presenting a splendid target to the German riflemen and machine gunners. The latter had set up their weapons on the parapets of their trench and cut the advancing British down with sustained bursts of fire. As a final blow, when the British infantry approached the German wire they found it uncut. Here, trapped in the open, they had little chance of survival.

In the first hour the 19th Brigade alone lost 857 men, with a high number of officers in the leading battalions becoming casualties; the 1st Middlesex Regiment lost sixteen out of seventeen officers and 439 men, the 2nd Argyll and Sutherland Highlanders fifteen officers and 315 men, the 2nd Royal Welch Fusiliers seven officers and 113 men. Only eleven men of the 2nd Argylls returned to their own lines that night; all the rest were killed or captured. The 6th Brigade, advancing on the bank of the La Bassée canal north of the 19th Brigade, met a similar fate, and the 5th Brigade north of the canal had made no progress whatsoever.

This brigade had elected to attack in two places a kilometre apart, one near the canal and the other near Givenchy. Once again the gas failed to reach the German trenches and machine guns flayed the advancing infantry. On the right, the attack of the 1st/9th Highland

Light Infantry petered out within minutes with the loss of eight officers and 350 men killed or wounded. The left-hand attack, put in at 0600 hours, half an hour before the main assault, was made by the 5th Brigade's other three battalions, heading for a line between the villages of Canteleux and Chapelle-St-Roch, about a kilometre in front of their overnight position.

These battalions reached the German wire without undue loss and found it well cut but again the front-line German trench was empty, negating any effect of the third mine, which had exploded under it before the attack. The Germans were waiting in their support line, from which they greeted the advancing British infantry with mortar bombs, machine-gun fire and showers of grenades. They then mounted a counter-attack down the communication trenches and forced the British back into no man's land, where the enemy guns could work upon them.

By 0830 hours the 2nd Division's attack was stalled in front of the German wire and casualties were rapidly mounting. General Horne therefore ordered the artillery to bombard the German line for another half-hour before the infantry tried again, but reports from the battalions stated that even after another twenty minutes of shellfire the German strongpoints and machine-gun posts were untouched. Horne was a man who listened to his subordinate officers, and at 0945 hours the attacks were halted until further orders; the 2nd Division attack had failed. Although the South Staffordshires of the 6th Brigade along the canal towpath made some progress, they were soon driven back by showers of grenades and intense machine-gun fire.

Attacks against the German positions continued all along the front for most of the day, but no further advantage was gained and losses continued to mount. Even so, it could be argued that this day had produced some solid gains, the various divisions accomplishing many of the tasks required in the original plan. The 47th Division had established a protecting flank in the south and the 15th (Scottish) Division had captured the Loos defences and overrun that village and Hill 70. The division had even proceeded beyond Hill 70, if not in the right direction.

Farther north, both the 1st and 7th Divisions had reached the Lens–La Bassée road while the 9th (Scottish) Division had taken the

Hohenzollern Redoubt, Fosse 8 and the Dump and even got through the German second-line position at Haisnes. The 2nd Division had not been well handled and was now back in its original trenches, but the other assault divisions had penetrated the German front line and in many cases advanced a short distance beyond it. The requirement now was to hang on to these costly gains and if possible exploit them by the rapid commitment of reserves.

To balance this result it is necessary to look at the cost. Over fifteen thousand men from these six divisions had been killed or wounded – about one sixth of the force engaged that morning – and many of those wounded now lay out in no man's land in urgent need of rescue. Granted, if these losses are compared with the losses suffered for far less territorial gain at Neuve Chapelle and Aubers Ridge, they might be regarded as 'acceptable', at least in the context of the normal losses of the Western Front, but for the moment they had not produced a worthwhile result. Whatever happened now, this costly engagement on 25 September was not going to yield any strategic return. Indeed, such a return was not part of the main intention; this was a 'bite and hold' attack, as yet uncompleted – the final outcome largely depended on what happened to the French attacks in Artois and Champagne.

In Artois the results were not encouraging. The losses in the French Tenth Army at Vimy on 25 September were as horrendous as those of the British First Army opposite Loos and had met with less success. The French assault, a large affair with nineteen divisions supported by 1,090 guns, had gone in at 1255 hours. The results may be summed up in the Tenth Army communiqué: 'Insignificant on the right of Tenth Army, slight in the centre but very satisfactory on the left where the 70th Division and the XXI Corps reached all their objectives. On the other hand the British offensive had been very successful.'

It is hard to see where that final scrap of misinformation came from, and the descriptions of the French performance seem optimistic in the extreme. Any ground taken by the French XXI Corps was retaken by the Germans before the end of the day, and elsewhere the German line held firm. By that evening General Joffre was asking Foch whether it was worthwhile renewing the attack on the following day or whether reserve divisions on the Artois front should not be switched to Champagne, though the attack there had not been significantly more successful.

Foch therefore went to see Field Marshal French, who told him that he intended to resume the attack at first light with a push by his three reserve divisions, and Foch therefore decided to renew his attack with another push on Vimy Ridge. There seems to be some disagreement as to who actually took the initiative in deciding to resume the attack, but since both Allied generals were in agreement the battle of Loos was duly renewed on 26 September.

13

The Battle of Loos, 26 September 1915

We did not understand what it would be like . . . but we will do all right next time . . .

Survivors of the 24th Division, *British Official History, 1915,* Vol. II, p. 335

GIVEN THE GRIEVOUS losses of 25 September and the shallow penetrations in the enemy line achieved on that day a question arises: why was the Loos attack not called off? The short answer seems to be that on the evening of 25 September General Sir Douglas Haig was convinced that victory was either just within his grasp or had just been snatched from him by the action – or inaction – of his direct superior, Field Marshal French.

For the first belief there was a certain amount of evidence. As far as could be ascertained, some advances had certainly been made, although at great cost. Loos village had been taken; some units had crossed the Lens–La Bassée road and at one point even reached the edge of the Bois Hugo, a kilometre beyond that road. On the other hand, the troops of the 2nd Division were back in their own trenches after suffering a total defeat, in general the advance had stalled before, or just beyond, the German front-line trench, and the losses among all the assault battalions had been terrible.

With the exceptions noted in the previous chapter, however, the troops had generally been well handled. Although there had been the usual and inevitable amount of battlefield confusion, Haig's plan had achieved some successes and there remained the underlying fact that the entire purpose of the British assault at Loos had been to assist

the French push at Vimy. If that push on to Vimy by the Tenth
Army succeeded, the sacrifices of the First Army would not have been
in vain.

Unfortunately, the French had done no better than the British on
the first day of this combined offensive. Great losses had been sustained
at Vimy and Arras and little ground taken by the Tenth Army. Even so,
as related in the previous chapter, on the evening of 25 September,
Field Marshal French and General Foch had made the decision to keep
up the attack on the following day, and Haig supported this intention
with orders for a further advance. This meant reinforcing those battalions now embedded in the German defences, pushing up the reserves
and – or so it was hoped – entering the exploitation phase of the battle
with an advance to the Haute Deule canal.

At this point it is necessary to leave the Loos front on the evening
of 25 September and go back a little in time and place, not least to
recall the battles at Neuve Chapelle and Aubers Ridge. This will show
that among the reasons these attacks petered out with great losses for
no territorial gain was a failure to commit the reserves as soon as possible after the initial attack. If any lesson was glaringly obvious to all
after those previous encounters in 1915, it was the need to commit
the reserves *on time*.

'On time' in this context meant *quickly and early*, while the enemy
was still reeling from the surprise and violence of the initial assault and
before he could bring up his own reserves and seal off the front-line
breach. In considering this point we arrive at one lesson of these
Western Front battles that the commanders should certainly have
learned by now. In order to achieve exploitation of the initial breakthrough, the reserves had to be close at hand, able to move and under
the direct control of the assault commander when or even before the
initial assault began. This basic rule seems to have escaped the notice
of Field Marshal French.

To see what happened to the reserves at Loos on 26 September,
therefore, we must now turn to the actions of the BEF reserve formation, Lieutenant General R. C. B. Haking's XI Corps. With the
Cavalry Corps (the 1st, 2nd and 3rd Cavalry Divisions), Haking's
corps formed the formation known as the GHQ Reserve, and to

understand their situation it is necessary to trace their actions during the days before 25 September. The GHQ Reserve was the reserve of the entire BEF and therefore under the direct control of the commander-in-chief, Field Marshal French. XI Corps consisted of the newly formed Guards Division and the 21st and 24th (New Army) Infantry Divisions, largely composed of post-August 1914 volunteers, men who were new to France and completely without any experience of the front line, let alone of all-out battle.

The deployment of the GHQ Reserve divisions and the timing of their release to First Army were to be the cause of much argument between French and Haig in the weeks after the battle. This being so, it is essential to track the path of XI Corps in the days before the battle and especially on 25 September, and so get a firm grasp of the salient facts before discussing this high-level dispute in the next chapter.

These divisions began their march towards Loos on the night of 20 September when the 21st Division left its billets near St-Omer in the Pas de Calais; the 24th Division and the Guards Division left St-Omer a day later. Night marches, between 1800 hours and 0500 hours the next day, were always tiring, but were employed by the BEF and indeed by the Germans at this time, to screen the movement of troops from scouting aircraft.

This movement may have been necessary but the men should have rested in billets during the day. But it took time to find suitable billets, feed the men, inspect their feet and get them turned in. Throughout the day there would be the regular call for fatigue parties and this, plus the general daily bustle of a French village, would keep the men awake. Long before dark those asleep must be woken and rousted out, fallen in, inspected, fed and readied to march on again. This march up from St-Omer took three full nights, 30 kilometres a night for the first two nights before the divisions arrived at Lillers on 24 September. They were still 26 kilometres, a good day's march, from the British front line and not yet under General Haig's command, even on the eve of the battle.

By that time the men of XI Corps were very tired and in some disarray. The weather had been vile, with two nights of heavy rain to soak the men to the skin, and cobbled roads to blister their feet. The staff work had not been good either; many units had not been adequately fed or sheltered and the daily arrangements for rest had either not been made or not been enforced. These divisions were still a considerable distance from the start line and by any standard the men were in sore need of a good night's rest before going into action. Unfortunately, the battle of Loos was about to start and General Haig was most anxious to employ these divisions . . . provided he could prise XI Corps from Field Marshal French's tenacious grasp.

Before the battle, lengthy discussions had taken place between Haig and French on the vexed question of deploying these reserves. As related, the previous battles of 1915 had underlined the fact that the prior deployment of reserve formations close to the front was crucial to the continuation of the battle after the assault divisions had shot their bolt.

Crucial, perhaps, but not easy. If the reserve divisions were placed far enough forward to permit swift deployment, they might be within range of the enemy artillery – or become tangled up with the rear echelons of the front-line divisions. Nor was it easy to keep them supplied, for their logistical requirements – food, water and billets – would add to the logistical difficulties facing the assault divisions, which must have prior call on the available roads, transport and supplies.

This logistical problem was no light matter; in 1915 an infantry division on the march took up some 27 kilometres of narrow, cobbled French road – which meant that over 80 kilometres of road immediately behind the BEF front line would be full of men and horse transport for XI Corps alone. Getting the brigades and battalions of the six assault divisions through to the forward area and so into battle would require skilled staff work by the divisional staffs and the minimum amount of congestion on the approach roads.

Better, then, perhaps, to keep the reserves well back and away from the shellfire until they could be committed to the action at some suitable time and point. But this was no easy solution either; the problem then lay with getting these reserves to the front up roads crammed with wounded men coming the other way and jammed with ambulances, staff vehicles, horse artillery, ammunition limbers and supply wagons. The *Official History* describes this task as 'Like trying to push the Lord Mayor's Show procession through the streets of London without clearing the route and holding up the traffic.'[1]

Far better, maybe, to revert to the first plan and position these reserves well forward before the battle began? Decisions were called for but there was no established staff college or textbook answer. This was a judgement call, a problem to which there was no easy solution. The problem was further compounded by the chronic difficulties of communication, of getting orders back to the reserve's divisional commanders, telling them when they were needed, where to go and how to get there.

This last problem was enhanced if the reserves were not under the direct command of the field commander (General Haig) or could not be committed without the express permission of higher authority (Field Marshal French). General Haig had brooded on these various difficulties and possible solutions and had finally decided that he wanted his reserves as close to the front as possible and under his command from the start of the battle – if not before.

Field Marshal French disagreed with this conclusion. He declined to hand XI Corps over to Haig, stating in his orders to Haig on 7 August that 'The troops available for the operations will be those of your own Army plus the Cavalry Corps and two divisions held in general reserve under the orders of the Commander-in-Chief.' Available, perhaps, but not directly under First Army control.

Haig was unhappy about this and said so. The two men then reached an understanding by which French would control the reserve but would place it under Haig's command – as soon as he considered it was required. This was highly unsatisfactory to Haig, who continued to press for command of XI Corps, but French, ever stubborn, flatly disagreed.

The field marshal continued to disagree even at a meeting on 26 August when General Foch also pointed out that, in his opinion, reserve formations should indeed be placed no more than 3 kilometres behind the assault divisions and should be there before the battle started. All previous experience had shown that unless the reserves could be brought into action within three hours of the initial assault, the Germans would have time to man their rear defences and bring any advance to a standstill.[2]

Matters of command and control were not helped by the fact that just before the battle French moved his headquarters to the Château Philomel, three miles south of Lillers. This chateau not only had no telephone communications with the outside world, it was also deep in the countryside and very hard to find. At this time there was no wireless link with First Army HQ and GHQ so messages went to and fro by staff car or dispatch rider. If Haig needed those GHQ reserves in a hurry, his first problem would be finding Field Marshal French.

So this dispute continued; Haig continued to press for the prior commitment of reserves to First Army while French remained adamant about retaining them under GHQ control. On 18 September French told Haig that the divisions of First Army were more than sufficient for the attack and that he still intended to keep these reserve divisions at Lillers, under direct GHQ command and some 26 kilometres behind the front. Haig kept up the pressure for a prior commitment of these divisions, and indeed he had to do so. He had committed all the divisions of I and IV Corps to the initial assault and had no available reserves of his own for exploitation.

He therefore replied at once to French's statement of 18 September, asking the field marshal to put the leading troops of XI Corps as far forward as Noeux-les-Mines, 5 kilometres from the front. This last appeal clearly had some effect, for on the evening of 19 September Haig was informed that the 21st and 24th Divisions would be assembled 'in the area mentioned in your letter, by dawn on the 25th'. Haig therefore began the battle of Loos believing that his view had finally prevailed, that these two divisions would be at his disposal, ready for instant deployment when the battle began.

This was not so. Field Marshal French retained control of these divisions even after moving them forward. The issue remains confused, for French clearly intended to make them available to Haig some time soon, as he then issued orders to Haking, ordering that the 21st and 24th Divisions should be at Noeux-les-Mines and Beuvry respectively by daybreak on the 25th, and the Guards Division should be a short distance behind them, in the country south of Lillers.

Beuvry, a village just south of the La Bassée canal, is some 8 kilometres west of the front line, while Noeux-les-Mines, on the railway line west of Vermelles, is a little farther away. This move therefore represents only a partial success for the First Army commander; Haig had succeeded in getting these divisions moved forward – but they were still under the field marshal's direct command when the attack at Loos began.

The march forward began at 1900 hours on 24 September. It should have been an easy march of a mere 18 kilometres, but movement proved extremely difficult over congested roads, and it took six or seven hours for the forward elements to reach Noeux and Beuvry. The battalions had lost contact with their transport and cookers and their rations were not reaching them. As a result these reserve divisions arrived at their destinations in the early morning of 25 September, exhausted, hungry and in some disorder. A few hours later, at dawn, the battle of Loos began, and their travails continued.

At around 0700 hours, hearing that elements of IV Corps and I Corps had already breached the German line, Haig sent a staff officer to the Château Philomel to report this success and urge the immediate commitment of XI Corps. At 0845 hours, believing that the attack of I and IV Corps was forging ahead, he again requested that the reserve divisions should be placed under his direct command and the battalions moved into the British front-line trenches, which should by now be clear of the attacking units.

According to Haig's policy, the British front-line and reserve divisions should make their respective moves forward as one, rather like a train, the reserves pulled forward into the British front line as the assault troops left it. This proposal was never implemented; two hours had already been lost since the attack began and the true situation of the attacking battalions was as previously described, successful in some parts but in many cases verging on the perilous . . . and the reserves were still not available.

The next act began at 0930 hours when French finally gave way to Haig's importuning and sent orders to move the reserve divisions forward to the front line. French still retained the command function and the field marshal's orders for this move were typically ambivalent:

'21st and 24th Divisions will move forward to First Army trenches as soon as situation requires and admits. On arrival, they will come under the orders of First Army, arrange move in accordance with First Army. Guards Division will move up to ground vacated by 21st Division. XI Corps, less 21st and 24th Divisions, will remain in general reserve.'

This order contains at least two problems. First, who would decide when the situation 'requires and admits' the forward movement of the two infantry divisions? This part of the order leaves the whole question of when these divisions would move completely in the air. Second, Haig wanted the entire XI Corps and was getting only part of it – and then by divisions, without the corps staff to handle either the forward movement or any subsequent commitment to the battle.

This order from French was another setback for the First Army commander. Haig had intended to put the two divisions into battle under Haking's command; now he might have to commit them, together or separately, under some other corps commander, a difficult move to make in the current situation and in the middle of the battle.

Haig got this news at 0950 hours. At 1130 hours Field Marshal French arrived at Haig's headquarters and finally agreed that the entire XI Corps, less the Guards Division, should be put under Haig's command. That done, French went to see Haking at Noeux-les-Mines and pass on this change of plan. And so, finally, at 1320 hours on 25 September, when the battle of Loos was already in train, Haig heard that XI Corps was under his orders and on the move . . . but was now being delayed by heavy traffic congestion.

The march of these two new divisions to the front line on the first day of the battle was a horrific experience for these young, inexperienced, New Army soldiers. They marched past ambulances crammed with muddy, bloodstained wounded. For the first time they saw corpses torn by shellfire. Then they came under shellfire themselves as they marched east, towards the ever louder rumble of the guns. The two divisions marched on towards the Loos sector and halted just forward of Vermelles, 4 kilometres from the old front line, with the 24th Division deployed to the north and the 21st to the south, both formations waiting for further orders.

Believing that he would not have the use of the XI Corps HQ, during the morning Haig had placed the leading brigade, the 73rd Brigade of the 24th Division, under Gough of I Corps, and at 1315 hours he put the entire 21st Division under the control of Rawlinson's IV Corps. This last order was cancelled at 1435 hours but the cancellation arrived too late; by that time Rawlinson had ordered the leading 62nd Brigade of the 21st Division to support the 15th (Scottish) Division at Loos. This brigade marched into battle at Loos and Hill 70 and was duly chopped to pieces.

The situation into which these inexperienced troops were advancing has already been described but Haig or his corps commanders had not yet grasped the true situation; the usual communication difficulties were now taking effect. They believed that, given another push, victory was on hand and a breakthrough imminent. These beliefs were based on reports which, as the *Official History* points out, 'had overestimated the successes, and the great losses suffered were scarcely mentioned'.[3]

The situation at mid-morning was revealed in the actions of the 3rd Cavalry Division, commanded by Major General C. J. Briggs, a formation that was already in First Army Reserve before the battle and therefore spared the debate over the movement of XI Corps. At 1030 hours, convinced that the enemy front was crumbling and perhaps despairing of ever getting command of XI Corps, Haig ordered this division forward, with orders to pass through the assault infantry and capture the high ground between Harnes and Pont-à-Vendin on the Haute Deule canal, 10 kilometres behind the German lines.

Fortunately, Major General Briggs was an intelligent officer, very different from the popular image of a Great War cavalry general. Mounting his horse, Briggs rode to the headquarters of the 1st, 7th and 15th (Scottish) Divisions. There he discovered a far from rosy picture and so, leaving officer patrols to stay in contact with the front-line formations and report on events, he returned to his headquarters and ordered his division to stay put. Therefore at 1240 hours, when Haig ordered the 3rd Cavalry Division to advance, Briggs told him that the current situation made an advance impossible – but that he would move when and if it was possible to do so.

Haig appears to have taken this response well, without changing his belief that the advance was proceeding well and would go even better when the 21st and 24th Divisions went forward. Therefore, at 1435 hours, having retrieved the 24th Division from General Rawlinson, he ordered General Haking to 'push forward at once between Hulluch and Cité-St-Auguste and occupy the high ground between Haisnes and Pont-à-Vendin, both inclusive, and secure the passage of the Haute Deule canal at both places'.

The aim now was to penetrate the German second-line position, which lay well behind their front-line position and was overlooked by untaken German positions in the north and south. Any advance towards the second line would therefore be countered by enfilade fire, even before the thick German wire in front of the second-line position held it up – study of the map on page 206 will be helpful at this point.

Had the situation been anywhere as favourable as Haig believed, these orders would have made good sense on the afternoon of the first day, 25 September – in theory he was pushing fresh formations forward on to high ground and securing his front for a further advance. Unfortunately, the situation was far from good; some advances had been made but the battle was already proving extremely costly and the advance had stalled.

The problem, yet again, was poor communications, aggravated by optimism. Haking made out his orders for this advance fully believing that Hill 70 and Hulluch were already in British hands and that his flanks would therefore be secure from enfilade fire. In this belief he ordered the two brigades of each division – the 73rd and 62nd Brigades having already been lost to I and IV Corps – to advance across the open ground in the centre, between Loos village and the Vermelles–Hulluch road, and carry out Haig's orders. This optimism spread farther down the line; these divisions went forward fully convinced they were passing through previously captured positions and pursuing a beaten foe.

All these actions took time. The orders to advance were issued at 1435 hours but the divisions did not move forward until 1700 hours or later, and it was after 1800 hours before the leading elements were in position east of the Vermelles–Grenay road. General Haking reported this delay to First Army HQ and was advised that, in view of the coming darkness, General Haig considered that, for the moment at least, the advance should not go beyond the Lens–La Bassée road, though night patrols should move up to the Haute Deule canal.

Asked about the condition of his men, Haking stated that they were tired but ready to proceed. The latter point is certainly correct, but the men were more than tired – they were exhausted. They had not had a decent night's sleep for days and many of the units had not been fed for the last twenty-four hours. They had spent most of this long day marching forward or standing about and needed a good rest before any further burdens were placed upon them.

Rest was not available on the evening of 25 September; at 1810 hours, the divisions were ordered forward to 'gain the Hulluch–Lens road as the first objective. Be prepared to move if the moon gives sufficient light. GOCs of 72nd and 63rd Brigades should consult at junction of Lens–Hulluch road and Lone Tree–Hulluch track at 0100hrs, regarding arrangements for further advance.'[4] Clearly, another long and sleepless night was in prospect for these bone-weary soldiers. And finally, as the troops moved forward in the gathering dusk towards the Lens–Hulluch road 5 kilometres to the east, it began to pour with rain.

The night advance of the 21st and 24th Divisions into the Loos valley on 25/26 September was a nightmare. Heavy rain, uneven, shell-torn ground littered with corpses and wounded men, belts of wire, abandoned trenches, mud, scores of men from other units wandering about seeking comrades lost in the battle, traffic congestion on the available roads and tracks . . . and bad news – all added to the gloom.

Reports coming back from leading patrols revealed that Hulluch was still in German hands and the enemy dug in to the east was both active and aggressive. At that meeting by Lone Tree at 0100 hours, the commanders of the leading brigades elected to stay where they were in the German trenches and wait for the dawn. Haig had wanted these reserve divisions on hand at daylight on 25 September; now they were waiting for dawn on 26 September – a full day had already been lost.

The story of the 21st and 24th Divisions on 26 September, the second day of the battle of Loos, now becomes confused. Two infantry brigades, the 62nd and 73rd, one from each division, had already been detached for service with I and IV Corps and the fate of these needs to be described separately. The point to note is that, as a result, these two divisions were reduced to just two brigades, each with a rifle strength of around four thousand men. These brigades comprised the main body of the 21st and 24th Divisions; what happened to them became the main event on 26 September and the cause of much future dissension between the two BEF commanders.

Fighting and patrol activity continued all along the line throughout the night, with German patrols probing the British advanced positions. One such counter-attack, at 0100 hours, forced its way into the lines of I Corps, and another succeeded in recapturing the Quarries strongpoint. By dawn the brigades were in position by the Lens–Hulluch road and were preparing to push on when orders arrived from divisional HQ, telling the brigadiers that a general attack had been ordered for 1100 hours.

Meanwhile we can return to the activities of the 62nd Brigade, which had been detached to IV Corps and sent to assist the 15th (Scottish) Division on Hill 70. The situation there was so unclear that the 62nd Brigade's commander told his battalion commanders: 'We do not know what has happened on Hill 70. You must go and find out. If our people are there, support them. If the Germans hold it, attack them. If no one is there, dig in.' The situation was further confused because the battalions had inadequate maps and no clear idea what portion of the rising ground beyond Loos was Hill 70.

Two battalions, the 8th East Yorkshire and the 10th Green Howards, went forward at 1500 hours on the 25th, coming under heavy machine-gun fire from Chalk Pit Wood, just west of the road, as they advanced. Their advance halted on the outskirts of Loos, and when the last two battalions of the brigade came up they gradually took up positions between Hill 70 and Chalet Wood. German attacks were beaten off, so by dawn on 26 September the situation around Hill 70 was unchanged. The 47th Division had formed a front between the Double Crassier and the Loos Crassier and the 45th Brigade of the 15th Scottish, with two battalions of the 62nd Brigade (21st Division in support) held a line on the western side of Hill 70;

this line continued to Bois Hugo. This wood, and the crest and reverse slope of Hill 70, were in German hands.

Farther north, on the I Corps front, German attacks overnight had retaken the Quarries and captured Brigadier General Bruce of the 27th Brigade. After losing the Quarries and their brigadier, this brigade withdrew to the original British front-line trenches. Meanwhile, the German attack on Fosse 8 – another look at the map on page 206 will be helpful here – was forced back, though it came in when the 26th Brigade of the 9th (Scottish) Division was being replaced by the 73rd Brigade of the 24th Division. By dawn the Quarries and Fosse Alley had been lost. The sum total of the night's activities was that the open ground between Hulluch and Hill 70–Cité-St-Auguste was overlooked by the enemy, who was ideally placed to savage any force attempting to drive east towards the Haute Deule canal.

In an effort to limit the dire effects of this situation, General Rawlinson and General Haking decided that since any advance by the 21st and 24th Divisions would be hazardous, this advance should not take place before another attempt was made to take Hill 70. A preliminary attack to clear Hill 70 was therefore arranged for 0900 hours, two hours before the main advance in the centre, and the task was given to the 45th and 62nd Brigades. This attack duly went in, the advance watched by the Germans from their snug positions on the top of the hill. It was quickly broken by heavy machine-gun fire from the crest and artillery fire from Lens and Cité-St-Auguste.

By 1100 hours the attack was seen to have failed and was therefore broken off just as the 21st and 24th Divisions began their advance in the centre. The failure to take Hill 70 and the fact that the Germans held Hulluch did not lead General Haking to change his plans; indeed, it was too late for that. If the German line could not be penetrated today, the entire battle of Loos would be a failure.

As related, this attack took the form of a long advance over open ground into the jaws of the enemy line between Lens and Hulluch, a 1.5-kilometre front enfiladed from both flanks and from the Bois Hugo in the south-centre of the line. The prime objective was the German second-line trench, which was protected by a barbed-wire thicket more than a metre high and 5 to 6 metres deep. This position had been strengthened overnight by the arrival of six fresh battalions from the German 153rd, 157th and 22nd Reserve Regiments. As the *Official History* points out,[5] this second-line position was held in greater strength than the first line had been held on the previous day.

The attack was supported by a preliminary bombardment lasting an hour in which the heavy guns were restricted to 200 rounds of 6-inch ammunition and 90 rounds of 9.2-inch. This was hardly adequate for the task, but this fire was supported by the field guns of the divisional artillery also pounding the enemy line between the Bois Hugo and the southern edge of Hulluch. Both bombardments met with an immediate response from German counter-battery fire, and the shelling of the German second line was inaccurate and ineffective, the wire remaining uncut. The Germans also attempted a pre-emptive strike, counter-attacking from their second line between Cité-St-Auguste and Hulluch at 1000 hours. This attack was driven off, but not before considerable confusion had developed among the 63rd Brigade and Brigadier General Nickalls had been killed.

The rising death toll among the senior officers, brigadier generals and above, is another notable feature of the Loos battle. Before this battle ended in October, Major General Sir T. Capper of the 7th Division, Major General G. H. Thesiger of the 9th Scottish and Major General F. D. Wing of the 12th Division had been killed, as had three brigadier generals, Wormald, Pollard and Nickalls, while Brigadier General Bruce had been captured and Brigadier General Pereira had been wounded. The popular notion that the British generals stayed well away from the front line is refuted by these figures.

And so the second day's attacks and the slaughter of the two reserve divisions duly began around noon on 26 September. On this day there would be no gas discharge, no smoke cover, no four-day prior bombardment, no trained, experienced, well-rested troops, no surprise: any long-term gain from the battle of Loos now depended on two tired divisions of inexperienced infantry tasked to break through on a narrow front between Bois Hugo and Hulluch and then advance some 8 kilometres to the Haute Deule canal – over ground where no British troops had yet advanced more than 1,000 metres, and then only at great cost.

The assault was launched, the men moving forward in broad daylight across shell-pitted ground carpeted with the dead and wounded from the day before. Before them stood uncut German wire, plentifully draped with British corpses, a sight to quell the most dauntless spirit, but the infantry still went forward and the enemy machine guns duly flayed their ranks with fire.

All the attacks made that day failed. The 15th (Scottish) Division failed to retake Hill 70 and the 1st Division failed to capture Hulluch. As for the 21st and 24th Divisions on this, their first day of battle, their men were slaughtered as they advanced across the Lens–La Bassée road and into the gaping jaws of the trap.

This attack began with a setback when two battalions of the Durham Light Infantry in the 64th Brigade (21st Division) came under heavy flanking fire from the Bois Hugo. This fire killed the commanding officer and seventeen other officers, including all four company commanders, and 220 men in the 14th Durhams, and the 15th Durhams, coming up behind, were quickly brought to a halt, lost their CO and many other officers and were driven back from the foot of Hill 70. By just after 1100 hours, the 64th Brigade was falling back, apparently broken.

The 24th Division, having lost one brigade to I Corps and with other battalions on detached tasks, was reduced to six battalions for the main attack, and this attack was launched from their overnight positions a kilometre west of the Lens–Hulluch road. Their lines crossed the road at about 1200 hours when, according to a German account, 'Masses of infantry, estimated at about a division, began to advance in about twenty waves on a front between Loos and Chalk Pit Wood, towards Hill 70.'

This was the 21st Division, a most wonderful target, and machine-gun fire from Bois Hugo and Chalk Pit Wood promptly caught their advancing lines in enfilade. Led by their company officers, a mixed force from the 63rd and 64th Brigades advanced across the Loos–Hulluch road and up the slopes of Hill 70, their lines constantly swept by heavy machine-gun fire from Chalet Wood and the Bois Hugo.

The battalions pressed on but, as the *Official History* recounts: 'Before the men reached the Lens–La Bassée road they had passed the limit of endurance and though some held on most fell back in an orderly manner across the Loos–Hulluch road.'[6] The 'limit of endurance' can for once be quantified; that morning the 21st Division lost 4,051 officers and men, killed, wounded or missing, about 50 per cent of the force committed, during this advance.

Just to the north, the 24th Division were also going in to the attack north of Chalk Pit Wood, under shell, mortar and machine-gun fire from the moment they rose from cover. Their attack, like that of the 21st Division, was pressed home with great resolution, but again without success. The 24th Division lost 4,178 men before the German wire that morning, slightly more than 50 per cent of the men committed.

Here the fate of the 72nd Brigade, typical and terrible, can stand as an example of what happened to the rest. This brigade consisted of four Home Counties battalions, the 8th Queen's, the 8th Buffs, the 9th East Surrey and the 8th Royal West Kents, good, solid infantry units from the cream of Britain's county regiments. They came under enfilade fire as they crossed the Lens–Hulluch road and then ran into frontal fire as they approached the German second-line wire. They were in the open and on their own, fully exposed to the full weight of fire from positions in Hulluch, the Bois Hugo and their immediate front. Then, adding to this rifle and machine-gun fire, came artillery fire from two German batteries concealed on the outskirts of Hulluch.

Shedding men at every step, the battalions crested the low ridge and saw before them the thick barbed-wire fence before the German second line – from which another terrible blast of fire was then directed on to them. Still, incredibly, they pressed on, 'never wavering, in short rushes',[7] until the leading lines were within 50 metres of the German wire. Even then some men attempted to get forward, crawling up to the undamaged entanglement – the German account states that 'our men fired standing up, as fast as they could pull the triggers. No Englishman got through the wire entanglement and the ground in front was covered with bodies.'

The slaughter here was so terrible, and the situation of the advancing troops so hopeless, that at around 1400 hours the German soldiers ceased firing along part of the front to let the survivors fall back and British stretcher-bearers come up to clear away some of the thousands of wounded. Later in the day, German doctors and stretcher-bearers went forward to assist them.

The survivors of this brigade and the other units of the 24th Division now began to fall back; shortly after 1300 hours the 21st and 24th Divisions were in full retreat and falling back across the Lens–La Bassée road. This was not a rout or even a panic-stricken retreat; the men fell back steadily and at their own pace, but they retreated, still under fire, to the road and beyond, finally reorganizing in the trenches they had left just a few hours before.

When the news that these two divisions had broken first reached XI Corps HQ, it was not believed. It took a direct report from the staff of the 24th Division to convince General Haking that his attack had been a disastrous failure. General Haig, who was at XI Corps headquarters when this report came in, at first believed that these reports of a major reverse had been exaggerated; later reports confirmed that it was all too true and Haig promptly applied to French for the use of the Guards Division, which was then moving up from Noeux-les-Mines. This division was ordered to relieve the 21st and 24th Divisions when it arrived that evening. Meanwhile attempts would be made to discover the true situation on the Lens–Hulluch part of the line.

Staff officers were sent forward to round up the men of the 21st and 24th Divisions and form a new line on Lone Tree Ridge. One pleasant aspect of this disastrous day is that no attempt was made to blame the officers and men of these divisions for this reverse. Their courage and sacrifice were quickly recognized and Major General J. E. Capper, who took over the 24th Division from Major General Ramsay soon after Loos, wrote in his subsequent report that 'The division had undertaken a task under conditions in which the best-trained troops in the British or any other Army would have found it difficult to succeed. Until Hulluch should be taken there was little chance of success.'

Certainly no one could say that these raw New Army divisions had not tried. Their casualty figures alone would refute such a suggestion.

The 21st Division had lost 4,051 men, killed, wounded and missing, the 24th Division 4,178, more terrible losses to add to those sustained on the first day.

By nightfall on 26 September the attack had clearly stalled, but the battle of Loos was not over. The Guards Division had now come forward and shored up the line, facing the scene of that morning's debacle, and fighting continued all along the line, most notably at the Hohenzollern redoubt and the Quarries. This fighting at Loos would continue into mid-October, with steadily mounting losses and no significant gains.

There is no need to continue with this catastrophe for the final outcome is best expressed in the losses; there was no territorial gain. Total British casualties for this battle at Loos eventually numbered 2,466 officers and 59,247 other ranks. German losses totalled 441 officers and 19,395 other ranks, another example of that stark Western Front rule – the attacking force, advancing in the open, loses the greater number of men. The first assault at Loos on 25 September rapidly descended into a battle of attrition, the opposing armies, corps and divisions grinding away at each other, day after day into October, losing men in great numbers for no useful territorial gain.

As for the French, under whose constant pressure this Loos attack had been launched, they did no better either. In Champagne, where the French attack had been anticipated, the Germans let the French assault through their first-line position but held it on their second line and cut the trapped French divisions to pieces. In Artois it was a different story; the attack at Vimy, on the right of the British First Army, had long been anticipated, and the enemy were ready and waiting for it.

The Tenth Army assault took place on the first day, when there was no breakthrough of any kind. Indeed, one of the ironies of this joint Anglo-French offensive from Vimy to La Bassée is that the French reserve divisions, which had been brought up close to the front in anticipation of a rapid breakthrough, were savaged by the German guns and took heavy losses before they were withdrawn out of range.

As for the British First Army, the failure to break through on the first two days dictated the outcome of the Loos engagement and the results would be far reaching, but one of the curious aspects of the battle is Haig's claim that the first day had been 'a success'.

Writing to Lord Kitchener on 29 September, Haig claimed that 'My attack, as has been reported, was a complete success.' Haig is referring to his attack of 25 September, and after four days the adjective 'complete' seems excessive. Nor is it clear where these reports of 'success' were coming from, other than from Haig himself. Other reports, from those more closely involved in the action on that day, tended to disagree with this confident assessment.

Nor was his difference of opinion restricted to the units on the Western Front. As train-loads of muddy, bloodstained, wounded men from the 21st and 24th Divisions rolled into London's Victoria station, bearing news of all they had endured, rumours began to spread about the actions of the various commanders, most notably about the actions of Field Marshal French. Glory had died on 26 September, and the British public wanted to know why.

14

The Fall of Field Marshal French,
October–December 1915

The impression left by the events of the past year was that Sir
John French was unlikely to be equal to the task of command-
ing the larger armies which would be available in 1916.
British Official History, 1915, Vol. II, p. 408

THE BATTLE OF Loos ended officially on 8 October. The fighting
along the Lens–La Bassée line went on until 13 October but no
further advances were achieved. Losses continued to mount and in
the course of the fighting the Germans regained many of the front-
line positions lost in the early assault. Finally, on 4 November, Haig
informed French that he was compelled to give up any hope of continuing the offensive; winter was coming on and with the German
defences growing stronger every day, no further attacks could be
justified.

The battle of Loos was the ultimate, inevitable tragedy of 1915.
The steady escalation in BEF casualty figures since Neuve Chapelle
had demonstrated, time and again, that the only effect of expanding
an attack on traditional lines was to increase the casualty figures. Until
some new kit, new tactics and new thinking were applied to the problems of the Western Front, a wise commander would stay on the
defensive and defy eviction. Unfortunately, there were a number of
reasons, military and political, which prevented anyone following that
sensible course of action.

At Loos the overriding power of the defence had been demonstrated yet again. No means had been found to adequately quell the
combined effects of machine-gun fire, artillery and barbed wire. The

notion that a rapid commitment of more men to this dire situation would have produced some worthwhile results is at best debatable.

Steps to tackle those combined effects were certainly in hand, not least in the development of the tank and an improvement in battlefield communications, and further offensives must – or should – wait until the result of those developments was available some time in 1916. Up to a point, this happened, or would have happened, but for the intervention of the enemy two months into the New Year of 1916, at Verdun.

Heavy losses on the Western Front in 1915 were by no means confined to the BEF. The concurrent French battles in Artois and Champagne were equally unsuccessful and even bloodier. On 28 September, the leading troops of the Tenth Army reached Point 140 on Vimy Ridge in the German third line, but their advance was then stemmed by the arrival of the German Guard Corps. No further progress was made and by 15 October, when the Vimy offensive was broken off, Tenth Army losses amounted to 1,250 officers and 46,980 men.

The supporting offensive in Champagne was halted on 1 October but was then renewed on 6 October, when some of Pétain's Second Army divisions made limited gains. Other parts of the Second Army offensive and that of the Fourth Army in Champagne suffered a total check . . . and even more horrific casualties. Between 25 September and 7 October, French losses in the Champagne battle alone came to 3,743 officers and 139,824 men. The net result of the fighting in 1915 was to increase the number of casualties; the death toll of the combatant powers was now reaching close to 2 million men – and still the war continued.

By the end of 1915 the BEF had lost no fewer than 273,098 men, killed, wounded and missing, to add to the 89,804 of the original BEF who had fallen in the first four months of war from August 1914. All these men, Regular Army, territorials or New Army, were volunteers. After Loos, the flood of volunteers began to dry up, and by the spring of 1916 the British government found it necessary to introduce conscription.

Total German casualties from August 1914 to the end of 1915 came to a staggering 2,597,052, of which no fewer than 601,751 had been killed. French losses were soaring in pursuit of this German total and advanced steadily with every attack. None of this had been anticipated when the nations marched off joyfully to war in the summer of 1914.

The battle of Loos having ended, another battle, one between the generals, was about to begin. Even while this slaughter was going on an argument between Field Marshal French and General Sir Douglas Haig, on where to place the blame for the Loos disaster, had already begun in London. At first it appeared that the main thrust of their dispute was over who should carry the greater share of blame for the casualties among the two reserve divisions on 26 September.

This was indeed part of the dispute, as the extent of this catastrophe became public knowledge and the public argument struck at the competence of the generals and their staff. As the French–Haig wrangle over Loos continued, however, it became locked into a general argument over Field Marshal French's command capabilities and whether they were up to the demands of modern war.

The first strike went to General Haig, who, in that letter to Lord Kitchener of 29 September, raised the matter of the commitment of the two reserve divisions on 25 September. In this letter Haig reminded the secretary of state '. . . how earnestly I had pressed you to ensure an adequate reserve being close in rear of my attacking divisions and under my orders? It may interest you to know what happened. No reserve was placed under me. My attack, as reported, was a complete success . . .'

This last claim seems a little on the extravagant side; parts of the attack on 25 September had indeed enjoyed a limited success but others had failed completely. These failures had created the tactical situation that led to further disasters on the following day when all surprise had been lost and the enemy had been granted adequate time to reinforce his second-line position. This being so, it could be that the commitment of the reserve divisions a day after the initial assault was simply compounding the basic error and ensuring further losses. If so, then French and Haig were both culpable; reinforcing failure is a certain way of pushing up the casualty figures.

That, however, was not Haig's point, and he was clearly anxious to get his point across first. His argument was that his initial attack had indeed been a success and if the reserve divisions had been under his orders and deployed close at hand by 0630 hours on 25 September he would have committed them at once, exploited the breakthrough on the Lens–La Bassée road, a definite territorial gain, and so justified the losses. 'They [the reserve divisions]', Haig continued, 'came as quick as they could, poor fellows, but only crossed our old trench line with their heads at 6pm. We had captured Loos twelve hours previously and reserves should have been at hand *then*.'

This wrangle over the reserves soon came down to a matter of *time*, of exactly when the reserves were ordered to move and when XI Corps was handed over to First Army command on 25 September. On 2 October Haig notes a meeting with Robertson, the CGS, who had already tackled the field marshal about the commitment of reserves and received French's opinion that the right time to commit them was 'on the 2nd day of the battle and not the 1st'. Haig's riposte to this comment was that 'It seems impossible to discuss military problems with an unreasoning brain of this kind.'[1]

Bickering between the two generals over the continuation of the Loos attack on 26 September continued over the next few days, but on 8 October the events of 26 September surfaced again in the shape of a letter from Lord Kitchener asking for a detailed report on the handling of the 21st and 24th Divisions. The wounded men flooding into Britain's hospitals from Loos were reporting to friends and family – and the press – that they had been given impossible tasks and had not been fed, and their views were now appearing in the newspapers, national and local.

Nor was this all. On 9 October Sir John French's diary records that

Haldane [Lord Haldane, the Lord Chancellor and former Secretary of State for War, was visiting the BEF] has told me of reports which are current at home about the 21st and 24th Divisions. Comments have been made, as to my method of using them, by responsible members of the Cabinet. He has spent an hour or two this morning with Maurice [Colonel Frederick Maurice, then Director of Military Operations on the Imperial General Staff], and has obtained from him a correct version of the course of the battle. I have also written to K, in reply to his letter of October 6, explaining exactly when,

how and under what conditions the 21st and 24th Divisions were put
into the fight . . .

The arrival of that 'letter of October 6', from Kitchener, may account for the fact that Haig found French in 'a chastened mood' when
he visited the chief at St-Omer on 8 October. In any event, Haig
returned to the attack on the following day when Lord Haldane,
clearly pursuing his enquiries into the events at Loos, came to his
headquarters and asked for Haig's views on the action of the reserves
on 25/26 September.

Haig duly went over the entire business yet again, stating that his
main criticism was over the fact that the reserve divisions were not at
hand when wanted early on 25 September and that French's version
of events was not entirely correct on the matter of timings. To this he
added his personal views on the entire command set-up, not least that
during the battle Sir John French had established himself at the
Château Philomel near Lillers, over 30 kilometres from his headquarters at St-Omer. 'Many of us felt', said Haig, 'that if these conditions
continued it would be difficult ever to win!'

Haig's diary entry for this day, 9 October, concludes with the
comment that although Haldane stated that he was very glad to have
had this talk, on his return to England he averred that no blame for
failure could be attached to Sir John French. This left wide open the
question of who *was* to blame for the heavy losses, at Loos, and various
attempts to silence debate on this point now became evident.

In spite of the claims of 'success' for the advance on 25 September
made by Haig and French, 'cherry-picking' events or various parts of
the Loos battle to bolster their assertions, it was increasingly becoming apparent that the entire Loos operation had been a costly failure.
Haig had predicted just such an outcome from the first time he had
viewed the ground, and it remains something of a mystery why,
having resisted constant pressure from Joffre in July and early August,
he capitulated at once to the pleas of Lord Kitchener on 19 August.
He had indeed taken up the challenge of Loos with considerable
enthusiasm but the outcome, as he had always predicted, had been
disastrous. This fact could not be concealed; now, for the first time,

the competence of the BEF generals was being openly debated in the British press.

The wrangling between French and Haig therefore continued. On 16 October, French went over to the offensive, writing to Haig demanding an explanation for certain statements Haig had made 'in his report on the operations of September 25 and subsequent days, regarding the want of reserves at certain points' . . . and querying Haig's claim that his forces had breached the rear enemy line at certain points. To rebut these last queries Haig sent in reports from various battalion commanders and the diaries of prisoners.

Haig's diary entry for 17 October moves this matter on somewhat. On that day he claims that a proposal that he – Haig – should go to the Mediterranean to report on the Gallipoli campaign had been put on hold because of 'the possibility of requiring me in France to replace Sir John French'. This entry also claims that Lord Stamfordham, King George V's private secretary, had phoned Lieutenant General Sir William Robertson, the Chief of the BEF General Staff, and, at the king's command, had asked him whether the time was not right to replace Sir John French as commander of the BEF.

Moves to unseat Sir John French were clearly afoot at the highest level, fuelled by open public discontent in the press and murmurs of unhappiness in Parliament. Robertson declined to make any specific reply to Stamfordham's query but quickly raised the matter with Haig. Haig replied that he had always been loyal to Sir John French – a debatable claim in itself – and had always done his best to stop all criticisms of French or his methods. Now, however, in view of what had happened in the recent battle, especially over the reserves, and in view of the seriousness of the general military situation, he had come to the conclusion that it was not fair to the empire to retain French in command of the BEF. He added that none of his corps commanders had any faith in French either – in fact 'they have no confidence in him'.

Robertson relayed these views to the king via Stamfordham, while telling Haig that even those members of the cabinet who had previously supported French were now anxious to remove him. A week later, on 24 October, Haig dined with the king and gave His Majesty a frank and damning estimate of the field marshal's battlefield abilities.

Field Marshal French, said Haig, should have been removed after the retreat from Mons in 1914. During that retreat he had mismanaged matters, shown a total ignorance of the essential principles of war and declined at first to participate with the French in the battle of the Marne. In the recent Loos battle, especially over this question of reserves, French's obstinacy and conceit showed his incapacity, and it seemed impossible to stop him making the same mistakes again. Therefore – 'for the sake of the Empire' – French ought to be removed. As to who might replace French, Haig stated smoothly that he was willing to do his duty in any capacity and would, of course, serve under anyone chosen for his military skill to be C-in-C. As to who this military paragon might be, Sir Douglas ventured no opinion.

On 28 October, Haig's growing campaign to unseat Sir John French met with a personal setback. Riding Haig's own mare, the king was inspecting some corps troops at La Buissière, when the mare reared and threw the king heavily to the ground, causing injuries to his leg. This accident obliged the monarch to spend a few days in bed before being taken back to England on a stretcher. It also proved a considerable embarrassment to General Haig.

Then, on 2 November, the simmering quarrel between Haig and French burst into the open when French's dispatch on the battle of Loos was published in *The Times*. This dispatch was accompanied by a leading article from the paper's military correspondent, Colonel Charles Repington, no lover of Haig and a man who apparently had a high opinion of the field marshal; Repington had assisted French during the 'Shell Scandal' arguments after Neuve Chapelle. Repington's new article implied that the reverses at Loos were entirely Haig's fault and matters might have gone better if the field marshal had been in direct command of the attack.

Haig paid no particular attention to Repington's article but took serious exception to certain statements in the dispatch, notably over the timings. This dispatch, said Haig, was 'full of mis-statements of fact' concerning 25 September, and he set his staff to comparing the dispatch with the telegrams and messages received from GHQ on 25/26 September. This produced three telegrams confirming that the 21st and 24th Divisions had not been placed under Haig's command at the times claimed by Sir John French. Therefore, on 4 November, Haig wrote to French, asking that the paragraphs in the dispatch which referred to these matters be amended.

The dispatch is certainly contradictory and not without self-justification. French begins by stating that 'in view of the great length of the line along which the British troops were operating it was necessary to keep a strong reserve in my own hand. The Eleventh Corps was detailed for this purpose.'

Exactly what 'line' was French referring to? Does this mean he held on to XI Corps in case it should be needed by the Second Army at Ypres? Or is he referring to the 10 kilometres of front between Lens and La Bassée currently being attacked by First Army? In either case he reveals his deep-seated reluctance to hand XI Corps over to Haig, even though everyone else in France at this time – including Foch – thought that an early transfer of reserves to the assault commander was a basic essential of command.

French then goes on to clarify this matter somewhat, stating that 'in order to give speedy and effective support to the Ist and IVth Corps', the 21st and 24th Divisions had been moved to the line Beuvry–Noeux-les-Mines on the night of 24/25 September and that the 3rd Cavalry Division, less one brigade, had been assigned to First Army as a reserve and moved into the IV Corps area on 21/22 September. The crucial matter of who had command of these troops and could give them orders and what *precise* time they arrived at the front is not mentioned.

French's diary entries for the period 25–30 September[2] are also interesting. On 25 September, he states that 'I went to see Haig at eleven and decided to send him the 21st and 24th Divisions to support his attack. He told me he was holding the 3rd Cavalry Division [two brigades] in readiness to follow up any gap made between Hulluch and Loos. It was then arranged that the 21st and 24th Divisions were to move forward at once, under orders from Haig . . . the 21st and 24th Divisions only reached the old trench line after dark so were not available for attack today.'

It therefore appears, from the field marshal's private account, that the reserve was not placed under Haig's command and ordered to

move until 1100 hours on 25 September, well after the start of the battle. This reserve was not in the former British front-line trench until
eight or nine hours later. A whole day had indeed been lost before
these reserves could have been committed to the exploitation task; any
idea that they had been on hand at the start of the battle was clearly
wrong.

Even so, Field Marshal French's reply to Haig's request was peremp-
tory. On 8 November, two letters were received from GHQ. In the
first, French directed that all correspondence between them on the
actions at Loos was to cease forthwith. The second letter concerned Haig's request that French's dispatch of 2 November should
be amended. The field marshal declined to do this, declaring that
the statements in question were 'substantially true' and in no need of
amendment.

At any other time, Haig might have held his peace, but he now
knew that the field marshal's star was waning, both with the cabinet
and with the court. He therefore returned to the charge, stating
that he took exception to two paragraphs in the dispatch, one stating
that he had control of the 21st and 24th Divisions by 0930 hours on
25 September, and that he had charge of the Guards Division 'on the
morning of September 26', rather than the afternoon. Neither statement was correct, said Haig, and he requested that this fact be placed
on the record.

This argument was crucial, and neither officer could afford to lose
it. If there was an inquiry into the costly failure at Loos, and if that
inquiry revealed that the failure to have the reserves on hand and under
Haig's command was largely responsible for that failure, then the question of who had control of the reserves at the crucial time would be a
major factor in placing the blame.

Having failed to quell Haig with a direct order to drop the matter,
French then tried conciliation. On 10 November, Haig and French
met at St-Omer and French offered to send all Haig's letters on Loos
to the War Office, and let Haig see the covering letter, which would
accompany their joint correspondence. Haig said that all he wanted
was to have the true facts on record, that his only thoughts were
on how to win the war and he had no time for anything other than

commanding First Army . . . a statement that jars somewhat with his behind-the-scenes activities in recent weeks.

Matters then slowed down somewhat as Kitchener had departed to the Mediterranean to review the situation at Gallipoli and the prospects for an Anglo-French foray at Salonika while Field Marshal French was ill and confined to his bed.

Kitchener returned to London on 3 December, when this matter of command came rapidly to a conclusion. That day, at a meeting with Haig, Kitchener confirmed that he proposed writing to Asquith recommending that Haig should be appointed to succeed Sir John French. If this matter were not settled today, said Kitchener, it would be settled tomorrow, and in any event Haig was not to worry about it. In fact, Haig was given something else to worry about; after appointment, Haig was to regard Joffre as the C-in-C in France and 'do everything possible to meet the French C-in-C's wishes, whatever might be our personal feelings about the French Army and its commanders'.

This aside appeared to confirm that when Haig became commander of the BEF he would be under the same constraints and contradictions regarding the French as those inflicted on Field Marshal French in August 1914. When Haig took up his new post this was indeed the case, and the details were confirmed in his subsequent orders.

And so, on 10 December 1915, Douglas Haig came into his long-sought inheritance, when a letter arrived from Downing Street informing him that Sir John French had resigned his post with the BEF and the king had agreed that Sir Douglas Haig should replace him . . . 'Sir John French', said Asquith, 'has placed in my hands his resignation of the office of Commander-in-Chief of the Forces in France. Subject to the King's approval, I have the pleasure of proposing to you that you should be nominated as his successor.'

At noon on 19 December, Haig duly became commander of the BEF. Sir John French returned to Britain, as Commander-in-Chief, Home Forces, and General Sir Henry Rawlinson, currently commanding IV Corps, became the new GOC of First Army. General Sir William Robertson became CIGS in London and Henry Wilson was offered a corps in First Army under Rawlinson, though Haig knew that 'HW had been abusing me and other British Generals and insti-gated an article in *The Observer*, suggesting that the British Army in France should be placed under the command of General Foch!' (diary entry, 14 December).

Sir John French had finally been prised loose from the BEF, and his departure cannot be regretted. Although he was confronted with problems that would have taxed the abilities of more able men, his fail-ures were personal as well as professional. Personally, he was narrow minded, equivocal, indecisive, petulant and, as the case of Horace Smith-Dorrien reveals, extremely vindictive. Professionally he seems to have been totally unaware of the basic nature of the war in which his army was currently engaged and made little or no effort to under-stand the basic problems involved in the fighting.

His biggest failure, the one that affected his personal and profes-sional standing, was his unwillingness to stand up to the French and his constant vacillation over decisions and tendency to fall in with the views of the last person he spoke to, especially if that person was Joffre, Foch or Henry Wilson. The BEF were well rid of him and would have been better served in 1915 if his removal had taken place earlier. He was indeed a 'donkey'.

Now French had gone, and the appointment of Douglas Haig as BEF commander brings 1915 to a close. This being so, the time has come to review the events of that year and see whether the 'donkeys' allegation, which is largely based on those events and has smeared all the generals for several decades, has any real validity.

15

A Verdict on the Donkeys

1915 was the least successful year of the whole war for Allied arms; never again would the prospects for the Central Powers be so bright as at its close.

Alistair Horne, *Verdun: The Price of Glory*, p. 27

WERE THE GENERALS – and especially the British generals – fighting this war on the Western Front in 1915, all bone-headed incompetents and little better than donkeys? Taking the narrow view, concentrating exclusively on the events in the field in 1915, and considering the steady rise in BEF losses at Neuve Chapelle, Aubers Ridge, Second Ypres, Festubert and, above all, at Loos, it is certainly possible to argue that the allegations of incompetence and callousness made against the British generals have considerable validity.

It is also entirely fair to state that many of these actions might have been better handled, but the events on a battlefield – any battlefield – are often dictated by what has happened before the battle began, and so it was here.

The Great War did not produce any 'Great Captains'; few wars do. No Marlborough, no Wellington, appeared on the Great War scene to bring an element of genius to the problem of command in a new kind of war. At best, one can expect common sense, competence and a grasp of command in such a situation. These elements are often rare, and some of those officers who might have done better than the relevant incumbents – generals like Smith-Dorrien and Ian Hamilton – had either been sent to another front or had been disposed of by the end of 1915.

Nor, in spite of their ingrained beliefs and extravagant claims, can the French or German generals claim any military superiority. Their attacks too were costly failures; the harsh fact remains that no general of any nation emerges from the Great War with an enduring reputation for military expertise. *All* generals, whatever their nationality, were faced with the fact that the great armies of industrialized nations with all their equipment are difficult to handle, and with their mass and firepower they are hard to beat.

This relentless criticism of the generals, especially the British generals, can go too far. The generals were as much a victim of the times as the soldiers they commanded, and to seek a reason for the disasters of 1915 – the 'Year of the Donkeys' – it is necessary to go back to the time before the war began – not least because the war commenced just four months before the start of 1915 and an army cannot be re-formed in such a short time. The fumbling conduct of British military affairs in 1915 was largely caused by the pre-war neglect of the British Army and the failure to create a large munitions industry suitable for a continental war. To expect that those pre-war errors could have been corrected in the brief period of four months since the outbreak of war is simply unrealistic.

Four months – sixteen weeks – is not sufficient time to make up for the hesitations and indecisions of the pre-war years. Indeed, the war had already begun and had been in progress for some days before the British government decided to participate and order the departure of the BEF to France. That BEF consisted of just four infantry divisions and a cavalry division, a force of some 100,000 men to join a war where the armies of the other combatant nations were counted in millions. To expand this BEF contingent and the munitions industry needed to support it took *time*.

In 1914 the British Army could muster exactly eleven divisions, about the same as the army of Serbia. The British Army was a colonial force, quite capable of handling the defence of the empire but far too small to engage in a major European war. It would take time to raise the men and train the staff and manufacture the equipment those larger British armies would need.

By the end of 1914, that time had been assessed by Lord Kitchener as around two years. In other words, the British Empire would be fully capable of entering the European war some time in the summer of 1916 – as indeed it did, on the Somme in July. The question that therefore arises when considering the battles of 1915 is why were they fought at all when the means to conduct them successfully were so evidently lacking?

This question again raises the matter of time – and the problem of the French. By the end of August 1914 the German Army occupied Belgium and large industrial areas of northern France. Their armies now rested less than 160 kilometres from Paris, and the idea that the Germans should be allowed undisturbed enjoyment of this territory until the middle of 1916 is simply unrealistic . . . even had the French wished to do so. The French were not prepared to wait – they felt themselves infected by the presence of the German Army on French soil and wanted to expel that infection as quickly as possible, whatever the cost . . . and they expected the British to support them.

The British had entered this war on the side of the French and the instructions issued to Sir John French in August 1914 made the task of the BEF quite clear: 'The special task laid upon you is to assist the French and Belgian Governments in driving the German Armies from French and Belgian territory, and eventually to restore the neutrality of Belgium.'

There is nothing in this to suggest that the execution of this task could wait until 1916. As a result, the British commanders were pitch-forked into a large-scale continental war for which they lacked the manpower, the kit and the experience. The only thing they had in quantity was French pressure to do more. The BEF generals did the best they could with the resources they had, but since these resources were basically inadequate the BEF suffered a number of significant and costly reverses in 1915.

The causes of those reverses, not least in a shortage of such vital assets as artillery, extend back to the pre-war years. It will not do to place the entire blame for failures in 1915 on the shoulders of the front-line generals – or even on Field Marshal French. The conclusion of this author is that the 'donkeys' allegation has no general validity.

Certainly there were errors here that could, and should, have been quickly corrected. It was necessary to sort out the command structure in France and put some form of joint control in position, under a supreme Allied commander. It was also necessary to draw up some strategic plan for the conduct of the war worldwide, but the initiative for both steps rested with the politicians, not the generals.

It is interesting to note that when the USA entered the Second World War in December 1941 the first task of the politicians was to hold a conference in Washington – the Arcadia Conference – which drew up a high-command organization, the Combined Chiefs of Staff (CCS). Under political control from London and Washington, the CCS handled the strategic conduct of the war. This was not done without strain but the CCS worked, and its very existence made a major contribution to the ultimate victory.

No such organization was put in place during the Great War and Foch's appointment as supreme commander in 1918 applied to the Western Front alone. For most of the war the *Entente* commanders were fighting what amounted to separate wars with endless opportunities for bickering and buck-passing. And so, as we come to the end of 1915, what has been learned from that year of costly and indecisive conflict? The short answer is nothing – or nothing useful.

The most obvious step for the politicians of Europe to take at the end of 1915 was to bring the war to a conclusion as quickly as possible. What was the war about? Who had wanted such a holocaust among the European nations? A death toll of some 2 million men had not been contemplated when the nations of Europe marched joyfully off to war in August 1914. Surely this death toll alone should have inspired Europe's leaders to make a search for peace, calling on the good offices of the US government for arbitration?

Apparently not, however. As the death toll rose, the determination to press on with the war continued – on both sides of that corpse-littered Western Front line. In December 1915, two conferences took place in western Europe, one at Chantilly between the military commanders of the *Entente* powers, the other in Germany between the Kaiser and his military chief, General Erich von Falkenhayn. Each meeting reveals the state of political and military thinking after sixteen months of total war.

At the Chantilly conference, with General Joffre in the chair, the *Entente* leaders decided to mount simultaneous – but not combined – offensives in 1916, in France, Italy and Russia. The outlines of a strategic approach to this war can be dimly seen in the proceedings of the Chantilly conference, but these attacks were not coordinated; they depended, very largely, on goodwill.

As far as the British were concerned, however, Joffre was very much interested in the idea of a combined, Franco-British offensive, on a much larger scale than anything managed in 1915. As the ideal place for this combined offensive, Joffre selected the region in Picardy north of the River Somme, declaring that the ground there was very suitable for a major attack.

In this bland declaration Joffre appears to be replicating his faulty judgement on the ground at Loos. The rising ground beyond the River Ancre in the *département* of the Somme was, if anything, even less favourable for an attack than the open ground the BEF had encountered at Loos. The question of ground was not, in fact, the reason Joffre wanted to attack on the Somme; his real reason was that here, astride the River Somme, the BEF and the French armies met and here Joffre would be ideally placed to bend the new BEF commander to his will. So plans were laid for the next major battle and they led to another disaster, the July to November battle of the Somme, where British losses exceeded the combined BEF total for 1915.

Such slaughters were not confined to the battle on the Somme. The meeting between the Kaiser and von Falkenhayn had as its tragic outcome Operation Gericht, the devastating battle of Verdun, which lasted from February to December 1916 and caused combined casualties, French and German, amounting to some 700,000 men.

But it is von Falkenhayn's motivation, his reasons for proposing the Verdun attack, which arouses interest and betrays his thinking. Von Falkenhayn had been studying the Western Front battles of 1915; during that study he had come to realize that however little they offered by way of territorial gain, these offensives on the Western Front were highly effective in killing soldiers.

This being so, his proposal was to let this war do what it did best. Given the disparity in population – 37 million French to 66 million Germans – his nation could anyway afford higher losses, but his intention at Verdun was to create a battle that would result in the total destruction of the French Army.

'Within our reach', he told the Kaiser, 'behind the French sector of the Western Front there are objectives for which the French General Staff would be compelled to throw in every man they have. *If they do, the forces of France will bleed to death* – as there can be no question of a military withdrawal, whether we reach our goal or not.'

Von Falkenhayn was proposing a battle of attrition, and the Kaiser made no attempt to prevent him – indeed, he viewed the prospect of Verdun with delight. Attrition was duly achieved here, and in the course of 1916 all the armies on the Western Front – German, French and British – adopted that dire and costly strategy. As a consequence, by the end of 1916 the death toll in the Great War had doubled yet again, to 4 million men . . . and *still* the war continued.

This being so, 1915 cannot be seen as unique, a year when the blame for the losses can be placed entirely on the generals – the 'donkeys'; rather, it should be seen as another fatal year in a war that was now apparently beyond anyone's control and therefore could not be stopped. The reasons for this continual slaughter lay beyond the generals' powers to remedy. The politicians must share the blame for that, and the European electorate, who let this war continue and made no serious attempt to end it.

To say that peace was not an option at the end of 1915 and that therefore the war must continue is an abandonment of reason – but that is what happened. The result of this political blindness was Verdun and the Somme, but neither of those slaughters brought Europe to its senses. And so it went on, into the battles of 1917 and 1918. Exhaustion, and not reason, brought the First World War to a close in November 1918.

'At home', says the *Official History*,[1] 'there was profound disappointment at the ill-starred campaign of 1915; Neuve Chapelle, Second Ypres, Aubers Ridge, Festubert and Loos, had involved terrible loss of life without having shaken the enemy, far less broken his line. The difficulties of the task, the lack of adequate means, and the even greater failures and greater losses of our allies were an explanation that might well be urged.'

So it might, but 1915 ended with the BEF in much the same positions the soldiers had occupied at the end of 1914. These men had gone to war gladly and eager for victory, but the end of 1915 found them in the same place, in the trenches of Flanders, waiting in the mud and mire for whatever the spring might bring, having lost the dream of glory. In this at least they were right; 1915 had been a disaster and 1916, alas, would bring more of the same.

Appendix

Instructions from the Secretary of State for War to the Field Marshal Commander-in-Chief, British Armies in France, August 1914.

1. Owing to the infringement of the neutrality of Belgium by Germany, and in furtherance of the Entente which exists between this country and France, His Majesty's Government has decided, at the request of the French Government, to send an Expeditionary Force to France and to entrust the command of the troops to yourself.

2. The special motive of the Force under your control is to support and co-operate with the French Army against our common enemies. The peculiar task laid upon you is to assist the French Government in preventing or repelling the invasion by Germany of French and Belgian territory, and eventually to restore the neutrality of Belgium, on behalf of which, as guaranteed by treaty, Belgium has appealed to the French and to ourselves.

3. These are the reasons which have induced His Majesty's Government to declare war and these reasons constitute the primary objective you have before you.

4. The place of assembly, according to present arrangements, is Amiens and during the assembly of your troops you will have every opportunity for discussing with the Commander in Chief of the French army the military position in general and the special part which your Force is able and adapted to play. It must be recognized from the outset that the numerical strength of the British Force and its contingent reinforcement is strictly limited, and with this consideration kept steadily in view, it will be obvious that the

greatest care must be exercised towards a minimum of losses and wastage.

5. Therefore, while every effort must be made to coincide most sympathetically with the plans and wishes of our Ally, the gravest consideration will devolve upon you as to the participation in forward movements where large bodies of French troops are not engaged and where your Force may be unduly exposed to attack. Should a contingency of this sort be contemplated, I look to you to inform me fully and give me time to communicate to you any decision to which His Majesty's Government may come in the matter. In this connection I wish you to understand that your command is an entirely independent one and that in no case will you come in any sense under the orders of any Allied general.

6. In minor operations, you should be careful that your subordinates understand that risk of serious losses should only be taken where such risk is authoritatively considered to be commensurate with the object in view.

7. The high courage and discipline of your troops should, and certainly will, have a full and fair opportunity of display during the campaign, but officers are reminded that in this, their first experience of European warfare, a greater measure of caution must be employed than under former conditions of hostilities against an untrained adversary.

8. You will kindly keep up constant communication with the War Office, and you will be good enough to inform me as to all movements of the enemy reported to you as well as to those of the French Army.

9. I am sure you fully realize that you can rely with the utmost confidence on the whole hearted and unswerving support of the Government, of myself and of your compatriots, in carrying out the high duty which the King has entrusted to you and in maintaining the great tradition of His Majesty's Army.

Notes

About This Book

1. Sheffield, *Forgotten Victory*, p. 335.
2. *British Official History, 1915*, Vol. I, p. 1.

Chapter 1: Reflections on the War, August 1914–January 1915

1. Callwell, *Field-Marshal Sir Henry Wilson, His Life and Diaries*, Vol. I, p. 198.
2. Robbins, *The First World War*, p. 1.
3. Audoin-Rouzean et al., *France in the Great War*, p. 69.
4. Asprey, *The German High Command in War*, p. 163.
5. Robertson, *Soldiers and Statesmen*, p. 160.
6. Callwell, *Sir Henry Wilson*, Vol. I, p. 197.
7. *British Official History, 1915*, Vol. I, p. 2.

Chapter 2: The British Armies in France

1. *British Official History, 1915*, Vol. I, pp. 55–8.
2. For a full account of Wilson's pre-war activity, see *The Old Contemptibles* by Robin Neillands (London, 2004).
3. *British Official History*, 1915, Vol. I, p. 73.
4. James Marshall-Cornwall, *Haig as Military Commander*, London 1973.
5. Diary entry, 22 January 1915.
6. ibid., 11 August 1914.
7. *British Official History, 1915*, Vol. I, p. 66.
8. ibid, p. 65.

Chapter 3: Planning Neuve Chapelle, March 1915

1. Diary entry, 13 February 1915.
2. *British Official History, 1915*, Vol. I, p. 77.
3. Callwell, *Sir Henry Wilson*, Vol. I, p. 206.
4. Diary entry, 22 February 1915.
5. *British Official History, 1915*, Vol. I, p. 84.

Chapter 4: The Battle of Neuve Chapelle, 10–12 March 1915

1. *British Official History, 1915*, Vol. I, p. 96.
2. ibid., p. 115.
3. ibid., p. 123.
4. ibid., p. 125.
5. ibid., p. 180.
6. ibid., p. 133.
7. Diary entry, 16 March 1915.
8. *British Official History*, Vol. I, *1915*, p. 152.

Chapter 5: Gas! The Start of Second Ypres, 22–23 April, 1915

1. Callwell, *Sir Henry Wilson*, Vol. I, 13 March 1915.
2. *British Official History, 1915*, Vol. I, p. 203.

Chapter 6: The Fall of Smith-Dorrien, April 1915

1. Dan Dancocks, *Welcome to Flanders Fields*, Toronto, 1992, p. 193.
2. *British Official History, 1915*, Vol. I, p. 240.
3. ibid., p. 258.
4. ibid., p. 276.
5. ibid., p. 312.
6. ibid., p. 353.

Chapter 7: The Battle of Aubers Ridge, 9 May 1915

1. *British Official History, 1915*, Vol. II, p. 13.
2. ibid., p. 20.

3. ibid., p. 36.
4. French, *The Life of Field Marshal Sir John French*, pp. 298–320.

Chapter 8: Festubert, 15–27 May 1915

1. *British Official History, 1915*, Vol. II, p. 45.
2. See *The Old Contemptibles* by Robin Neillands (London, 2004).
3. See Appendix.
4. *British Official History, 1915*, Vol. II, p. 52.
5. Letter from French to Haig, recorded in *British Official History*, Vol. IV, p. 65.
6. *British Official History, 1915*, Vol. II, p. 79.

Chapter 9: Operations Elsewhere, 1915

1. Edmund Ions, *Woodrow Wilson: The Politics of Peace and War*, London, 1972, p. 52.
2. Liddell Hart, *A History of the First World War*, p. 160.
3. Quoted in ibid., p. 160.

Chapter 10: The Road to Loos, July–September 1915

1. *British Official History, 1915*, Vol. II, p. 116.
2. ibid., p. 122.
3. ibid., p. 123.
4. Blake, *Private Papers of Douglas Haig*, p. 101.
5. *British Official History, 1915*, Vol. II, p. 129.

Chapter 11: Planning Loos, 19 August–25 September 1915

1. Haig, *War Diaries and Letters*, pp. 137–143.
2. ibid., p. 144.
3. *British Official History, 1915*, p. 153.
4. Diary entry, 12 September.

Chapter 12: The First Day at Loos, 25 September 1915

1. *British Official History, 1915*, p. 243.

Chapter 13: The Battle of Loos, 26 September 1915

1. *British Official History, 1915*, Vol. II, p. 278.
2. ibid., p. 275.
3. ibid., p. 282.
4. ibid., p. 286.
5. ibid., p. 316.
6. ibid., p. 329.
7. ibid., p. 331.

Chapter 14: The Fall of Field Marshal French, October–December 1915

1. Haig, *War Diaries and Letters*, 2 October.
2. French, *The Life of Field Marshal Sir John French*, p. 321.

Chapter 15: A Verdict on the Donkeys

1. *British Official History, 1915*, Vol. II, p. 402.

Select Bibliography

Audoin-Rouzeau, Stephane, Annette Becker and Leonard V. Smith, *France in the Great War, 1914–1918*, Cambridge, 2003

Blake, Robert, *The Private Papers of Douglas Haig, 1914–1918*, London, 1952

Brown, Malcolm, *The Western Front*, London, 1993

Callwell, C. E., *Field-Marshal Sir Henry Wilson: His Life and Diaries*, London, 1927

Cave, Nigel, *Vimy Ridge*, Barnsley, 1996

Clark, Alan, *The Donkeys*, London, 1961

Dancocks, Dan, *Welcome to Flanders Field*, Toronto, 1992

Edmonds, Brigadier General Sir James, *History of the Great War, Military Operations, France and Belgium, 1915*, Vols 1 & 2, London, 1928

French, Major the Hon. Gerald, *The Life of Field Marshal Sir John French, First Earl of Ypres*, London, 1931

Griffiths, Paddy, *Battle Tactics of the Western Front*, London, 1994

Home, Brigadier General Sir Archibald, *The Diary of a World War I Cavalry Officer*, Tunbridge Wells, 1985

Liddell Hart, B. H., *A History of the First World War*, London, 1970

Marshall-Cornwall, James, *Haig as Military Commander*, London, 1973

Neillands, Robin, *The Great War Generals on the Western Front*, London, 1999

Robbins, Keith, *The First World War*, Oxford, 1984

Sheffield, Gary, *Forgotten Victory: The First World War, Myths and Realities*, London, 2001

Sheffield, Gary and John Bourne (eds), *Douglas Haig – War Diaries and Letters, 1914–1918*, London, 2005

Travers, Tim, *The Killing Ground: The British Army, the Western Front and the Emergence of Modern Warfare*, London, 1990

Warner, Philip, *The Battle of Loos*, London, 1976

Index

Index

Ranks and titles are generally the highest mentioned in the text

Millerand, Alexandre, 198, 200, 202
Mitteleurope: creation proposed, 171
Moltke, General Helmuth von: relieved
  of duty, 4, 7
Monro, Lieutenant General Sir Charles,
  157–9, 181, 195
Montgomery, Colonel H. M. de F., 112
Mordacq, Colonel Jean Henri, 106
Mouse Trap Farm (Ypres salient), 123
Munitions, Ministry of (British):
  established, 145
Murray, Major General Sir Archibald,
  17–18
Murray, John (publisher): *Drill and Field
  Training*, 24

Naismith, Colonel, 92
Nancy, 39–40
Neuve Chapelle, battle of: conduct of,
  xx, 61, 62–77; British endeavour at,
  26; French and Haig plan offensive at,
  40, 46, 55–60; British attack, 46,
  47–8, 50–2; position and territory,
  48–9; artillery plan and use, 54–61,
  63, 69–70, 73–4, 80; casualties, 64,
  68, 72–3, 76, 78, 132, 236, 273;
  German defences and counter-attack
  at, 67–71, 73–4; Haig cancels further
  attacks, 77–8; effects and
  achievements, 78–81, 162, 273; and
  battle of Aubers Ridge, 126–7, 132;
  lessons from, 127–8; aims, 173; as
  support for French, 188; reserves not
  committed, 239
Neuville-la-Targette, 131
Nicholas, Grand Duke of Russia, 178
Nickalls, Brigadier General N. T., 251
Noeux-les-Mines, 213–14, 243–5, 264
Notre Dame de Lorette, 129, 149
Noyon salient, 12, 38–9, 126, 188–9

Observer, The (newspaper), 267
Ocean, HMS, 180
Official History: assessment of Neuve
  Chapelle, 79–80; on attack on
  Geddes Force in second battle of
  Ypres, 99–100; on failed attack in
  second battle of Ypres, 108; and
  Lahore Division in second battle of
  Ypres, 111; on John French's orders

to Plumer to withdraw, 114–15; on
  BEF defence position at second battle
  of Ypres, 119; on French view of
  British passion for counter-attacks,
  123; on offensive against Aubers
  Ridge, 132; on artillery support at
  Aubers Ridge, 134; on battle of
  Festubert, 153; on BEF's incapacity to
  break through, 162; on Kitchener's
  agreeing to cooperate with Joffre's
  offensive plan, 199; on unfavourable
  ground at Loos, 205; on battle of
  Loos, 216, 218, 233, 246, 252; on
  logistical problems at Loos, 242; on
  John French's inadequacies, 257; on
  disappointment of 1915 battles, 273
O'Gowan, Brigadier General Wanless,
  99–100
Oh, What a Lovely War (musical and film),
  xvii
Omdurman, battle of (1898), 30
Ostend, 38

Passchendaele, 84, 117
Pereira, Brigadier General C. E., 251
Pétain, General Philippe, 258
Philomel, Château, 243–4, 261
Pilckem, 94–5, 97–9, 112
Pilckem Ridge, 87
Pinney, Brigadier General R. J., 143
Plumer, Lieutenant General Sir Herbert
  Charles Onslow: commands V Corps,
  21, 85, 92; warned of German use of
  poison gas, 83; in second battle of
  Ypres, 94, 99, 101, 105–6, 119, 122,
  125; takes over command from Smith-
  Dorrien at Ypres, 102, 114, 116;
  ordered to withdraw from Ypres
  salient, 114–15; qualities, 117;
  shortage of shells, 122
Poelcappelle, 97
Poincaré, Raymond: war aims, 9
Poland: Germany occupies, 183
Pollard, Brigadier General J. H. W., 251
Polygon Wood, 84–5
Pont-à-Vendin, 197, 246–7
Poperinghe, 107
Pope's Nose Redoubt, 229
Port Arthur, 78, 161
Porton Down, 203